Social conflict and
educational change in
England and France
1789–1848

Social conflict and educational change in England and France 1789-1848

by

MICHALINA VAUGHAN

Senior Lecturer in Sociology
The London School of Economics and Political Science

and

MARGARET SCOTFORD ARCHER

Lecturer in Sociology, University of Reading

CAMBRIDGE
AT THE UNIVERSITY PRESS 1971

Published by the Syndics of the Cambridge University Press
Bentley House, 200 Euston Road, London NW1 2DB
American Branch: 32 East 57th Street, New York, N.Y.10022

© Cambridge University Press 1971

Library of Congress Catalogue Card Number: 70-155581

ISBN: 0 521 08190 4

Printed in Great Britain by
C. Tinling & Co. Ltd   London and Prescot

Contents

Contents

Preface

This book is not of the kind historians would have produced – but excellent histories of English and French education already exist for the period we have dealt with. Nor is it of the type educationalists would have written – for this field too has been adequately covered. Our purpose is neither to describe historical events nor to investigate educational provisions. Instead we have attempted, by using the comparative method, to make a sociological contribution to the understanding of educational change.

Despite our differential experience of the two countries and their educational traditions, this book is a joint effort. We have shared equally in the research in England and in France, as well as in the writing, and accept joint responsibility for all chapters.

We would like to thank firstly our students, the classes of '68 and '69 at L.S.E. and Reading, on whom many of the preliminary ideas were tried out and with whom some of the conclusions were thrashed out. Nor were our colleagues spared and among them our greatest debt is to Michael Burrage for playing devil's advocate with the first draft. We are very grateful for all the encouragement we have been given by Ernest Gellner and Salvador Giner. We also thank our friends from École Pratique des Hautes Études, particularly for our Café Richelieu meetings. Finally, we are indebted to Donald MacRae for the constant interest he has shown in this work and for his sympathy with its perspective.

M.V. and M.S.A.

April 1971

Behind all the present discussions of the foundations of the educational system, the struggle of the 'specialist type of man' against the older type of 'cultivated man' is hidden at some decisive point.

Max Weber, Wirtschaft and Gesellschaft

1. Introduction

One of the most important and most neglected problems in the field of education concerns its structural relations with other social institutions and the factors leading to change in them. No major nineteenth-century sociologist gave more than cursory attention to the historical relationships between formal educational institutions and other social processes. While a skeletal approach to the problem can be constructed from scattered insights in the work of both Marx and Weber, theorists like Mannheim and Durkheim tended to treat contemporary education prescriptively, as a function in the process of social integration, rather than analytically. In the twentieth century, the macroscopic study of educational systems is still the weakest part of the sociology of education. Research in this field concentrates almost exclusively on contemporary institutional relations in advanced economies (or on the quickest ways to copy them). Furthermore, such limitations in the historical perspective of studies preclude the development of a theory of institutional change. It is a small step from accentuating the importance of education in the structure of technological society to the assumption that 'industrialism gives rise to – or at least justifies – the sociology of education as a specialised field of study'.[1]

The complexity of the multiple integrations between education and other institutions in advanced industrial societies is of course undeniable, but three related assumptions made from it can be challenged. Firstly, certain sociologists have established a strict pre- and post-industrial dichotomy corresponding to simple and complex structural relations involving education. This is clear in Floud and Halsey's descriptive statement that 'the relationship between education and social structure remains in principle relatively simple until the onset of industrialism'.[2] Secondly, it is frequently assumed that some aspect of the industrialisation process itself accounts for the transition from simplicity to complexity. The same authors point to the widespread nature of this approach when discussing the changing role of colleges and universities – 'The staple of sociological analysis here is the dialectical interplay of a distinctive corporate organisation with the rationalising pressures of advancing industrialism.'[3] In other words, a general theory of structural change is advanced although the specific agency responsible for effecting the integration of education with the economy can be and has been interpreted variously – technological need for skills, changing cultural values, class conflict, etc. Thirdly, since integration with the economy involved removing education from the control of the church, the processes of industrialisation and institutional secularisation are necessarily viewed as concurrent.[4] Such an approach may stress 'the secularising potency of capitalistic industrial rationalisation',[5] but might only stress its influence on institutions, not on the wider culture.

It is these three assumptions, held under a variety of theoretical guises and implicit rather than explicit in many studies, that the present work seeks to query through comparative analysis. Educational change in England and France recommended itself for study of structural relations on several distinct grounds. Firstly, in both countries (as in the rest of eighteenth-century Europe), education was a semi-integrated institution articulated only with the church and sharing many common features – curriculum, goals, input and output. Secondly, their dissimilar rates of industrialisation and institutional secularisation represent differential changes in social structure whose relationship to education is problematic. Finally, their emerging educational systems indicated different institutional relationships in the two societies, during the nineteenth century.

It is our contention that no adequate theory can be developed to cover these two countries which accepts any of the three assumptions outlined above. Any general theory of institutional change must be compatible with the diversity of structural relations involving education during the first part of the nineteenth century. The occurrence of change in a social institution can be primarily attributed either to factors external to the given society, to antecedent historical events or to forces present within the contemporary social structure – or to a conjunction of these elements. In the case of both England and France, external influences appear to have had a negligible impact on educational change during this period. In the main they can be classed as intervening variables, capable of delaying certain developments and accelerating others. For example, the Napoleonic wars whose financial repercussions inhibited government investment in the Imperial University, conceded in theory but postponed in practice. Similarly the diffusion of foreign pedagogical ideas and practices hastened the implementation of existing policies. Thus imitation of the Lancastrian method in France during the Restoration stimulated the growth of state primary schooling. In such cases, external forces merely affected the pace of change, not its direction.

On the other hand, historical antecedents in the field of education appear to have been very similar in the two countries. In the eighteenth century, English and French education was integrated with the same social institutions – primarily with established religion and accessorily with the prevailing system of social stratification. In each country the church exercised an unchallenged domination over education, was the major owner of school buildings and, in so far as teacher-training existed, its only provider. As established churches, whose educational role was sanctioned by the state, they both possessed limited legal constraits to reinforce their domination. Hence the major dissimilarities between Anglican and Catholic education can be related to the differences in religious dogma of the two churches. The similarities however tended to outweigh the differences.

Thus in terms of organisation, both sets of establishments were voluntaristic, while their administration was local and their financing private. In structure, both were integrated only at the secondary and higher level. Since the two teaching professions were clerical, their members were partially trained in the main subjects taught. Pupil selection at the various levels of instruction mirrored the prevailing system of social stratification in each country. Although curricula were not formally standardised in either, they hardly diverged from a catechismal pattern in primary and a classical one in secondary and higher education. In England and France, the goal of the instruction given was predominantly religious and its conceptual framework was traditionalistic. Thus a high degree of structural similarity prevailed between English and French education towards the close of the eighteenth century. Hence subsequent educational changes and the growing disparities between the two countries in this field cannot be attributed to antecedent integration of education with other social institutions or to major differences between the two former dominant groups.

Therefore the main source of change in both countries in the early nineteenth century seems likely to be found in factors pertaining to their contemporary social structures. During this period the previous integration of education with the established churches was steadily eroded to be replaced by new institutional relationships. In this context, two sociological theories will be considered firstly in terms of their ability to account for change in educational institutions in general and, secondly, for the specific development of these institutions in England and France during the period considered. It is hoped to show that the interpretative weaknesses characterising theories of institutional adaptation to changing social needs and of institutional reflection of socio-economic conflict are related to endorsement of at least some of the assumptions outlined earlier.

STRUCTURAL FUNCTIONALISM AND EDUCATION

Structural-functionalist explanations of the development of educational institutions depend more or less explicitly upon the end assigned to the process of education. This end can be described in shorthand as 'cultural transmission' or in longhand as socialisation and instruction for future roles. Education 'functions to internalize in its pupils both the commitments and capacities for successful performance of their future adult roles, and . . . functions to allocate these human resources within the role-structure of the adult society'.[6] Two assumptions are implicit in this approach: firstly, that education is made up of two components, the cognitive and the moral; secondly, that all educative societies possess a system of well-defined roles and expectations, with norms governing them. A correspondence is thus being posited between the functions of education and the structure of society; successful educational socialisation will ensure cultural unity and social order. 'Preparation for, and regulation of, social life determines the content of education. Schools are agencies of socialisation operating alongside the family, religion, the social services and the local community.'[7] While it is only in primitive societies that this correspondence is perfect, that is to say free from conflict, clashes of values occurring in modern educational systems are not construed as causes of change, which is attributed to an adaptive response to changing social needs – such value conflict may be indicative of imminent change, but it is symptomatic, not deterministic. The influence of educationalists and pressure groups is thus dismissed unless their ideas were congruent with the requirements of their contemporary social structure. Historically the growth and specialization of schools was, therefore, a response to social needs. The form which education took was influenced by the educationalists, but within the limits set by the existing social framework. Frequently the ideas of pioneers have only been influential after their death, once social conditions have changed in a direction which has made them relevant.[8]

Thus the selective mechanism determining educational change is located in the broad and undefined area of social needs. While all European countries underwent the same type of social change involved by industrialisation, they nevertheless developed several distinct patterns of educational institutions. The structural-functionalist theory can only offer two explanations for this diversity of educational development. On the one hand, it can be argued that the social changes brought about by industrialisation in each country implied similar social needs, which were met by functionally alternative adaptations in various countries. However, arguments in terms of a range of functional alternatives do not allow one to assert that this range is finite. They do not themselves invalidate the proposition that *any* educational system devoting more attention to scientific or technical subjects would have failed to fulfil the 'needs' of industrial society. In fact, if the possibility of an infinite range of alternatives is admitted or at least cannot be denied, the theory is deprived of all explanatory power. If the only statement made is that with more industry in society there will be more science in schools, this is better reduced to a causal, but unoriginal, proposition. On the other hand, an alternative funct-ionalist argument could be that social needs are distinct from those of industry. However, since the whole concept of 'need' is undefined, their deterministic influence on educational development can only be detected *ex post*. This deprives the theory of predictive potential.

While social needs remain undefined, some mechanisms for their transmission to educational institutions are asserted while others are denied. The possibility of transmission by the agency of individuals or groups is rejected. The influence of individual educationalists is discounted since their ideas are ignored by society unless they coincide with its needs. Similarly, pressure groups are alleged to be deprived of influence on education unless their aims coincide with these needs. If neither individual nor group action is held to account for educational change, some other mechanism must be posited which guides legisla-tion. This is generally considered to be the dominant norms and values of society at a given time. Thus for some, schools are 'the agencies for preserving and handing on culture, [which] tend to reflect the para-

mount values of the society they serve. An industrial society develops
its own values, although these are frequently opposed by residues from
the non-industrial past'. [9] To Turner, who is most explicit on this
theme, the agency responsible for this reflection is the 'organising folk
norm'.

Such organizing norms do not correspond perfectly with the objective characteristics of the societies in which they exist, nor are they completely independent of
them. Out of the complex interplay of social and economic conditions and ideologies,
the people in a society come to develop a highly simplified conception of the way
in which events take place. This conception of the 'natural' becomes what 'ought'
to be – and in turn imposes a strain towards consistency upon relevant aspects of
the society. Thus, the norm reacts upon the objective conditions to which it refers
and has ramifying effects upon directly and indirectly related features of the
society. [10]

While dealing specifically with the relation between such organising
folk norms and modes of upward mobility, Turner is positing a more
general process by which such norms directly affect the school system.
Though avowedly unconcerned with the origins of educational systems,
the essay in seeking to account for educational continuity has nevertheless to admit the possibility of change. In so far as one organising
norm presides in a society,

there will be a constant strain to shape the educational system into conformity
with that norm. These strains will operate in two fashions: directly, through
blinding people to alternatives and through colouring their judgements of what are
successful and unsuccessful solutions to recurring educational problems; and
indirectly, through the functional interrelationships between school systems and
other aspects of the class structure, systems of social control and many features of
the social structure. [11]

Thus continuity in an educational system is attributed to the continuity
of an organising folk norm and conversely educational change can
presumably be said to reflect a change in the content of this norm.

Apart from the obvious indefiniteness of the concept 'folk norm',
there is a fundamental objection to positing the necessary ascendancy
of any one norm in a society at a given time. While Turner himself
acknowledges the plurality of norms in any society and the existence
of contradictions between them, he argues that 'predominant norms
usually compete with less ascendant norms engendered by changes
and inconsistencies in the underlying social structure'. [12] However, to
posit educational continuity – as he does for England from the nineteenth century onwards – implies that the ascendancy of one set of

norms is continuous. The two forms of supportive evidence are inconclusive: firstly, that critics of an educational system do not transcend the predominant norm on which it is based and, secondly, that the functional interrelationships between school enrolment and social class largely prevent the occurrence of conflict in education. Since one can point to the presence of profound philosophical criticism and to the existence of bitter social conflict over education during that period, the whole concept of norm ascendancy in terms of a generally accepted set of evaluations is untenable. When one considers Turner's central case of 'sponsored mobility', this appears an excellent description not of social unanimity, but of the social control of one group over the educational opportunities of others. The fact that it was in the interest of the educationally dominant group to propagate the tenet that education and leadership were the prerogatives of the well-born does not confirm the existence of such a folk norm. On the contrary, the efforts required and displayed to instil this view in the other sections of society witness to its non-universality. The only sense in which ideas of sponsored mobility in education could be said to be ascendant was that they alone were reflected in legislation, whereas all competing views could only find expression through substitutive activities – the foundation of separate institutions. This relates ascendancy to social control rather than to value consensus. Turner's theory can only account for educational conflict between ideas, groups or institutions, if these are regarded as a mere legacy of the past, or as 'inconsistencies in the underlying social structure', or as the temporary characteristics of a transition period.

Structural functionalism and educational development in England and France

The postulate of institutional adaptation to 'needs' of the social structure requires restating before its assessment is possible. Concentrating upon the large process of industrialisation, attempts have been made to formulate the specific requirements of institutional adaptation which it 'imposes' upon education.

An industrial, urban society has the following characteristics:
 1. Rapidly changing productive techniques, requiring an advanced division of labour in large-scale organisations.
 2. A class and prestige structure, resulting from the new relationships between occupations, accompanied by a new distribution of power.

3. Values which are increasingly rational and materialistic.
4. An acceptance of change as normal.
Each of these influences the schools which are a vital part of this industrial system.[13]

Accordingly, education becomes more concerned with training, occupational structure with qualifications, curricula with science and teaching with research. The thesis of institutional adaptation has now been reformulated as the testable proposition that – 'The greater the extent to which society A possesses the attributes, x, of an industrial society, the greater the probability that its educational system will display y characteristics.' A comparison of England and France in either 1800 or 1850, employing a multiplicity of indices – percentage of manpower engaged in industry, contribution of industrial production to G.N.P., number or size of factories – shows England to have been the outstanding leader in industrialisation. Contrary to the prediction, however, it is France whose educational institutions bear the characteristics attributed to industrial society – specialised training for the professions and administration, social mobility through school achievement, a rationalistic educational philosophy and an incorporation of recent scientific developments in these curricula. England's industrial 'needs' were not immediately satisfied by educational institutions, remaining largely unchanged from the eighteenth century. Institutional adaptation to structural requirements is clearly far from being automatic. It remains to be seen whether any of the postulated reasons for delayed or non-adaptation apply in this case. It should be remarked that while these may account for British delayed adaptation, they are logically incapable of explaining the industrial 'pre-adaptation' of French educational institutions.

The mechanism leading to adaptation, the organising folk norm, should possess two characteristics in relation to educational development in England and France. Since such evolution was consistenty different throughout the period considered, two dissimilar value systems should be identifiable in the two countries and each should be consistently 'ascendant'. While no precise criteria for the identification of organising norms have been provided, the fact that England during this period experienced very few educational reforms, while the French system was completely reorganised, is presumably taken as evidence of the existence of norms whose respective effects on institutions were conservative and reformist. Already the adaptive nature of such norms has been severely challenged with reference to industrialisation, but this does not in itself constitute a denial of the *influence* of norms on educational development – only a denial of their *adaptive* influence. However, to point to conservatism or to reform of an institution is to describe the legislation applied to it; it may be necessary, but it is not sufficient evidence for the existence of organising folk norms. Any attempt to investigate the values guiding French educational legislation reveals normative diversity rather than consistency. While some provisions reappear in both revolutionary and Napoleonic laws, for example the provision of scholarships for deserving primary-school pupils to proceed to secondary establishments, they depend upon different values – the revolutionaries wished to equalise educational opportunity and Napoleon to maximise state efficiency by encouraging merit. In neither case could the philosophical assumptions behind those provisions be considered as an ascendant organising norm – they were never sufficiently widespread to be considered popular norms rather than official policies, nor sufficiently devoid of vocal and often successful opposition to be called 'ascendant'. Similarly, the minimal educational legislation in England merely testifies to enduring clerical domination, not to the philosophical ascendance of 'sponsorship' values – the conflict between educational ideologies was as rich in England as in France. Therefore in neither country can one identify the continuous impact of an ascendant norm since both underwent constant normative conflict. Hence the presence or absence of institutional change cannot be related to norm ascendancy. This is not to deny that norms and values influence educational development, but merely to reject them as its exclusive determinants.

Value conflict is, however, only one of many recurrent conflicts which characterised English and French education during this period, including that between groups and classes, within politics and over legislation. As previously indicated, three possible accounts have been offered which would render conflict peripheric rather than central to institutional development. These correspond to the location of conflict in the past–the partial endurance of superseded 'traditions'; in the present structural discontinuities of society; and in the future – contemporary disaccord representing a period of transition to a new equilibrium. All three are also employed to explain slow institutional adaptation. Frequently the 'religious difficulty', an obstacle to educational reform in both its English and French versions, has been represented as a clash between 'traditional' and 'dominant' values which time has solved. Essentially this account seems to confuse present evaluations of historical institutions and ideas with an objective analysis of their influence at the time and since. The churches continue to function as interest groups influencing institutional development after their ideological supremacy has been challenged. Their prestige may be considered traditional; their influence must always be empirically assessed in the present and its effects are not self-evident. The deposition of a group from a previous position of institutional domination does not spell its ultimate decline. The group will continue for as long as adherence to it offers either objective or subjective advantages to its members. As an interest group it will interact with others; while it is unlikely to dominate social institutions, it is still capable of influencing them.

The second and third accounts – structural discontinuities and periods of transition – may be considered together, since while they are logically distinguishable, the distinction is impossible in practice. If profound conflict represents cultural discontinuities leading to the imposition of contradictory demands upon and expectations of a particular institution, one would anticipate no legislative consistency in the provisions governing education. More seriously the intensity and endurance of educational conflict in England and France involves positing a lasting state of cultural discontinuity from the late eighteenth century onwards, showing little sign of a resolution in the twentieth. The argument that such conflicts represented the vanguard of transition movements to a new state of institutional adaptation would seem, unless restricting itself to *post hoc* explanations, to confuse trends with laws. Thus the concept of functional adaptation fails to adequately explain the differences between educational development in England and France during the period considered.

MARXISM – CONFLICT THEORY OF EDUCATION

The Marxist theory accounting for the development of educational institutions can briefly be summarised in 3 interrelated propositions:

(1) educational institutions and ideas are part of the superstructure which reflects the economic infrastructure;
(2) therefore educational ideals and philosophies reflect economic interests;
(3) since economic conflict is represented by conflict between classes, so educational conflict is merely an aspect of the general class conflict.

Superficially this interpretation appears to provide a more adequate

framework for the analysis of the outstanding and observable characteristics of educational development in England and France than does
structural functionalism. Thus profound educational conflict, the use
of instruction for indoctrination, the denial of educational parity to
certain groups and the prestige accorded to certain establishments
and types of instruction – could all be derived from relationships of
class domination and subjection. However, in explaining educational
change in both countries, fundamental difficulties arise from the main
proposition concerning superstructure and subsidiary ones from the
other two tenets of the theory. The postulate that education belongs
to the superstructure renders educational ideas and debates as illusory
as they are alleged to be by structural functionalists. Marx was committed to a sociology of knowledge based on the assumption that it is
not men's consciousness that determines reality, but rather social
reality that shapes their consciousness.[14] By corollary, the ideas,
classifications and theories developed by any group are merely reflec-
tive of the social relations they express. 'The ruling ideas are nothing
more than the ideal expression of the dominant material relationships,
grasped as ideas'.[15] Such an ideological relativism precludes not only
the truth content of ideas, but also their efficacy, since they are denied
the character of independent variables. Yet, when applied to educational institutions, the distinction between infra- and superstructure
is untenable. If the infrastructure refers specifically to the economy,
that is, its forces and relations of production, then it is difficult to see
how knowledge, skills and science – which are essential to them – can
be regarded as their mere reflection.

All the technical apparatus of a civilization is inseparable from scientific knowledge;
and the latter, in turn, seems to belong to the realm of ideas, of knowledge, and
these last elements should derive from the superstructure, at least to the extent that
scientific knowledge is, in many societies, inseparable from the way of thinking,
from philosophy and ideology. In other words, there are already present in the
infrastructure, defined as forces of production, elements which should derive from
the superstructure.[16]

Thus, since the economy depends upon some of the knowledge
accumulated and the skills inculated by educational institutions, it is
difficult to consign them to the superstructure and to imply a unilateral
determinism.

The second difficulty stems from proposition (2) which ascribes
ideas to modes of production and identifies false consciousness with
class consciousness. The resultant view of each class being limited to

its *Weltanschaaung* by its situation in relation to production only escapes complete relativism by endowing proletarian ideology with an exclusive prerogative of truly representing reality. This would imply the absence of any truth transcending class barriers, the impossibility of any knowledge, scientific, literary or artistic, being universal, and the perniciousness of any education for the working class propagating a common or national culture. If any of these contentions is rejected, then the process of education is distinguished from the transmission of false consciousness. In fact, if – as it has been argued – all knowledge cannot be defined as superstructural, at least some elements of education must be separated from either intentional or unintentional indoctrination.

It is clearly untenable to regard mathematics, logic, language and various intellectual techniques as the purely transitory efflux of a particular historical and class (false) consciousness: by the very fact that they outlast any particular epoch they are of universal validity. They must therefore represent true knowledge quite independently of the uses to which it is put, or indeed how it originates . . . similarly with great works of art . . . or again with inventions like the wheel, the compass, or the theory of the circulation of the blood. If we are to regard all these forms of consciousness as having been called forth from a certain economic structure for the purpose of sustaining the social order to which they belong then the entire sphere of intellectual activity becomes incomprehensible.[17]

Conflicts over access to and acquisition of this type of universal information – provided it is acknowledged as objectively valuable – will reflect true interests and not false consciousness.

The last proposition (3) is associated with certain difficulties related to Marx's varying use of the term 'class'. While his structural theory of class designates two great antagonists, the bourgeoisie and the proletariat, his historical observation of both Germany and France encompasses a plurality of social groups. In fact, Marx insisted that many of these groups did not have the character of classes. At the same time, they engaged in educational conflict. Just as the participation of these groups in social conflicts deprives class conflict of its bipolarity, their activities in connection with education prevent educational conflict from being bipolar.

It is impossible to reduce the development of educational institutions to the outcome of the struggle between the two great structural classes without either overlooking or misinterpreting the role and effects of certain participants, in particular the churches. These cannot be assimilated to either opponent since they can pursue autonomous goals – they may conflict with social classes, but are not themselves a class. Increasingly throughout the nineteenth century the church in England and France sought to defend its own interests in education and MacIntyre rightly rejects the view 'that in fact the clergy were at this point servants of one class against another'.[18] Moreover the ultimate outcome of educational debates can be influenced by the activities of various groups which cannot even be termed quasi-classes. Groups of educational reformers cutting across their contemporary social hierarchy can only be assimilated to the proletariat in so far as supporters of reform participate in true consciousness by wishing to increase the workers' share in education. Simultaneously they can be regarded as representatives of the ruling class in their wish to extend education to the working class and thereby imbue it with false consciousness. This ambivalence corresponds to the deeper uncertainty with which Marx viewed the role of 'enlightened intellectuals', among whom progressive educationalists would be prominent.

The logical outcome of the three propositions summarised above would be the complete educational hegemony of the class which dominated the economy at a given time. Therefore the group controlling the infrastructure would automatically command the superstructure.[19] However, this fails to explain the endurance of institutional patterns and pedagogical practices initiated under previous modes of production and unrelated to the requirements of a changed economy. An outstanding example is provided by the universities in England. The occurrence of situations in which the economically dominant group was educationally under-privileged by being debarred from certain institutions is not accounted for by his theory unless a fairly considerable time-lag is assumed. Such an assumption would necessarily distort the basic relationship posited between infrastructure and superstructure. Secondly, educational institutions can be transformed while economic factors remain constant and the relations of production unaltered. Thus the predominant mode of French production remained agriculture during the Revolution and the Empire, and educational reforms of the time must therefore be attributed to other causes. Although the influence of the economy on political institutions is not denied, political action cannot be construed as a completely dependent variable. Its independent influence over educational development suggests that the hypothesis of an infrastructure determining institutional change can only be maintained if the definition of this infrastructure ceases to be exclusively economic.

Marxism and educational development in England and France

As a sociological theory, Marxism does not satisfactorily explain the differences in educational development between the two countries. In neither case does the economic infrastructure appear to have determined institutional change. The rapid pace of industrialisation in England with the accompanying economic ascendancy of the middle class was not matched by a corresponding set of educational reforms which would have rendered access, structure and content more consistent with the requirements of this class. Although the agricultural mode of production associated with the landowning class declined in importance, and their supremacy in some institutions, including Parliament, receded accordingly, the aristocracy retained a virtual monopoly of access to church-dominated higher education. The traditional syllabus content remained unchanged until 1850.

The typical transition of Universities from their earlier functional emphasis was not a simple story of extension in provision for secular professional training as a response to the demands of developing industrialism. On the contrary, there was an overlapping and, in England at least, still observable phase in which the Universities were dominated by their function as preserves of the aristocratic and gentry classes. Indeed the history of . . . universities in the age of coal and steam industrialism is one of successful resistance, by ideological and other elements in the 'superstructure', to the pressures set up by economic change.[20]

In France, rapid political change in the context of a stable mode of production led to the educational transformations culminating in the creation of the Imperial University. This reform reflected the priority assigned to political rather than economic imperatives. Thus in one country the economic supremacy of a class did not entail educational parity, let alone domination, while in the other the educational hegemony of the bourgeoisie was achieved through its control of the political superstructure, not the economic, agricultural infrastructure.

The assumed response of educational institutions to changes in the mode of production entails an untested postulate that educational development is necessarily integrated with the economic structure of society. However 'the European universities were, in their medieval origins, an organic part of religious rather than economic life'.[21] In England, the complete control of the church over education gradually gave way during the later nineteenth century. In France, Catholic control was forcibly restricted by state monopoly over education, which integrated the educational system with the administrative structure, using religion as a source of control over the lower orders.

In neither case was domination of the economic structure sufficient to guarantee educational control. This implied that English higher education continued to favour an aristocratic group while the corresponding French establishments were biased towards the state bureaucracy in their intake and their curricula. 'In this sense higher education has been essentially a phenomenon of status rather than class; a process directed "against the market".'[22]

A Marxist model is relevant to an interpretation of educational development in both England and France in the first half of the nineteenth century in so far as it posits the central concept of institutional conflict to account for change. It would, however, be unduly restrictive in designating the forces of production as the only source of conflict and the relations of production as the sole determinant structuring the antagonistic groups. This monocausal approach fails to account for influences other than economic and for the interplay between groups other than classes.

2. Domination and assertion

Any theory capable of interpreting educational change in England and France can neither assume that complex institutional relations are only characteristic of the post-industrial period nor posit any factor related to the economy as essential to change. Similarly, it must be able to account for the occurrence of institutional secularisation unrelated to economic development. Finally it should take account of profound educational conflict without either assimilating the parties involved to conflicting social classes or attributing to the ideas involved some order of ascendancy and subordination according to social needs.

FROM MAX WEBER

While Weber does not develop a systematic theory of education in his work, his studies of bureaucracy, religion and status provide the main elements from which it can be extracted, and which meet the above conditions. Thus in his discussion of Confucianism, he suggests a tripartite classification of educational types based on the two characteristics of control and content of instruction:

TYPE	A	B	C
Content	Heroic/magical	Cultivation	Specialised expert training
Control	Charismatic	Traditional	Rational-bureaucratic

SOURCE: H. H. Gerth and C. Wright Mills (eds.), *From Max Weber* (London, 1967), pp. 240–4 and 426–34.

At one polar extreme, the education which corresponds to the charismatic structure of domination seeks to awaken various latent possibilities – heroic qualities or magical gifts, for these can neither be inculcated by teaching nor developed by training. The intermediate pattern 'attempts to educate a cultivated type of man, whose nature depends on the decisive stratum's respective ideal of cultivation'.[1] The traditional group which dominates this form of education may be either religious or secular. At the other extreme, the bureaucratic structure of domination develops 'specialised and expert schooling [which] attempts to *train* the pupil for practical usefulness for administrative purpose – in the organisation of public authorities, business offices, workshops, scientific or industrial laboratories, disciplined armies'.[2] All three are ideal types which may overlap and rarely occur in a pure form.

English education in the first half of the nineteenth century approximated to the second type (B) and aimed at producing conventional members of the ruling elite.

The goal of education consists in the quality of a man's bearing in life which was *considered* 'cultivated', rather than in a specialized training for expertness. The 'cultivated' personality formed the educational ideal, which was stamped by the structure of domination and by the social condition for membership in the ruling stratum. Such education aimed at a chivalrous or an ascetic type; or, at a literary type, as in China; a gymnastic-humanist type, as in Hellas, or it aimed at a conventional type, as in the case of the Anglo-Saxon gentleman.[3]

While the English educational ideal was the cultivated gentleman, the French was far more career-orientated and school achievement was highly formalised. The examination system in the Imperial University tallies with Weber's characterisation of the vocational training inseparable from rational-bureaucratic control (type C). The evolution of this system confirmed his hypothesis that degrees and diplomas tend to perpetuate themselves because of the economic advantages they represent for their holders and of the social prestige attached to them.

Such certificates support their holders' claims for intermarriages with notable families – claims to be admitted into the circles that adhere to 'codes of honour', claims for a 'respectable' remuneration rather than remuneration for work done, claims to monopolize socially and economically advantageous positions.[4]

Weber attributes the transition from 'cultivation' to 'specialised expert training' to 'the irresistibly expanding bureaucratization of all public and private relations of authority'.[5] However, while this expansion is presented as unavoidable, it can be delayed and modified by either the prevalence of a democratic ideology hostile to meritocratic selection and to the status distinctions it entails, or by an intensification of in-service training as a substitute for educational reform. Rather than providing an explanation of the differences in the educational development of England and France, the postulate that it is determined by differential bureaucratisation requires testing. The establishment of ideal types has merely shown a logical consistency between bureaucratic organisation and the hierarchical, centralised, integrated and vocational nature of the French educational system on the one hand, and, on the other, between the domination of a traditional elite in English society and a voluntaristic, unintegrated education mainly aimed at character formation. The hypothesis could be expressed as follows: 'The rate of administrative bureaucratization will determine the degree of rationality in education.' Since France made the educational transition to specialised expert training faster than England, it should be possible to identify for the relevant period a more rational form of social and ideological domination in the former than in the latter. The fact that France passed from type B to type C should, according to Weber, have implied the successful overthrowal of a previously dominant group and of its supportive philosophy by a new group and its ideology. Thus it should be possible to detect an older traditional structure of domination whose members endorsed non-rational values and its replacement by a more recent bureaucratic structure associated with rationalistic values. In fact, the dominant religious group under the *ancien régime*, whose traditional values predominated in education, was displaced in the Napoleonic state by a bourgeois bureaucracy adapting the eighteenth-century rationalism to an ideal of administrative efficiency. The endurance in England of educational type B would imply the continuation of a traditional structure of domination and its non-rational values. This continuity is not synonymous with the absence of any challenge to the control or the content of education; it merely signifies that during the period studied no challenge proved successful against church control and against the religious-traditional values implied in the ideal of the Christian gentleman.

However, the processes by which domination over education is removed from the church and this institution becomes integrated with the bureaucratic structure are left unclear. Indeed Weber himself acknowledged that in establishing the compatibility between bureaucratic structure and specialised education he has not provided a complete theory of educational change. 'Behind all the present discussions of the foundations of the educational system, the struggle of the "specialised type of man" against the older type of "cultivated man" *is hidden at some decisive point*.'[6] The essential aspect of educational change is thus to be found in conflict, in 'struggle' between groups and between ideas. Any attempt to explain educational differences between England and France must therefore be preceded by an account of the relations of stability or change in the domination of groups and of the value systems associated with them.

Weber attributes institutional change to the interplay of groups and ideas within a social structure. The contribution of both these elements is regarded as partially independent – their relationship to one another is thus one of interaction. Such interaction is inextricably bound up with a process of struggle for domination[7] in society. Either a dominant group and its ideology seek to retain their position by controlling other groups and by attempting to eradicate their ideas through the universalisation of its own. Or alternatively the supremacy of a dominant group and its ideology is being successfully challenged by competing groups advancing different ideas. These alternatives are epitomised in Weber's contrast between the ancient Chinese and Indian societies, on the one hand, and that of ancient Palestine, on the other.

Various types of groups can achieve institutional domination – ranging from classes and status groups to political groupings, organisations and associations. Such groups may overlap and may be characterised as voluntary or compulsory, as communal or aggregate. This plurality negates the polarisation of conflict posited by Marx, as well as its uniquely economic content, and is therefore better able to account for the multiple forms of educational conflict. The essential characteristic of any group dominating an institution or a society is the possession of a monopoly. Hence the economically dominant class enjoys unique opportunities for capital accumulation by virtue of its monopoly of property.

It is the most elemental economic fact that the way in which the disposition over material property is distributed among a plurality of people meeting competitively in the market for the purpose of exchange, in itself creates specific life chances. According to the law of marginal utility this mode of distribution excludes the non-owners from competing for highly valued goods; it favours the owners and, in fact, gives them a monopoly to acquire such goods. Other things being equal, this mode of distribution monopolizes the opportunities for profitable deals for all those who, provided with goods, do not necessarily have to exchange them.[8]

However, property is merely a special case of the acquisition of a monopoly in an economic context.

Monopoly exists as soon as a group imposes a closed-door policy, within variable limits, in order to enhance its opportunities as against those on the outside ... The idea of monopoly, therefore, should not be taken in the current polemical and ideological sense, as used by those whose purpose is to discredit a certain form of capitalism. For the trend toward monopoly is not bound up with any particular historical economic and social structure.[9]

The very existence of status groups is dependent upon the monopolisation of attributes, albeit valued on irrational grounds, which confer upon their members the exclusive right to social honour.

Stratification by status goes hand in hand with monopolization of ideal and material goods or opportunities, in a manner we have come to know as typical. Besides the specific status honour, which always rests upon distance and exclusiveness, we find all sorts of material monopolies . . . This monopolization occurs positively when the status group is exclusively entitled to own and manage them; and negatively when, in order to maintain its specific way of life, the status group must *not* own and manage them.[10]

Similarly the very definition given to a state is based upon a monopoly: 'a compulsory political association with a continuous organization will be called a "State" if, and in so far as, its administrative staff successfully claims the monopolization of the legitimate use of physical force in the enforcement of its authority'.[11] In all these cases, the monopoly on which domination is based should be distinguished from further monopolisation derived from it. Domination unavoidably results in constraints and the counterpart of the monopoly enjoyed by some is the exclusion of others. The imposition of constraints and the enforcement of exclusion are the objects of social control, which is, when unsuccessful, the source of conflict in relation to specific institutions. In both cases, conflict may consist in either communal or societal action.[12]

However, while monopolies can be successfully exploited through reliance on force, domination will be more secure and more efficient if a general justifying ideology can be invoked by the dominating and accepted by the subordinate group, thus transforming power into authority. In fact Weber uses the terms 'authority' and 'domination' as largely synonymous and differentiates them from the power arising from an unlegitimated monopoly.[13]

Thus Weber emphasized both the organization that implements and the beliefs that sustain a given system . . . His study of domination stresses the importance of group formation *and* of beliefs. In Weber's view beliefs in the legitimacy of a system of domination are not merely philosophical matters. They can contribute to the stability of an authoritarian relationship, and they indicate very real differences between systems of domination.[14]

Not only can ideas serve to consolidate domination, but also to further the assertive claims of a competing group.

Each society is a composite of positively or negatively privileged status groups that are engaged in efforts to preserve or enhance their present 'style of life' by means of social distance and exclusiveness and by the monopolisation of economic opportunities. In order to understand the stability and dynamics of a society we should attempt to understand these efforts in relation to the ideas and values that are prevalent in the society; or, conversely, for every given idea or value that we observe we should seek out the status group whose material and ideal way of life it seeks to enhance.[15]

While they are far from being determined by material environment, the ideas adopted by a particular group are influenced by it and are necessarily related to the interests at stake. As groups compete for domination either in society or over an institution, so their ideas clash and any universally accepted ethic merely represents the outcome of past struggles.

Thus conflict is the obverse aspect of control over a social institution and both are part of a continuous process of interplay between the interests and ideas of competing groups, summarised as follows:

ASSERTION	TRANSITION	DOMINATION	ASSERTION
Status group A & its ideas compete with other groups & their ideas →	Status group A gains power & seeks to institu- tionalise its ideas →	Status group A becomes dominant & its ideas uni- versal →	Status group B & its ideas challenge dominant group A and its ideas

This table is an over-simplification of the process, since assertion does not necessarily culminate in domination, which in turn can prove remarkably stable and resist counter-assertion for centuries. Similarly periods of transition may be very long.

While retrospectively the interplay of groups and their ideas competing for domination over educational institutions can be reconstructed on the basis of Weber's notions of monopoly and ideology, these do not allow for any predictive statement and do not constitute a theory of change. His historical studies describe the unfolding of conflict culminating either in the overthrowal or in the continuation of domination over an institution. A theory with predictive power would need to specify and quantify the main prerequisites of successful domination and successful assertion. In the forthcoming pages it is hoped to supplement the elements supplied by Weber to specify more closely the factors involved in successful domination and assertion.

This can perhaps be seen as a mid-way stage between his formulation and the development of a predictive theory of institutional change.

DOMINATION AND ASSERTION: TOWARDS A THEORY OF EDUCATIONAL CHANGE

In seeking to extend Weber's insights into institutional change it should be borne in mind that at the macro level this is inextricably related to a study of the structural relations of education. This derives from the simple, but often forgotten, fact that education is never a completely autonomous social institution – it is always, to the best of our knowledge, related to at least one other. The earliest types of informal instruction were integrated with the family and tribe while the emergence of formal education throughout Europe involved its integration with religion. This means that it would be exceptional to detect in history, a group dominating education which itself was strictly 'educational' – in the same sense that at different times the groups dominating religious, legal and military institutions have often been the clerical, juridical and army elites. The very fact that the concept of giving education 'for its own sake' emerged so late in European history witnesses to its perpetual subordination to other social institutions and to the aims of their dominant groups.

As education is never completely autonomous, a theory of educational change of necessity goes beyond this institution to the extent to which it is integrated with others. Similarly, the groups dominating education will not be narrowly educational any more than will those which challenge them through assertion. While the main concern is to specify the factors ensuring the domination of a group over the social institution of education, these may at times coincide, as they do in modern England and France, with those required for social domination – defined as domination over the main institutions of society. However, when education is semi-integrated (largely unarticulated with various such institutions), the group dominating it will tend to be distinct from the ruling group in society. Correspondingly, assertion need not then involve attacks upon the ruling group and may even be aided by it, where the goals of assertion are perceived as approximating more closely to national needs than those of the dominant group.

It should also be remembered that the notion of an educational system, involving hierarchically-integrated levels of institutions, is comparatively recent. Before such a system is established, domination may be pluralistic, different groups controlling different levels or types of institutions. In this case various levels may be integrated with a diversity of social institutions, and assertive groups may only attempt to gain control over one rather than all levels. Thus it is only when an integrated educational system exists that domination must be unitary, although of course a single group can control all levels without these being regarded as operating as a system in the usual sense of the word.

In this brief discussion of education and its relationships to social structure, the area in which analyses of domination and assertion are applicable has also been defined. As has been seen, when an educational system exists, the dominant group must be unitary and, when the factors required for its domination coincide with those ensuring social domination, the analysis of educational control in these terms ceases to be relevant. In other words, when an educational system becomes integrated with the state, it is irrelevant to discuss domination and assertion since both activities become subsumed under a broader model of changes in political power of different groups and parties.

It must be underlined that the possession of political power by a group is not synonomous with their educational domination, since education may not be integrated to the state for two major reasons. Firstly, the dominant political group may see no advantages to be derived from controlling education. They may either view the education dispensed by a separate dominant group as perfectly adequate – as most political elites during the middle ages considered instruction given by the church – or they may be willing to allow educational control to be decided by the free interplay of domination and assertion. There are even certain advantages accruing to the state from the latter policy in that competing groups may considerably extend educational provisions in the process, and do so from their own funds. Secondly, the political elite may seek to integrate education with the state, but lack the facilities required for deposing the existing dominant group and constituting a state educational system. Therefore it is only upon the emergence of a state system of education that changes in political power subsume those of domination and assertion.

Following Max Weber, domination in this context has been defined as the opportunity to have a command concerning education obeyed by a given group of persons. By assertion is meant the sum of efforts made by another group – denied the opportunity of making commands concerning education – to challenge the existing form of domination. The dominant group is successful both when it remains unchallenged and when it overcomes challenge. Although the former situation is characterised by the absence of educational conflict, it is not necessarily identical with the unanimity described as consensus. Prolonged educational stability corresponds to the lasting domination of a particular group and the successful resolution of conflict in its favour. While minor forms of educational change may be initiated independently by the dominant group in accordance with its changing interests, major changes in goals and content result from the conflict between dominant and assertive groups – either through the success of the latter or the concessions gained from the former. However, the changing structural relations of education with other social institutions usually results from successful assertion against an existing form of domination. It is therefore by investigating the main prerequisites of successful domination and assertion that one can account for educational stability and change at the macro-sociological level.

A group whose domination over education proves lasting is characterised by three main factors. Firstly the dominant group must possess a *monopoly* of certain scarce resources in society, scarcity being relative to time and place. Monopoly is used in the Weberian sense and does not carry exclusively economic connotations. When education is a semi-integrated institution, this monopoly will be connected with owning and providing the facilities – material and human – for imparting instruction. However when education is multiply integrated with other social institutions, the resources monopolised will tend to become less specifically educational, but it is not until an educational system is fully integrated with the state that the monopoly requisite for its domination coincides with the legal right of control vested in the governing political group or party. Here, of course, this group will not own or provide educational facilities either corporately or through its members.

The second feature of successful domination is that, for monopolies to be fully advantageous, they must be allied to *constraints* ensuring the acquiescence of other groups to their existence and exercise. Such constraints may range from economic or legal sanctions to the use of coercive or repressive force. While these constraints need not be specifically educational their consequences reinforce domination over this institution. Again, the more integrated education is with other social institutions, the more general will be the types of constraints employed. The nature of the dominant group's monopoly will act as a predisposition towards the types of negative sanctions available and employed. Hence a church, unless established, will tend to rely solely on symbolic constraints to protect its educational domination. Some constraints, however, are common or available to all dominant groups and these are constituted by the ways in which educational institutions themselves can be manipulated. Discrimination against other groups or their exclusion from education, the use of instruction for indoctrination and the imposition of non-academic requirements for entry or examination can all serve to consolidate the dominance of a particular group by promoting its supporters and penalising its potential critics or those likely to challenge its monopoly. Legal constraints will only be available to those groups either whose educational dominance is sanctioned by the state or who themselves also control the state machinery. While methods of constraint need not actually be employed, it is unlikely for a group to remain dominant over time without at least threatening to use such methods. It would be even more rare to identify a dominant group not manipulating the educational institutions to reinforce its own position.

Thirdly, a complementary *ideology* legitimating the monopolistic claims of a group and justifying pressures for the maintenance of its domination is indispensable to gaining the willing conformity rather than the forced compliance of others. It is always in the interest of the dominant group to gain willing collaboration from those they dominate, since this ensures greater efficiency as well as stability. The universalisation of an ideology will transform a system of control by power into one of legitimate authority. A dominant group can be legitimated by reference to any type of ideology but, following Weber, the justifying ideas endorsed by a dominant group will be consonant with its interests, and with its monopoly. The very fact of controlling the educational institutions facilitates the dissemination of an ideology – thus in the same way that the church had taught the Catechism in schools, so Napoleon placed the Imperial Catechism on the curricula. It is, however, rare to find a newly dominant group relying solely on this method of dissemination since its results are too long-term. It was the realisation of this which led the French revolutionary educationalists to stress the importance of *fêtes nationales*, meetings at which Republican philosophy could be spread to adults in the provinces. Ideologies presenting a dominant group as the embodiment of national interests, class interests or religious interests buttress its position. They either replace the use of constraint or, if they are less successful, justify its employment.

B

In outlining the three factors, *Monopoly*, *Constraint* and *Ideology*, an attempt has been made to specify the necessary conditions for successful institutional domination. Successful domination is measured by the ability to resolve conflict or quell opposition, and therefore to endure. While only monopoly appears essential to the *achievement* of domination, constraint and ideology seem vital to its *maintenance*. Indeed, the latter two elements may in some cases only be developed or acquired after a group has become dominant. For example, it is rare for a status group to possess any formal powers of constraint until it has established its control over a particular institution. Similarly other groups, such as military ones, do not develop or at least refine an idology until domination has been established. Monopoly is also related to the other two factors in that it always affects, though it does not determine, the forms taken by constraint and ideology, and in turn is supported by them. In addition, constraint and ideology will tend to be mutually reinforcing where the dominant group is successful – the type of constraints employed will be compatible with at least the fundamental ideological postulates, while the ideology will seek to legitimate not only the dominant group but also the methods it uses or may have to use to maintain its position. These relationships can be expressed as follows:

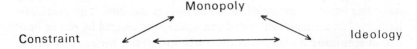

It should be stressed that the connecting lines represent influences, not determinants, and that these factors, even when interrelated in this ideal form, are probably far from constituting the sufficient conditions of successful institutional domination.

Conflict over a social institution need not prove ultimately damaging to the dominant group or modify the targets of its policy. Constraints and ideological pressures may be sufficient to contain or eliminate opposition. If they fail to do so, changed institutional relations will be the outcome. Obviously, change within the institution is not always produced by inter-group conflict within a society; it may be prompted by forces external to it, or by natural phenomena, or be initiated independently by the dominant group itself. However excluding these cases, institutional change will be effected through conflict with an opposing group possessing certain attributes. Again, only the necessary conditions of successful assertion are advanced. Any form of assertion by a group implies a position of subordination within the institution concerned – successful challengers to the dominant group must overcome the three factors on which its supremacy rests. To assert itself successfully the subordinate group must engage in activities *instrumental* in devaluing the existing monopoly, either by restricting it or replacing it. Thus the instrumental activities of an assertive group are defined as the sum of actions in which it can or does engage to devalue the particular monopoly on which domination is based in the given institution. This devaluation can take two forms, substitution or restriction. The former consists in replacing the scarce resource which the institutionally dominant group monopolised by an alternative resource or by discovering another source of supply. Where education is a semi-integrated social institution, and consequently the dominant group's monopoly is largely educational, this substitution takes the form of providing alternative educational facilities. Thus the creation of such establishments as denominational schools, commercial schools and mechanics' institutes challenged the previous monopoly of the established church. Similarly the development of the Lancastrian teaching method, enabling more pupils to be educated at a lower *per capita* cost, represented a new supply of a previously scarce resource – teaching staff. Where education is highly integrated with other institutions, and consequently the dominant group's monopoly is largely supra-educational, substitution can occur in a greater variety of fields, according to the area in which this monopoly is located.

However, instrumental activities alone do not suffice for successful assertion. A group must not only engage in instrumental activities, but should also possess *bargaining power* in order to be successful. Bargaining power is an alternative to the use of violence and yet implies a degree of organisation which would make revolt effective if reform were denied. The prospect of success or failure is related to the two components of bargaining power – numerical strength and organisation. The conjuncture of those two elements is indispensable to the success of pressures upon the dominant group, in order to make it relinquish some of the advantages related to its position. Although bargaining power is dependent upon the instrumental character of the subordinate group's activities, it cannot be deduced from this, as it involves both the possibility and the desire for concerted action. Sufficiently strong social control would prevent the development of either factor, constraint would limit the possibility and ideology would eradicate the desire. Thus, where the assertive group has limited numbers willing to engage in concerted action and a low degree of internal organisation, while the dominant group has a strong and highly organised portion of its membership engaged in applying constraints, domination is likely to prove stable. Numerical and organisational variations in both groups partially account for their relative degrees of success. However, this interplay is influenced by the alliances either group can form in order to acquire wider support for either domination or assertion.

Finally, the ideology of the dominant group has to be challenged and replaced by a separate philosophy legitimating the claims and activities of the assertive group. Hence this new *ideology* must be both a negation and an affirmation.

This is necessary because goal-objectives and purposes must be defined and theo-retically justified. Such justification involves attacking counter-ideologies, counter-ing social control mechanisms which may be enforced against it, within the collectivity it requires competing with alternative rival interpretations of the problem situation.[16]

The general acceptance of an ideology by an assertive group will be related to its interests and will influence the form taken by its instru-mental activities, as well as the degree of intensity of its members' participation. Like that of the dominant group, the assertive ideology can be derived either from the supernatural or natural premises. Thus, in both England and France, the educational domination of the church was supported by a religious ideology, while the assertive activities of the competing group advanced a secular philosophy – enlightenment in France, Utilitarianism in England.

These three factors, *Instrumental Activities*, *Bargaining Power* and *Ideology* are necessary, rather than sufficient, conditions of successful assertion. While some advantages may be gained from the existence of the first two, ideology is required both to inform the movement of its goals and to provide its members with a justification for the use of the bargaining power at their disposal. By definition the development of an assertive ideology implies a recession in the philosophy informing social control, since this means that the latter is no longer universal. Such a recession results in a weakening of constraint, as the legiti-mation of assertive bargaining power strengthens opposition to the monopolistic group. Thus in assertive action instrumental activities, bargaining power and supportive ideology are related as follows:

Instrumental Activities

Bargaining Power   Ideology

The outcome of a confrontation between a dominant and an assertive group depends upon the balance of factors present on both sides. There are two limiting cases: an unchallenged domination under which none of the factors of assertion exist in other groups and, on the other hand, a situation in which the three factors of domination are matched by the three factors of assertion. These extremes correspond to institutional stability and overt institutional conflict. They also probably represent the limits of the predictive power deriving from this preliminary attempt at a theory of educational change. When only some of the factors of successful assertion exist, for instance when the dominant group dependent on a particular monopoly possesses both means of constraint and an ideology, while the assertive group has only ideology, the outcome is clearly in favour of the former. Organised conflict rather than unco-ordinated violence will result from a situation in which the three factors of domination are confronted by those of assertion. Such phases can be illustrated as shown below.

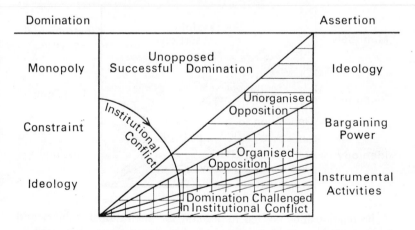

When institutional domination is challenged, the first factor to weaken is ideology. This is self-evident since the existence of such a challenge implies that the dominant ideology no longer provides a universally acceptable legitimation of the *status quo*. However, the full

crystallisation of an alternative ideology need neither precede nor accompany this negation; while there may be a time-lag, this will not be a long one, since assertive activities require justification, both to those who engage in them and to onlookers. The second respect in which domination weakens is the power of constraint, which is no longer feared and increasingly challenged once its use does not appear to be legitimate. This stage cannot be reached unless the assertive group possesses a degree of organisation, enabling it effectively to use its bargaining power. The activities of the subordinate group must be instrumental in severely devaluing the monopoly of the dominant group for changes in institutional relations to take place. The final phase of this challenge is marked by a modification in the relationship between the monopoly of the dominant group and its institutional position. Depending on the restrictive or substitutive character of the assertive group's instrumental activities, their success will consist in either reducing or replacing this institutional domination. In the former case educational change will result, in the latter a change in institutional relations is also likely to occur. These relationships can be expressed as shown below.

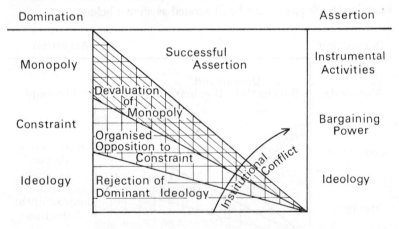

The relationships posited to account for institutional stability and change constitute no more than hypotheses requiring to be tested by reference to events. Thus their adequacy will be assessed in relation to their ability to account for the differences between the development of education in England and France. Even if this study appears to corroborate the initial hypotheses, it would do nothing to establish group conflict for educational domination as the universal cause of educational change. Such development may not be a unitary variable – the factors accounting for it may differ with time and place. Even as concerns the countries and the period studied, limitations inseparable from investigation of the past will necessarily affect the material considered relevant or extraneous. As has already been stressed, this discussion of domination and assertion, in only seeking to outline necessary, not sufficient, conditions for educational change, is far from constituting a fully predictive set of hypotheses. It cannot be said to do more than to provide a preliminary interpretation rather than explanation of educational change at the macro-sociological level.

THE IMPORTANCE OF EDUCATIONAL IDEOLOGIES

Even if it were assumed that the factors mentioned above are indeed the necessary conditions for stability and change in educational domination, special attention would have to be paid to *ideology* to account for the form and content given to education by the dominant group. As Clarke has indicated, the use of this term is peculiarly appropriate in the field of education –

If the word 'ideology' had not already been ruined for any precise use (having been employed so much recently as equivalent to 'creed' or 'doctrine'), we might cite English writers on education as illuminating examples of it. For strictly, it would seem, the word applies to exactly this phenomenon – the undetected influence upon what is supposed to be generalised thought of the interests and attitudes of national, class and other groups by which the writer or thinker has been formed.[17]

However, the interests of a dominant group could be served and its position maintained by a variety of internal institutional arrangements and practices and the actual choice between them is not dictated by the nature of the group's monopoly. Similarly the claims of an assertive group in respect to the content of educational reform advocated are not fully determined by the nature of their instrumental activities. In both cases it is by reference to the ideologies held that the more specific aspects of educational policy are defined.

Thus ideology is not only a component of successful domination and assertion, but also defines the means by which educational goals can be implemented. Therefore it not only functions as a source of legitimation for domination and assertion, but also as a wider educational philosophy for the dominant and assertive group. Bearing these points in mind, the ideology adopted by either type of group can be said to serve three distinct purposes – those of *legitimation*, *negation* and *specification*. While each of these may not be stressed to the same degree, they must be consistently related to one another within a given educational ideology.

As has been seen, both the dominant and assertive groups must seek to *legitimate* their position to their followers as well as to a wider audience. This involves an appeal to certain principles consonant with the interests the group represents, but not derived automatically from them. Secondly, the same principles must be extended to constitute a *negation* of the sources of legitimation advanced by other groups. With an assertive group this happens immediately, since the claims of domination must be undermined before challenge is possible. It is because of this that assertive groups in their earliest stages may concentrate almost exclusively upon negation, that is upon unmasking or condemning the interests concealed by the ideology of the dominant group. However, a group whose domination has been unopposed over a long period may only begin to develop this negative function in proportion to the attacks launched at it. This is why the typical response of a well-established dominant group to new assertion is an immediate reformulation of its ideology, intended to strengthen its source of legitimation by extending it to negate the claims of other groups. Thirdly, a *specification* of the blueprint to be implemented within educational establishments, their goals, curricula and intake, must be derived from the same ideological principles.

This third purpose of ideology again means that the precise educational blueprint advocated by a group cannot be derived from its interests alone. Those interests neither dictate the exact content of the ideology adopted nor, after its adoption, do they determine the exact formulation of its educational programmes. Thus, in order to account for the educational institutions and practices corresponding to the domination of a particular group or advocated as part of an assertive programme, the content of its ideology must be fully analysed. Consequently the following sections of this book are divided between analyses of relationships of domination and assertion in primary, secondary and higher education in England and France, in order to interpret changes in the structural relations of education and, on the other hand, outlines of the ideologies advanced by both types of groups, to help account for the types of internal educational change initiated.

3. Change in English Primary Education

Primary education in nineteenth-century England was a semi-integrated institution articulated mainly with the Anglican church. Furthermore it was small in quantity and low in quality, the church at this time seeing little need to increase its enrolment or to extend its curricula beyond biblical teaching. With the exception of dame schools and schools of industry, the majority of educational resources at this level, represented by the parish schools and by the endowments to charity schools, were under religious control. However, the church's neglect of elementary instruction as compared with secondary and higher – corresponding to the prevalent acceptance that the poor had no need of tuition – meant that no efforts were devoted to developing supportive constraints. If the Anglican church was dominant during this period, it was only because it was unopposed.

Opposition grew throughout the latter part of the eighteenth century from two sources, both related to the industrialisation/urbanisation process. On the one hand, the spread of dissent in urban communities strengthened a group to whom the content of Anglican instruction was doctrinally unacceptable. On the other, the growing differentiation of the middle from the working classes extended a group to whom such instruction was impractical from the viewpoint of prospective employment.

Since primary education was semi-integrated, both dissenters and secularists could create and operate educational establishments, thus challenging the domination of the Anglican church. The use of voluntary subscriptions and the monitorial method represented new supplies of educational resources which enabled both groups to become instrumental in devaluing the Anglican monopoly. Thus the integration between primary education and the established church was weakened by being subdivided between competing denominations, whose philosophies were unidentical. However, the unintended consequence of such assertive activities was the stimulation of Anglican efforts to retain control at this level. The foundation of the National Society for Promoting the Education of the Poor represented such an attempt to defend Anglican domination. Two years later the launching of the British and Foreign Schools Society for 'undenominational' or non-Anglican schooling indicated that dissenters and radicals had acquired the requisite organisational bargaining power to support their instrumental activities in devaluing the monopoly of the established church.

The religious difficulty whereby both Anglicans and dissenters resisted state intervention for different reasons constituted a refusal to integrate primary education with the political structure. As state action was limited to the enforcement of parity between the established church and the denominations by the voluntaristic principle of financing schools through the two rival societies, it left the question of domination to be determined by success or failure in controlling educational facilities.

In the first half of the nineteenth century the middle class gradually acquired the elements for successful domination over primary education. It partially devalued the previous Anglican monopoly of educational facilities by creating its own alternative networks of establishments. Its economic wealth permitted the acquisition of buildings and the recruitment of teaching staff. Employers had effective control over the type and amount of instruction which working children could receive – a situation institutionalised by the Factory Act of 1833. Within primary schools themselves, instruction could be used for indoctrination in a particular economic and social philosophy. Lastly, the middle class had an economic philosophy in classical economic theory, a social philosophy in Utilitarianism and a religious philosophy in dissent. Despite the fundamental incompatibility between the latter two, their supporters coalesced in advocating social control through education and both philosophies were used to legitimate it.

However, while the middle class possessed the factors necessary for successful assertion, its progress towards displacing the dominant Anglican group was directly proportional to the facilities and funds made available to increase instrumental activities of substitution. Two main factors appear to have limited progress after the Reform Bill. Firstly, the unwillingness of the entrepreneurial element to reduce profits by taking full advantage of the educational provisions in the Factory Act of 1833. Secondly, the growing distrust with which its dissenting and radical elements alike were viewed by the working class after the First Reform Bill. Such distrust had the double effect of preventing middle-class takeover of facilities provided by the working class (as had been the case with the mechanics' institutes) and also of turning the leaders of this class away from the provisions made for them, particularly in adult education.

Increasingly working-class activities in elementary education had to be viewed as a distinct form of assertion, directed against radical and dissenting schools as much as against Anglican. Chartism and early socialism supplied a refutation of classical economics and a legitimation of assertive action. The existence of such ideologies was indicative of the failure encountered by the middle class in attempting to universalise its source of educational legitimation. However, the element of bargaining power was lacking in education as in politics. While the signing of petitions and the joining of demonstrations indicated the numerical strength of working-class assertion, its organisational deficiencies were only to be overcome much later.

Thus, towards the middle of the nineteenth century, an unstable situation had developed, representing a new balance of forces. The middle class still fought to depose Anglican domination, without however being able to make dramatic interventions to further devalue the church's monopoly. The voluntaristic principle had largely introduced a situation of stalemate between the two parties. At the same time, the disenchantment of the working class and its emergence as an assertive group in its own right constituted a major limitation on middle-class advance, both through reducing its facilities and discrediting its ideology.

THE MIDDLE CLASS AND PRIMARY EDUCATION

Since the church presented stations in life as pre-ordained, the education it dispensed was socially conservative, but as elementary instruction was not highly valued by the political elite, no attempts were made to integrate it with the state and assume parliamentary control over it. The semi-integrated character of education meant that the scarce resources monopolised by the educationally dominant group, the Anglican church, consisted in the exclusive possession of facilities such as buildings and staff. As competing denominations, emphasising scriptural knowledge, realised the need for developing their own schools, they gradually could and did acquire similar facilities. The utilisation of chapels for Sunday school gave place to the provision of special buildings.[1] This development of dissenting education gave the middle class an opportunity to influence popular instruction in direct proportion to its educational resources, material and human. Similarly, when another section of the middle class, the Philosophical Radicals, sought to institute secular schooling, their schools were established by voluntary subscriptions. This double incursion of the middle class in primary education challenged the former Anglican domination by encroaching on its monopoly. While control over primary establishments was no longer unitary, this did not imply that the content of instruction was any less conservative, although the ideologies seeking to legitimate it became more diverse. Dissenters, like Anglicans, justified the *status quo* by reference to divine will, whereas radicals found in classical economics a new philosophical justification for the perpetuation of social inequalities.

The context in which dissent and secularism began to challenge Anglican domination over primary instruction was one of very limited educational provisions. At the turn of the century, this instruction was given by dame schools, common day schools, charity schools, established by religious philanthropists, and schools of industry. While the first two provided a rudimentary instruction for those who could afford small fees, it was calculated in 1792 that a further 40,000[2] gained some tuition in charity schools. The first attempted estimate of attendance rates for primary schools was provided in Henry Brougham's Royal Commission in 1820. This calculated that one child in fifteen of the appropriate age was undergoing primary schooling – one discovery among many which led him to declare England the worst educated country in Europe.[3] This numerically inadequate instruction mirrored the theme of training the poor to poverty. The people were handicapped by long working hours, lack of schools and cost of tuition. Moreover, the irrelevance of the curricula to their future occupational activities, and their own inability to alter this, acted as further deterrents. None of the elements limiting working-class entrance had been considered undesirable by the aristocracy, who viewed any extension of education among the workers as socially disruptive. Indeed the dominant educational theme of the landed aristocracy was that exclusion represented the best form of constraint. This postulate was clearly reflected in a constant opposition to state education in later years and a steady rejection of measures intended to increase the schooling of the people. This accounts for the enduring semi-integrated character of primary education over which the domination of the church in the early nineteenth century received no state support in the form of legal constraints. It also helps to explain the greater ease with which assertive forces developed at this level than at secondary and higher.

Initially there was little impetus for educational reform at the beginning of the century, except on denominational grounds of providing primary schooling in order to propagate biblical teaching, which in turn stimulated greater Anglican activity at this level. It was estimated in 1803 that 800,000 children were catered for by Sunday schools.[4] However, the growth of the Sunday school movements often led to the closing of day schools and released child labour.[5] Parliament explicitly opposed any addition to purely scriptural teaching, on the grounds that schooling would make the poor contemptuous of their lot and would thus threaten social stability. Criticism was meted even to the predominantly religious education proposed by Hannah More, in whose Anglican schools 'they learn on weekdays such coarse works as may fit them for servants. I allow no writing for the poor, my object is not to make them fanatics, but to train the lower orders to industry and piety'.[6] Parliamentary bills which might have conceded a modicum of education were dismissed as contentious.

While the political elite positively dissociated itself from educational extension, the church was forced to engage in greater educational activity by the increasing pressures of dissent. The spread of industrialisation was accompanied by a strengthening of non-conformism, and the church of England, fearing the growth of dissenter participation in education, was for the first time on the defensive. It condoned the religious and social indoctrination of Hannah More, considered more effective than exclusion not only from the point of view of religious orthodoxy, but also of social stability. The increasing use made of the monitorial method in dissenting and secular schools enabled them to augment their intake and constituted an additional threat to Anglican educational domination. As a response, the National Society for Promoting the Education of the Poor in the Principles of the Established Church throughout England and Wales was created in 1811. Not only was this creation prompted by a concern for religious orthodoxy, it also reflected the Whig Party's growing distrust in the efficacy of repression. The education which was to be dispensed would emphasise neither knowledge nor utility, but instead 'it may suffice to teach the generality on an economical plan to read their Bible and understand the doctrines of our holy religion'.[7] Implicit in this new approach was a belief in the formative power of education, a belief that social control is more easily effected by providing an appropriate form of schooling fitting individuals for their future station in life rather than by the crude method of total deprivation.

Increased Anglican activity in primary education was paralleled by greater middle-class efforts, represented by the foundation in 1813 of the British and Foreign School Society, an extension of the Royal Lancastrian Society, devoted to popular education. This institution reflected both the utilitarian postulate that the workers' discontent resulted from their lack of enlightenment and the industrial demands for an increasingly literate labour force. This joint concern indicates from the start the indissoluble connection between the industrial interests and the social philosophy of the middle class. The content of the instruction dispensed by the British and Foreign School Society was adapted to its aims in devoting a greater part of the curriculum to useful accomplishments – geometry, arithmetic and geography – and in departing from the traditional emphasis on religious tuition. It was this deviation from biblical teaching which led to the schism between the quaker and the secularist trends in the society, ultimately leaving the movement in dissenting hands and destroying the West London Lancastrian Association.[8] The education provided was intentionally cheap, in order to minimise the middle-class investments in its creation and working-class expenditure in fees. Low costs could be maintained thanks to the utilisation of the monitorial system,[9] based on a low teacher – pupil ratio.

The gradual impoverishment of skilled workers brought about by industrialisation made it increasingly important to appeal to their reason, if property were to be respected. First attempts made in this direction depended upon parliamentary action. Successive bills were introduced with Whig support, advocating for the first time universal, compulsory and cheap elementary education for the people. The introduction in 1807 of Samuel Whitbread's Parochial Schools Bill represented Whig tolerance of the liberal group in their midst and intended to secure popular support by making concessions to working-class educational aspirations. After its failure, a similar bill was presented by Brougham in 1820 and, although endeavouring to meet Anglican objections, nevertheless advocated a state system. The rejection of this proposal by Parliament reflected pressures of the aristocracy and the church, who feared secular power in education, and that of the middle class, who feared the reduction of working hours. (The latter reflected the conflict between Utilitarian philosophy and the immediate interests of factory owners.)

This parliamentary failure, coupled with increased working-class discontent in 1815-17, led to a second series of attempts designed to have a direct impact on the working class by adapting existing forms of adult education rather than creating new elementary schools for workers' children. A double endeavour was made to solve the problem of providing elementary education for working adults. The large diffusion of mechanics' institutes[10] after 1823 represented the extent of working-class self-help, but at the same time provided a ready platform and a captive audience for middle-class intervention. Not only were considerable funds supplied by industry for this purpose, but lecturers were increasingly drawn from the middle class, thus gradually superseding working-class control of institutes. Free discussion was replaced by tuition in classical economies, which inculcated the ideological postulates of the middle class. Economic orthodoxy was strictly preserved, and early socialist reinterpretations rejected, as the pressures to prevent Hodgskin lecturing illustrate.[11] The partial success of this ideological control was shown by the widespread acceptance of classical economics and its endorsement as being favourable to the working class:

The political economists are the great enlighteners of the people. Look at their works from the time of the great man Adam Smith . . . and see if they have not, all along, deprecated everything which was in any way calculated to do injury to the people; see if they have not been pre-eminently the advocates for increasing the knowledge of the working classes in every possible way, and then let any man say, if he can, that they have not been as pre-eminently the best friends of these classes.[12]

However, this acceptance of classical economic tenets was challenged by the growing proliferation of radical publications, addressing themselves to the working class.[13] The reaction to this attack was the formation of the Society for the Diffusion of Useful Knowledge in 1826.[14] Supported by Whigs and Utilitarians, this society was devoted firstly to the propagation of abstract scientific treaties and latterly to the diffusion of pamphlets refuting the claims of labour against capital.[15]

Until the First Reform Bill, the tone of middle-class interventions in primary education was protective, preventive and paternalistic. Such interventions were prompted by the desire to maintain industrial advantages, while at the same time ensuring working-class political support. Moreover, these attempts were necessarily limited by the context of an economic approach to social policy: the cost of Poor Law Relief was considered as a financial liability and stimulating workers' self-help was a form of indirect saving. Prior to 1832, the efforts made to persuade the working class that their interests coincided with those of the middle class were largely successful, as was evidenced by popular participation in the campaign for enfranchisement. The passing of the First Reform Bill, conferring the vote on the middle class and denying it to the working class because of the property qualifications, brought about a political realignment which influenced educational policies. The disenchantment of the working class extended to middle-class educational ideology, whose content was questioned from then on and increasingly rejected as contrary to the workers' interests. Conversely the middle class displayed a gradual disengagement from radical policies and activities, after its political ambitions had been fulfilled in 1832. The only principle to which they remained attached was the connection postulated by Utilitarianism between popular ignorance and the danger of social unrest.

The compromise between the ebbing radicalism of the middle class and the increasing militancy of the working class crystallised around the debate on the Ten Hours Bill. The Factory Act of 1833, without imposing any restrictions on adult working hours and therefore without challenging laissez-faire ideology, constituted the first legislation on compulsory school attendance – two hours of schooling per day became compulsory for child labour.[16] While factory inspectors were appointed to ensure the observance of such regulations, no funds were provided to organise this instruction and no provisions made to standardise its content. A more coherent attempt at social control was expressed in Parliament by Roebuck, who advocated a universal education system, since he recognised growing political unrest and thought instruction was the way 'this new force may be made efficient to the purpose of good, and how any of its probably mischievous results may be prevented'.[17] Thus recognition that the working class would unavoidably gain some access to political power increasingly led to an alliance between notions of formative education and of social control. In 1833, Roebuck stated the aims of his bill in claiming: 'I wish the people to be enlightened, that they may use the power well which they will inevitably obtain', but the underlying predominance of social control is clearly revealed by his enthusiasm for the Prussian educational system, with its distinctly authoritarian bias.[18]

The death of Bentham in 1832 and that of James Mill shortly afterwards, marked a new phase in middle-class ideology. As the working class increasingly joined the Chartist movement, the restraining power of classical economics was cast in doubt. The growth in working-class discontent and in its organised manifestations was met by the adjunction of religion to economics as an additional form of indoctrination. 'Political economy, though its object be to ascertain the means of increasing the wealth of nations, cannot accomplish its design, without at the same time regarding their happiness, and as its largest ingredient the cultivation of religion and morality'.[19] This implied a change in the ideology of the middle class which was contained in the writings of Kay-Shuttleworth. Economic indoctrination continued in the mechanics' institutes, but increasingly the secularist bias of Utilitarianism gave way to a religious approach to ethics. However, although such attitudes characterised the philosophical leaders of the middle class, the bulk of this class were more concerned with short-term profit than with the long-term prospect of social stability. Perhaps their largest miscalculation was that, although they had seen their own enfranchisement as imminent, that of the working class seemed distant and hence the need for preparatory and protective education appeared less imperative. Consequently the educational provisions under the Factory Acts were circumvented to a large extent and little improvement in the schooling of workers followed this legislation. Thus the contradiction between the requirements of industrial production and the prevailing middle-class ideology was exposed.

The First Reform Bill had not only given representation to industry, but also to dissent.

Primary education both lost and gained by the religious and denominational squabbles, characteristic of an age when Dissenters had become numerically formidable, but Churchmen were still unwilling to abate a jot of their privileges. On the one hand public money could not be obtained for education of the people, because the Church claimed that it must be spent under the aegis of the State religion, and the Dissenters would not agree to the use of public funds on such terms. On the other hand, the hostile denominations vied with each other in collecting money voluntarily for the erection of Day Schools and Sunday Schools.[20]

For all the activity displayed by denominational schools it could be argued that 'Religion, the keystone of education, is in this country the bar to progress'.[21] Thus dissent acted as the strongest brake on the formation of a state educational system, and instead accelerated the formation of a great denominational system, relatively independent of Parliament.

By imposing the voluntaristic principle through the allocation of state grants jointly to the National Society and to the British and Foreign Schools Society, Parliament forced an uneasy compromise upon the struggle for domination over primary education between the Anglican church and its dissenting or secularist opponents. This compromise solution implied the recognition that the middle class shared with the aristocracy and the established church a common interest in controlling working-class unrest and in propagating social quietism. Having gained important concessions from the Whig government after the First Reform Bill, the middle class no longer needed the political support of the working class and only required its compliance in industrial production. The introduction of the voluntaristic principle confirmed the semi-integrated character of primary education, which the continuation of the 'religious difficulty' was to perpetuate. The successful opposition of Anglicanism and dissent to state intervention during this period left the struggle for domination to be decided on the grounds of control over educational facilities. The Anglican monopoly of physical and human educational resources had been partially devalued through the substitutive activities of the dissenting and secularist middle class.

THE WORKING CLASS AND PRIMARY EDUCATION

At the end of the eighteenth century very little independent educational activity can be attributed to the working class, which – to form its own ideology – had first to free itself from the ideas thrust upon it by the Anglican church and the middle class. Until 1832 its support was largely given to the reformist aims of the latter, despite certain theoretical reservations which were the embryo of subsequent Chartist ideas. Although members of the two classes drew heavily upon the same pool of political and educational ideas, they arrived at diametrically different conclusions: the middle-class radicals through education would make the workers docile, the working-class leaders held that it would result in political emancipation.

During the period of the French Revolution the educational aspirations and political restlessness of urban workers were expressed in the activities of the London Corresponding Society and of similar bodies in the industrial towns of northern England. The originality of these organisations was that their membership consisted almost exclusively of artisans and skilled mechanics. Their main purpose was to educate these members and was allied to the quest for suffrage reform. It is in the latter context that Burke denounced the society in the House of Commons as 'the mother of all mischief'.[22] In 1799 all such societies were suppressed as imparting seditious instruction, but after the Napoleonic wars organisations pursuing similar ends, such as the Hampden clubs in northern England, resumed campaigns for parliamentary reform. Thus political and educational reformism were linked in working-class organisations from the start of the nineteenth century.

The mechanics' institutes differed from this pattern in concentrating initially on adult education for engineers and skilled workers. 'The men who made and mended the machines were the elite of the Industrial Revolution and its true bodyguard. They were better paid than their fellow workmen, they were on the average more intelligent, and they took the lead in educational movements'.[23] The content of the instruction given to them was predominantly scientific and technological, but with the gradual increase in middle-class control over such institutions, the curriculum became less vocational and included indoctrination in classical economics. This was unacceptable to early socialists such as Hodgskin who had written, 'Men had better be without education than be educated by their rulers; for then education is but the mere breaking in of the steer to the yoke'.[24] The progressive section of the working class tended to respond by substituting new less elitarian organisations which they could themselves manage. Although lack of funds often prevented them from fulfilling their aims, local schools were founded in urban areas and were integrated by the British Association for Promoting Co-operative Knowledge. The unstamped press championed by Cobbett provided a supply of information meant for the people and embodying a more radical interpretation of political events. Although the independent press threw doubts upon the wisdom of political coalition with the middle class, the overall attitudes before the First Reform Bill was an acceptance of this class as the friend of the people, and of their aims as universal and not particular. By not giving enfranchisement to the working class, the First Reform Bill changed the structure of political alliances and educational assertion. It demonstrated to the workers the exact limits of middle-class benevolence, teaching them to look to their own ranks for any improvements in their situation.

The post-reform era was characterised by the development of a separate educational ideology and new forms of political organisation for collective bargaining. The formation of the Grand National Consolidated Trade Union in 1834 sprang directly from disillusionment with the bill and although short-lived, due to deficiencies in its management, it fostered industrial agitation and stimulated the creation of the London Working Men's Association in 1835. Both these groups were organised on the national scale for the first time and were dedicated to class policy, if not class struggle. Both advocated the diffusion of education among their members, leading to the proliferation of halls of science and temples of instruction. The extent of this autonomous activity is illustrated by the £15,000 spent by Bristol parents on their children's education in the year 1840. Educational substitution was then given a new impetus by the wish to imbue the next generation with a new set of values.

The Chartist movement was the real expression of disenchantment with radical educationalists who were immediately dismissed as false friends of the people. Popular educationalists became involved in rebutting the interested claims of church, dissent, Tories, Whigs and radicals, showing that while the middle class might have accepted religious teaching for the masses, secular instruction was still at the forefront of the working-class ideal. In this period it was only in the Chartist schools and halls of science that secular and rationalist instruction was given. In the same spirit, educational material designed by the middle class for workers was dismissed and replaced by publications prepared and circulated by Chartists. While repression and the lack of united leadership caused the Chartist movement to decline after 1848, it had freed the English working class from ideas imposed upon it and endowed it with an ideology which, in the economic field, was to pass into trade unionism and, in the educational, into demands for secularism under a state system. Financial limitations had made its policy of substitution much weaker than that of the radical middle class as a method of devaluing the religious domination over primary education. Without being allied to a successful type of bargaining power, such instrumental activities represented self-help, not assertion. Thus the working class during this period had only acquired an educational ideology, but one whose importance lay in representing the only secular challenge to existing primary schools which, whether controlled by church or middle class, used religion to legitimate social control.

4. Change in English secondary and higher education

DOMINATION AND ASSERTION

Secondary and higher education at the beginning of the nineteenth century were semi-integrated and were articulated primarily with the Anglican church. However, the very fact of establishment implied a degree of integration between the church and the state which had direct repercussions on education at these levels. The three factors of successful educational domination pertained to the established church. The *monopoly* underpinning its domination was largely educational, as it acquired and developed a series of educational establishments and monopolised not only material facilities, but also the teaching body required to staff them. On the other hand, this historical situation was underwritten by parliamentary laws. Indeed the state had the right to confer university charters and to superintend the provision of school endowments at secondary level. Therefore the virtual monopoly of the established church over educational facilities originated from Anglican initiatives, but was reinforced and perpetuated by state intervention.

The *constraints* supporting this monopoly were part religious and part secular. The clerical teaching staff had at its disposal all the means of constraint available to educators, from indoctrination to the selective use of internal dicipline. At the same time, legal constraints derived from the state guaranteed the Anglican character of higher education, the most outstanding being the prevention of dissenters from graduation at either Oxford or Cambridge by the Test Acts. Therefore degrees were both certificates of competence and of religious affiliation. Since these acts served to debar the dissenting section of the middle class from universities, they contributed to the maintenance of a socially exclusive higher education, justified by the religious *ideology* prevailing both in and about education. By consecrating the concept of station in life, the church directly supported the existing system of social stratification.

By virtue of their middle-class background, both non-conformists and secularists resented the exclusiveness of Anglican education, as well as its religious content. While dissenters' attacks concentrated on the latter, without being exempt of resentment for the former, the Utilitarians negated the connection between heredity and intelligence, and therefore between birth and the right to higher education. By the time of the First Reform Bill, the expansion of these two forms of middle-class philosophy had deprived Anglican ideology of universality and therefore partly invalidated it as a component part of successful educational domination. In response to this double challenge, the various sections of Anglican opinion elaborated new justifications for the educational domination of the established church. While they were unanimous in defending Anglican education against dissenting and secularist alternatives, they differed about the extent to which it should be linked with social conservatism. The Oxford Movement, the Broad Church Party and Christian Socialism represented three interpretations of this connection.

Until the First Reform Bill, middle-class assertion in this field was confined to attempts at devaluing the Anglican monopoly of educational facilities. Hence at secondary level the foundation of denominational, commercial and experimental schools and at higher that of University College, London. These instrumental activities of substitution were of necessity limited by financial considerations. While independent alternatives to existing secondary schools could be devised, and indeed were in large numbers, the historical prestige of universities, as well as their legal right to confer degrees, made them difficult to challenge. It was the same features, differently interpreted, which left them open to attack; their traditionalism was construed as anachronism, their political position as unwarranted social privilege and their degrees as outmoded, mere titles rather than tokens of true learning. Hence criticisms were levelled at the related issues of the universities' collegiate structure, the social composition of their intake and the content of the studies given.

Awareness of the limits imposed on devaluation of the Anglican monopoly through substitution led middle-class leaders to recognise that their educational policies required parliamentary reform to restrict this monopoly. However, enfranchisement in 1832 did not immediately increase the bargaining power of this group, since middle-class representation followed slowly. Consequently, advance in educational assertion dependent on state intervention was delayed until the second half of the century. Thus during the period considered middle-class assertion in secondary and higher education remained at the ideological level, while the church retained its monopoly and constraints and attempted to redefine new forms of legitimation for them.

SECONDARY SCHOOLS

In the early nineteenth century secondary schools under Anglican control provided a preparatory course leading to university entrance. The social composition of their intake and the content of their curricula were similarly affected by this function. Hence, though many pupils did not actually proceed to university, secondary education was not regarded as an end in itself, but as an initial stage of higher education. Between charity schools for the poor and degrees for the privileged, hardly any intermediary level existed.

Secondary education was mainly dispensed by endowed schools which even at the time could be roughly divided into grammar and public schools – the criteria for distinguishing between the two being that the latter were not only more expensive, but also drew their pupils from the whole country rather than the locality. Many of these establishments, founded primarily as 'free grammar schools', had been conceived as charity institutions dispensing instruction to any pupils who resorted to them. This original intention was altered in two different ways. In many instances, schools intended to accept pupils without payment had reduced this intake in relation to the fee-paying students accepted on a boarding basis. This not only increased the profits of the establishments, but also had the effect that the school no longer served the locality for which it had been founded. Alternatively, 'where there was no local demand for instruction in "the tongues" a master might in effect close the school and yet retain the statutory stipend'.[1] The closing down of such schools reduced the original network and the location of those which survived was unrelated to the changing demographic pattern of an industrialising country. Furthermore, the restriction of free places made secondary education more socially exclusive and increasingly unfitted to the requirements of an expanding middle class.

A logical corollary of the function performed by secondary establishments was that they were placed under the same control as the universities – that of church and state. The state regulated the content of tuition since it constituted the only court of appeal against prevailing practice. The church officially controlled all teaching staffs since an ecclesiastical licence was required by all entering the profession.[2] As most secondary schools had been endowed by private founders, the terms of their constitutive acts enforced the predominance of classical subjects prevailing several centuries earlier. The state maintained this classical syllabus since it did not interfere with the founders' original intentions. The church imposed its forms of worship as well as its choice of teachers. Moreover, as the formation of clergymen had a classical bias, Anglicanism consistently supported classicism in secondary schools.

The origin of middle-class protest against the two assumptions governing secondary education – that it should be classical and Anglican – can be traced back to late eighteenth-century groups, such as the Birmingham Lunar and Manchester Philosophical Societies. As middle-class associations, these were promoted by the professions rather than industry, by dissenters rather than churchmen, scientists rather than classicists. Excluded through religion from education[3] and through class from political participation, self-help was the only available means for furthering their scientific interests. Hence Priestley's denounciation of classicism went hand in hand with the organisation of independent academies giving forms of instruction more appropriate to the age. As a non-conformist clergyman by profession and a scientist by inclination, Priestley personified the two types of discontent which were to direct middle-class educational assertion in the following century. These two forms of attack should be regarded as separate but related. Initially many individuals who had no objections to secondary schools on religious grounds, being churchmen themselves, objected to a classical schooling considered useless. Increasingly, however, as the claims of science became associated with those of Utilitarianism and progress, its advocates became supporters of a secular educational system.

Partial concessions to middle-class demands for more modern curricula were contained in Brougham's Bill of 1820. However his plan, being modelled on the Scottish parish school would have increased the part played by the local Anglican clergy in school government. Thus, while appealing to the modernistic trends in the middle class, it met with the resistance of dissent, as it would have strengthened the hands of the established church. Opposition from dissent was sufficiently feared for Parliament to reject the bill, which it had no scruples in throwing out, since the defence of classicism coincided with the protection of social privilege. A connection was thus posited between the liberal education and social leadership. Any dilution of the classical curriculum would automatically lead to the social debasement of an elitist education – it would become too popular.

The rich and those, who, if not rich, yet enjoy a competency, have parts to act in society, which the poor are neither required nor able to perform. To qualify them for these parts, the rich have usually the means of a more comprehensive education; that sort of education, which is termed liberal, and which is accorded at the grammar school. In the name of all that is Christian and humane, just and reasonable, let the poor be educated; but let them be educated, as they now are, in places, and according to institutions, appropriated to their peculiar exigencies and conditions. More would not only be superfluous but detrimental.[4]

Therefore, until the passing of the First Reform Bill, the middle class found themselves in the same relation to secondary education as the working class was in relation to primary until the Second Reform Bill. The reaction of the excluded group was identical in both cases – an attempt at substitution. Thus the development of private, denominational, commercial and proprietary schools outside the endowed network gradually came to represent the main form of modern studies. By definition such establishments lacked a common standard and were unevenly distributed throughout the country. They varied from religious schools catering for minorities, such as the Catholic institutions previously established in France and returning to England during the Revolution,[5] to experimental schools conducted on philosophical principles, such as Hazelwood, and proprietary ones founded by groups of parents for the tuition of their children.

One consequence of the existence of these privately established institutions was the foundation of a curriculum which first found a place for modern studies, and in the end made English grammar and history, elementary mathematics, geography, drawing and a branch of science (usually chemistry) the staple courses of study in schools of their type. They were not fettered by ancient statutes or traditional methods of teaching; but they were very susceptible to the opinions which ruled beyond the school walls, especially as these were held by parents. During the Nineteenth century the conception of what constituted secondary instruction underwent a profound change; so far as professional theory and practice influenced the change, it was due not to any Public School or Public School master but to the enterprise of the private schools.[6]

While such private schools catered for the requirements of the middle class with regard to professional training based on scientific instruction, dissenting academies satisfied their demands for religious freedom in education. Both types of school had their roots in late eighteenth-century thought; scientism produced private schools, revivalism multiplied religious schools. However, the first appeal of the sects had been to the lower rather than to the middle classes and therefore their active interest in secondary education was delayed until the widening of their social basis. The first Methodists' Grammar School was founded in 1838 with the object of providing primary-school teachers to offset the long exclusion of dissenters from teaching.[7] This not only gave a wider instruction to its trainees, acquainting them with the practical subjects taught in primary schools, but also opened the teaching profession to the middle class. However, limited resources prevented the rapid extension of denominational schools. It was the restrictions thus placed upon substitution which prompted the sects to re-enter the political arena and to seek a state education which would recognise religious differences. Thus voluntary schools appeared a provisional solution pending a reorganisation of the relationship between the state and the established church.[8]

The foundation of private and denominational schools was matched and its effects partially cancelled out by the revival of the public schools. At the beginning of the nineteenth century the standard of teaching, organisation and boarding arrangements in public schools were deficient in many ways. Their recovery began with the turn of the century; although the first twenty years were marked by pupil rebellions,[9] from 1830 their reputation and numbers grew. 'If the beginning of the Nineteenth century was a lean time for schools, the middle of it was one of unexampled expansion . . . In the forties came Marlborough, Cheltenham, Radley, Lancing, Rossall; in the fifties Wellington and Bradfield; in the sixties Clifton and Malvern'.[10] The pattern for their organisation was provided by Butler's reforms in Shrewsbury where he improved the standard of scholarship, but subordinated it to moral worth . . . 'If I train them to be honourable and virtuous men, I am conferring a greater benefit upon themselves and on society than by all the learning I can give them'.[11] These underlying principles of the nineteenth-century public school were codified in the works of Thomas Arnold. While some new schools were founded, others achieved their distinctive public character by becoming national boarding establishments instead of local day ones. Demand was increased by Arnold's success in Rugby.[12]

The common ideal of the public schools subordinated the instruction of the scholar to the education of the gentleman, and the education of the gentleman to the formation of the Christian. These aims coincided with the desires of aristocratic parents that their children should be trained to lead, in a society where leadership was awarded by virtue of birth rather than won in open competition. The closer the connection between the public schools and the university and the more socially restricted the intake of such schools, the safer was their privileged position in society. The first condition was met by insistence on a classical syllabus, the second by the increasing cost of the fees. Arnold, Butler and Thring defined education as training for leadership, not tuition for scholarship, and saw vocational tuition for the middle classes as completely separated from preparation for the universities. 'If professional education is the object, then by all means establish schools to give it. But they cannot be great schools that train for the Universities, for they go on the principle that education is the object'.[13]

Thus the development of the public schools sharpened the distinction between classes and precluded the notion of an educational ladder. As preparation for the universities became the virtual monopoly of public schools, the middle class, largely rejected from them on economic and social as well as, in many cases, religious grounds, relied on substitution for the instruction of its children. However, this method proved insufficient and the state increasingly appeared as the only agency which could free the middle class from educational domination of the established church.

In response to such pressures, which became effective after the First Reform Bill, the Grammar School Act of 1840 allowed endowed schools to consider not only the intentions of their founders, but also local conditions and demands.

However, an attempt to reconcile the middle class to Anglicanism was initiated by Woodard in 1847, in order to recover the church's position as educator of the nation. The Woodard schools, which multiplied rapidly, gave effective access to secondary tuition to those who could not afford public schools.[14] In its desire to retain educational domination and its awareness of a threat to its position, the church recognised this new right of the middle class more fully than the state. However, it used these boarding schools to propagate Anglicanism and hoped thereby to gain loyalty among the newly enfranchised.

THE UNIVERSITIES

'Until the State enforced reform in the fifties, Oxford history mirrored that of the church'.[15] The teaching body was entirely Anglican and largely clerical, the religious orthodoxy of the students being assured by the Test Acts.[16] The degree of clerical control was maintained through the system of closed fellowships,[17] to the detriment of scholarship, since for example in 1850, out of 545 fellowships within Oxford at that time, only 22 had been selected on the grounds of merit. This clerical oligarchy perpetuated itself since the church absorbed the majority of university graduates. During the first half of the nineteenth century, 25,000 matriculated from Oxford and over 10,000 of them were ordained.[18]

Thus all stages of a university career were under church control . . . beginning with

the Chapel system which in Oxford is regarded as an essential part or instrument of college discipline; next to the religious instruction which is regularly given, at least in form, and regarded as an equally essential part of the tutorial course of instruction; then there is the examination in the rudiments of religion, considered to be the most essential part of the examination for the degree of B.A., and lastly there is a sort of general recognition of religion as the leading principle in all university institutions and forms whatsoever.[19]

In this overwhelmingly clerical atmosphere, it is unsurprising that any theoretical debate about university reform should have been cast in a religious mould, and that the defence of church domination in education should have involved a redefinition of theology's role. It is more surprising that these issues were considered from a wider philosophical and social viewpoint.

Since both Oxford and Cambridge had been founded over time as an agglomeration of colleges with separate endowments, neither appeared to have a strong unitary character. The tendency of their authorities to regard colleges as private bodies involved frequent assertions of independence not only towards the state, but towards the university itself. 'The University as a national establishment is necessarily open to lieges in general: the colleges as private institutions, might universally do as some have actually done – close their gates upon all except their foundation members'.[20] The whole university structure rested upon the colleges since their heads comprised its most authoritative body, the Hebdomadal Board. Tuition was given principally by the tutorial system which was college based. Thus the academic policy as well as the administrative policies were decided separately in the common room of each college, giving rise to a considerable fund of variety in the university. The teaching functions of the university itself were restricted to public lectures by professors and, since the reforms of 1800 in Oxford and 1780 in Cambridge, public examinations. Any attempts to extend these functions were combated by the colleges who jealously guarded their power of direct influence over the students by the tutor and quoted the legal terms of their endowment in support of their claim. The tutor and the professor, therefore stood opposed in the internal struggle for power within higher education, but more particularly as they represented different interpretations of the formative power of instruction: for the character and the intellect. Although some professors gave lecture courses in 'modern' subjects, the first degree course was dominated by the classics and mathematics, Cambridge concentrating more on the latter. Consequently other subjects were neglected, as is evidenced by the fact that Oxford produced three medical graduates a year in the early nineteenth century, as against approximately 100 in Edinburgh.

The growth of both radicalism and dissent in the late eighteenth century challenged the privileged position of the established church and sought to destroy its educational domination. This supremacy and the social selectivity which accompanied it, became increasingly antiquated, as differentiation increased in society, rationalism in thought and technology in production. The former identification of church and state had implied that a uniform output of churchmen and statesmen would suffice in a predominantly agricultural economy. The growth of the middle class created a new group, largely excluded from higher education and increasingly critical of its curricula as irrelevant to modern society.

Both dissenting and Utilitarian groups, as representatives of the middle class, voiced similar objections to the educational position of the church. Asserting the equal rights of dissenters to participate in higher education and to influence curricula implied a theological dispute covering the whole field of Christian dogma. On the other hand, Utilitarian claims to a purely secular education demanded primarily the elimination of religion from programmes of instruction. Furthermore they asserted the claims of rationality against those of faith, as well as those of utility against those of tradition. Rather than launching a theological debate, the protagonists of secular philosophy challenged the relevance of theology – and attack required defence. Thus while discussion over the extension of primary education centred upon economics, that in secondary and university schooling was predominantly theological. Anglicanism was defended on two grounds, as religious truth in answer to the competing claims of dissent, and as socially relevant doctrine in reply to the Utilitarian accusation of its educational unsuitability.

In higher as in secondary education, middle-class assertion initially took the form of substitution. During the first thirty years of the century, Tory rule, accompanied by an intimate association between church and state, and loyally supported by the universities, precluded the possibility of reform in higher education. In fact the universities were part of the political establishment: 'the university of Oxford has long since ceased to exist except for the purpose of electioneering', claimed the *Westminster Review*.[21] While the established church and state presented a united front before the fall of the Tory ministry, Utilitarianism and dissent joined together to attack their educational monopoly. The first stage was the foundation of the University of London, planned from 1825 onwards, at the instigation of radicals and with the support of dissenting communions. Differing from Oxbridge in almost every respect, it was designed as professorial not tutorial, secular not religious, modern rather than classical, and furthermore non-residential. It was modelled on the Scottish universities and adopted their catholicity of intake. This venture was welcomed by the Whig Party, which 'gladly accepted the alliance of the Radicals and Dissenters, who, they hoped, might assist them in turn to arrive in power'.[22] Defence followed immediately upon this attack, and a new institution, to be called King's College, London, was devised. The instruction which it was to dispense in both classical and modern subjects would be imbued with Anglicanism. While this was a counterblast to secularism, it was nevertheless a departure from classicism, in providing facilities for professional training. Thus before 1832 higher education had been somewhat modernised, but its older institutions had not been reformed.

The passing of the First Reform Bill by the new Whig ministry opened the way to a second period of middle-class assertion aiming at restriction rather than substitution. For the first time Utilitarian leaders were in close contact with cabinet ministers: 'Brougham is Chancellor, and is more anxious than ever to consult Mill on all emergencies'.[23] For the first time since the Napoleonic Wars, the politics of the university differed from those of the parliamentary majority. 'In the first age of reform the university recapitulated the stormy history of the early days of the Hanoverian era. Now as then, Oxford was confronted with a sudden Whig triumph . . . Now as then a Whig triumph let loose a torrent of rationalist and non-conformist abuse against the university and its privileges'.[24] These privileges were embodied in the colleges perpetuating religious intolerance, social exclusivity and academic traditionalism.

In his series of articles on Oxford, 'of all academical institutions, at once the most imperfect and the most perfectible',[25] Sir William Hamilton stressed the undemocratic aspects of the collegiate system. Colleges were 'created, regulated and endowed by private munificence, for the interest of certain favoured individuals'.[26] However, they had exceeded their initial function and attempted to take over the whole university, transforming it into a clerical oligarchy. 'The privileges accorded by the nation to the system of public education legally organised in the university, cannot – without the consent of the nation . . . be lawfully transferred to the system of private education precariously organised in colleges, and over which neither the State nor the University have any control. They have, however, been unlawfully usurped.'[27] John Stuart Mill reinforced the demand for state oversight of colleges, by stating that the common law abhorred perpetuities and therefore all endowments should be periodically reviewed. Conservative replies followed immediately and are exemplified by Vaughan Thomas's riposte, 'The legality of the present academical system of the University of Oxford asserted against the new calumnies of the Edinburgh Review.'[28] However, it was not on legalistic grounds alone that Hamilton denounced colleges, he also accused tutors of debasing the standard of learning, advocated the professorial system and epitomised middle-class thought when he opposed the dominance of the classics. This attack stimulated, in turn, justifications for the existing system attempting to repel middle-class criticisms.[29]

However, the main obstacles to the democratisation of university intake and the secularisation of the syllabus were the Test Acts. A series of petitions from dissenters against these acts was received by the reformed Parliament. In both universities, the ecumenical party supported this claim in the interest of religious and national unity, rather than to advance the cause of any particular class. Strong counter-reactions were registered in Oxbridge in support of the domination of the established church. Thus Sewell wrote,

I deny the right of liberty of conscience wholly and utterly . . . I deny the right of any sect to depart one atom from the standard which I hold to be the truth of Christianity. And I deny the right of any legislative power, of any minister of God, of any individual on earth, to sanction or permit it, without using every means in my power to control and bring them back from their errors.[30]

Anglican domination prevailed as the bill to abolish the Test Acts was rejected by the Lords in 1834. It was also in response to Anglican pressures that the University of Durham was founded in 1837. In fact the only concession by the Whig Parliament in the first half of the century was the conferring of a Charter on London University, as an examining body for University and King's Colleges. This act constituted an admission of secular education – the first crack in the Anglican university monopoly.

In response to this series of attacks on the educational supremacy of Anglicanism, new justifications were devised for its domination which were necessarily inseparable from a debate on the political and intellectual position of the Anglican church. As criticism of educational institutions increased, the clergy could no longer rely upon tradition as sufficient legitimation and were forced to devise new forms of justification for their position, that is to redefine their educational ideology. Therefore the unity which had prevailed within the church, in so far as a concerted educational ideal existed, began to fragment, as different groups sought new justifications. As each of these outlined their educational proposals, with the overall aim of maintaining and consolidating the church's position, it became clear that they implied varying redefinitions of church-state relationships.

The main attempt was made by the Oxford Movement, which not only supported, but wished to consolidate further the monopoly of the established church in the state and in the universities by restoring its intellectual leadership. This Tractarian group became most influential in Oxford in the late thirties as defenders of Anglicanism, which it considered persecuted by the Melbourne government. The position adopted by Newman and his followers at this time emphasised the personal influence of the tutor to maintain the integrity of the university. In his advocacy of the collegiate system, he claimed that if presented with a choice between the professorial system leading to success in examinations and direct contact with the tutor who would provide the liberal education, he would have no hesitation in choosing the latter.[31] Such an outlook subordinated intellectual excellence to religious orthodoxy and encouraged theology, often to the detriment of other disciplines. The very success of the movement at the time demonstrated how damaging such a subordination could prove for other studies. Looking back, Mark Pattison voiced this criticism: 'It

was soon after 1830 that the Tracts desolated Oxford life, and suspended, for an indefinite period, all science, humane letters and
the first strivings of an intellectual freedom which had moved in the
bosom of Oriel.'[32] During the period of Tractarian influence, religious
domination prevailed in higher education, but university reform
gained some allies within Anglicanism, who feared dissent less than
Rome.

Tractarianism prevailed in the 1830s, but with Newman's conversion to Catholicism in the 1840s its influence was largely spent. In
addition, the threat of Chartism to social stability appeared greater
than that of liberalism to religion. This reaction against Tractarianism
gave a new strength to criticisms of the institutions and practices the
movement had supported. The Broad Church Party in Oxford were
the beneficiaries of this backwash. The liberals who formed this group
were known as the Rugby set, because of their admiration for Arnold.
Their activities in university reform mark the beginning of the third
period of assertion, one in which the middle class had allies within
higher education. Faithful to their Protestant ecumenicalism, the
Broad Churchmen wished to abolish the Test Acts, not to secularise
the universities. They assumed that 'a liberal education necessarily
means a religious one',[33] but considered dissenters should participate
in this if 'a public education worthy of the name'[34] were to exist.
Hence it was the dissenting groups within the middle class whom they
supported, not the utilitarians. Therefore the Broad Church Party
wished to adapt the universities to new requirements, but not to
destroy their religious character or classical bias.

There is nothing I less wish to see than Oxford turned into a German or a London
University, on the other hand, is it at all probable that we shall be able to remain as
we are for twenty years longer, the one solitary, exclusive, unnatural corporation –
our enormous wealth without any manifest utilitarian purpose; a place, the studies
of which belong to the past, and unfortunately seem to have no power of incorporating new branches of knowledge; so exclusively that it is scarcely capable of opening
to the wants of the Church itself.[35]

This was written by Jowett to the dissenting M.P., Christie, in an
outline of the main reforms required. The connection between dissent
and the middle class was not lost to the Rugby set, who saw that the
abolition of the Test Acts would 'provide the means for many more
persons of the middling class to find their way through the University
into professions'.[36] However, in this their main purpose was ecumenical. Stanley saw the university as a melting pot 'where the healing

c

genius of the place . . . shall unite the long estrangements of Judah and Ephraim, of Jerusalem and Samaria'.[37]

The counterpart of plans to widen recruitment was a desire to reduce the powers of the colleges, which the history of the Tractarian movement had shown to be divisive in religious matters as well as conservative in academic changes. The Oxford Broad Churchmen supported the professorial system, not only to raise standards of scholarship but to undermine strongholds of privilege. Indeed, according to Sewell, a partisan of colleges, 'a tutorial system of education has always been connected with monarchical principles and institutions – a professorial almost always with democracy'.[38] Reform of the examination system intended to increase the part played by professorial lecturing was suggested by Tait and Stanley in 1839, and repeated by Stanley and Jowett in a pamphlet published nine years later. This also contained proposals for the widening and integration of the syllabus, since Jowett saw that 'the great evil at Oxford is the narrowness and isolation of one study from the other. We are so far below the level of the German ocean that I fear one day we shall be utterly deluged'.[39]

These pressures culminated in the establishment by Lord John Russell in 1850 of the Royal Commissions investigating the two old universities. Both Tait and Stanley were among the Oxford Commissioners despite strong opposition from the university itself.[40] The acts following this investigation reflect their participation; in 1854 the Test Acts were abolished for students, fellowships and studentships opened to free competition, the professoriat strengthened by the creation of new chairs and the curriculum broadened to include modern languages and natural science. While this satisfied the claims of dissenters, it did not comply with the requirements of a secular education advocated within some sections of the middle class.

Such reforms marked the beginning of state intervention in higher education in the 1850s; in the 1860s, it was to spread to the public and endowed secondary schools. Thus the period after enfranchisement and the death of the leading Utilitarians had been one in which the middle class increasingly recognised the difficulties of devaluing the Anglican monopoly by substitution and accordingly turned to policies of restriction through the use of their newly acquired bargaining power. It coincided with a time at which the leading party within Anglicanism welcomed educational reform, so as to increase their influence over the sectarian forces of dissent. Paradoxically both the assertive and dominant groups thus felt that their positions would be furthered through state intervention – an attitude which accounts for their otherwise surprising collaboration during the 1850s. This undoubtedly hastened the integration of secondary and higher education with the political structure and through it with other social institutions.

5. Assertive ideologies in English education

The existence of educational theories in a country where schooling had previously been governed by expediency rather than philosophy was largely a manifestation of the late eighteenth century. The extension and reappraisal of such ideas throughout the first half of the nineteenth century originated from groups who had no influence over existing establishments. The divergence of interests between the middle and the working class precluded a lasting identification between their educational goals and shaped two distinct bodies of thought reflecting their respective positions. Moreover the exclusion of both groups from political participation accounted for the association between the political ambitions and the educational aspirations held by each. The connection thus established between politics and education led to a general examination of democratic ideals, inseparable from their redefinition by any group dissatisfied with the position assigned to its members by virtue of the prevailing definition. This discontent stimulated interest in the new republican ideas prevailing in France and in the enlightened philosophy from which they originated.

The fund of ideas provided by republican France was by no means homogeneous and its various aspects could be used towards different ends. Since property was the factor which characterised the middle class, the theories they accepted uniformly accentuated the legitimacy of ownership and therefore were predominantly economic. These were the pre-revolutionary theories emphasising the social role of property and claiming that political rights should be inseparable from it.[1] The possession of capital without corresponding rights, either political or educational, constituted a ground for demanding reforms, but represented at the same time a limitation of the number of proposed beneficiaries. Thus educational reform became restrictive rather than universal and political radicalism was tempered into liberalism rather than socialism. Conversely, the working class, in so far as it differed from the bourgeosie in the formulation of its aims and in their justification, drew on revolutionary principles relating political claims to human rights rather than economic services. Freedom and equality were interpreted as pertaining to the individual, regardless of economic considerations. The generality of the rights postulated logically led to the universality of the reforms advocated. This applied to schooling as much as to the franchise. Since property was an obstacle to both educational equality and political reform, working-class thought gradually incorporated socialist tenets. Thus the middle class were influenced by the economic approach to a theory of differential rights, whereas the working class endorsed a philosophical theory of universal equality. The middle class concentrated on the exigencies of political economy, while the working class stressed the more abstract demands of social philosophy.

MIDDLE CLASS EDUCATIONAL THOUGHT

The indispensability of education to laissez-faire policy

As education represented only one of the institutional relationships which various sectors of the rapidly growing and differentiating middle classes sought to adapt to their activities, it is unsurprising that the source of legitimation for assertion in this also derived from economic theories purporting to demonstrate a correspondence between group and general interests. The intellectual origin of middle-class economic theories which underpin their educational thought can be traced to the works of eighteenth-century Physiocrats.[2] The main exponents of this school – Quesnay, Mercier de la Rivière, Mirabeau, Baudeau and to a certain extent Turgot – are important influences in two ways: firstly, for having revolutionised economic thinking by breaking away from the mercantilists' insistence on foreign trade as the source of national wealth, and secondly, for establishing the association between education and economic development. In this connection the second is more significant since their economic propositions concerned the contribution of agriculture to general prosperity. Thus their basic sociological preconceptions about relations between social institutions were more influential in England than the actual content of their economic doctrine. This selective acceptance may be explained by the more rapid rate of industrialisation in England, particularly from the beginning of the nineteenth century onwards. In addition, the Physiocrats' postulate that all social phenomena are regulated by laws which social sciences aim to discover and formulate, was in accord with the secular rationalistic spirit prevailing among English radicals at the time.

Of particular importance for later British thought was the concept of 'natural order'. On the one hand, it is a descriptive concept showing the interdependence of all groups in society and stressing their ultimate dependence on nature; on the other, it is normative not only as an embodiment of a divine order pre-ordained for human happiness, but also since it is the duty of individuals to maximise the 'natural order' by regulating their behaviour accordingly. Such conduct is held possible because the knowledge of the ideal state, is considered self-evident and therefore the 'natural order' is familiar to every individual. Thus all individuals are equally involved in the general good, to which they unwittingly contribute and which they can consciously increase. Secondly, the existence of the 'natural order' does not constrain individual freedom, but rather stems from it. 'The laws of the natural order do not in any way restrain the liberty of mankind, for the great advantage which they possess is that they make for greater liberty',[3] since the particular interests of individuals are never in conflict with the common interests of all. Thirdly, the means whereby 'natural order' is best assured is the free interplay of individual interests, a system of 'laissez-faire'. While such a view reflects the belief in the concordance between individual liberty and general good, it appears contradictory in specifying a particular system needed to engineer this complementarity. This is because the tasks assigned to a laissez-faire government include the protection of private property and also individual liberty – two elements potentially conflicting. Hence hedonism is confined to operating in the narrow limits of the existing property distribution. This apparent inconsistency is overridden by the Physiocrats in their very definition of the 'natural order': 'Property, security, and liberty constitute the whole of the social order.'[4] Fourthly, it is due to this definition that the importance of education is stressed. It is considered the duty of a laissez-faire government to instruct in the laws of the 'natural order'. Again it is paradoxical that the 'natural order' should have to be taught and that state intervention should be required to that effect. The statement that 'education is the first and only social tie'[5] modifies the initial tenet whereby 'natural order' was intuitively perceived. In addition, order itself ceases to be the spontaneous product of individual hedonism, since the perception and the pursuit of enlightened self-interest have to be taught. Thus the introduction of universal education as a prerequisite for the 'natural order' robs it of its natural character and its spontaneous orderliness. Thus the claim that the institution of private property and of liberty would secure perfect order without the help of any other law[6] clearly requires qualification after the introduction of education as an additional prerequisite. Therefore property is regarded as insufficient in itself to guarantee social stability and other factors have to supplement it. A related ambiguity surrounds the Physiocratic exposition of laissez-faire policy. The sphere of state intervention should logically be limited to a strict minimum in order to avoid interference with the free interplay of individual interests. However such interests will be directed towards a common end – defined as the 'natural order' – by a state educational system. Not only is the existence of such a system synonymous with a departure from the minimalistic view of state functions, it further accentuates the need for an external agency, transcending the individual, to inculcate personal desires appropriate to the general welfare. By a gradual transition order ceases to be considered as the outcome of nature and increasingly nature is viewed as a product of order. Likewise education is designed to inculcate an awareness of enlightened self-interest – equated with freedom – instead of instruction being acquired voluntarily.

Since the prevalent mode of stratification was regarded as a reflection of the 'natural order', education was designed to maintain it. In view of the connection posited between education and the maintenance of the natural order, the educational process was seen as a means of social control, which justified its constraint of individuals by reference to the common good of all. These elements of the Physiocratic system are almost identical with those found in later Utilitarian thought. Both the transmission of Physiocratic doctrines and also their adaptation to the economic circumstances prevailing in England at the outset of the Industrial Revolution, are provided in the writings of Adam Smith. Since he was personally acquainted with the main exponents of Physiocratic economics, particularly Quesnay and Turgot, and commenced *The Wealth of Nations* in France while in communication with them, the book bears the imprint of their notions. Indeed Adam Smith describes the Physiocratic system as 'the nearest approximation to the truth that has yet been published'.[7] While its main tenets are reflected in Smith's theories, they are reinterpreted in the light of industrialising England rather than the predominantly rural nature of the French economy.

In positing that the 'spontaneous order' already exists, Smith avoids the contradiction whereby the Physiocrats postulated the 'natural order' as given and ideal, but at the same time sought to perfect it. Smith's belief in the inevitability of progress cannot be construed as a similar contradiction since he considers legislative and institutional deficiencies as restrictions upon the underlying 'spontaneous order'.

The uniform, constant, and uninterrupted effort of every man to better his condition, the principle from which public and national as well as private opulence is originally derived, is frequently powerful enough to maintain the natural progress of things toward improvement, in spite both of the extravagance of government, and of the greatest errors of administration. Like the unknown principle of animal life, it frequently restores health and vigor to the constitution, in spite, not only of the disease, but of the absurd prescriptions of the doctor.[8]

In so far as the 'order is already achieved' the goal of political economy is reduced by Smith to a description of existing economic relationships and is stripped of the prescriptive role which the Physiocrats could attribute to it by virtue of their notion of perfectability. In his description Smith is therefore committed to emphasise the concordance between the interests of different groups as his theory postulates a unity of interests among all sections of society. Therefore all inequalities of distribution, observed throughout the population, are construed as necessary concomitants of production, which by definition is organised in the way most conducive to the general good. To Smith individual happiness is linked to productive efficiency, rather than distributive justice.

Unlike the Physiocrats, Adam Smith defines human labour and not natural resources as the source of wealth. Hence the importance of production as creative of wealth and its foundation upon the division of labour. Successive subdivisions of productive processes and the specialisation arising from differentiation of tasks, increased national wealth through stimulating productivity.[9] The occupational hierarchy inseparable from the division of labour is not only beneficial to the community as a means of increasing wealth, but favourable to all the individuals involved since individual interests cannot conflict with the general good. Thus social stratification contributes more to the common good than does individual equality. The wealth of nations is the product of individual interests, but the general welfare is not conducive to equality between individuals. Nevertheless, since all existing economic institutions are regarded as natural because they spring from individual hedonism rather than being superimposed, they must be viewed as beneficient and not oppressive.

However the division of labour implies certain disadvantages for some of the strata it creates. While increasing specialisation promotes skill, those who are engaged in purely repetitive operations merely acquire a time saving dexterity which improves output, but

The man whose whole life is spent in performing a few simple operations, of which the effects are, perhaps, always the same, or very nearly the same, has no occasion to exert his understanding, or to exercise his invention in finding out expedients for removing difficulties which never occur. He naturally loses, therefore, the habit of such exertion, and generally becomes as stupid and ignorant as it is possible for a human creature to become.[10]

This ignorance to which workers are reduced as a result of their role in production entails an inability to perceive that their true interests are fulfilled by the existing order. Instead they become receptive to 'the interested complaints of faction and sedition'[11] which attack the existing distribution of property.

To advocate a redistribution of wealth is in Adam Smith's terms to act counter to the real interests of society as a whole. It is in the interests of the community as well as that of the apparently under-privileged individuals for the discontented to recognise that the redistribution of property would worsen rather than improve their lot. Smith proposes to cure and prevent discontent by education.

It is important to note that Adam Smith's argument for education violates his main principle, that of the natural identity of interests of all sections in society. In general he treats the division of labour as an expression of the unity of interest of all individuals in society; since each contributes in his own field to provide the sum of goods and services the community needs, all are dependent on each other and have a community of interest in the society of which they are an essential part. Yet considering the effect on the factory worker he is bound to advocate a system of popular education specifically in order to counter the adverse effect of the division of labour.[12]

The role of instruction as a means of social control is illustrated by the fact that the state is to contribute towards the maintenance of local schools. Popular education is to be confined to reading, writing and arithmetic and not to be extended beyond them. Such a limited syllabus is presumed adequate to expose the inadvisability of changing the economic system, the social structure and the political regime, and to reconcile individuals with the existing order. That such elementary instruction should be seen to have such far-reaching consequences can only be explained by reference to the assumption that with the application of reason true interests become self evident. An additional contradiction within the theory emerges at this point. No longer is individual hedonism considered sufficient to guarantee the 'spontaneous order' once a distinction has been made between an individual's true and apparent interests – particularly when reason is identified with true interests and untrained drives endorse apparent ones. This contradiction precipitates Smith to what is heresy from the standpoint of laissez-faire principles. To suggest state intervention into education for the purpose of social control is to contravene the fundamental tenet of minimal intervention as well as that of social unity.

Thus Smith's extension of Physiocratic economics to industrial production expresses a similar view on the indispensibility of state education to laissez-faire economic policy, despite the fact that this represents almost a contradiction in terms. This need to integrate education with the economy does not rest upon any recognition of the productive role of instruction in training manpower; education is essential however in preventing the spread of ideas detrimental to production and thus plays a negative, protective role. A firm connection is therefore established between advancing laissez-faire and the need to control the education of industrial operatives. Middle-class economic theory is thus firmly tied to seeking educational domination.

The indispensability of education to economic advance: classical economics

Adam's Smith's retention of the Physiocratic tenet that agriculture represents a special source of wealth was an obstacle to the immediate assimilation of his theories by middle-class radicals whose main political objective was to overthrow agricultural privilege. It was Ricardo, who by reversing the priorities assigned to the different sectors of production, made political economy increasingly acceptable to the radical reformers in politics and education. Since to Ricardo all value is founded upon labour, the cultivation of land is not the sole or even the main source of wealth. He distinguishes between the rent of land, the profits of capital and the wages of labour, and demonstrates the conflicts of interests between them.

The antagonism posited between different sectors of the economy is located by Ricardo in the conflict of the manufacturers with land-owners. Due to the connection between agricultural prices and wages, described as an economic law, price fluctuations affect only the nominal wage but not the standard of living of the wage labourer. However such fluctuations have a real effect upon the profits of the manufacturer, therefore positing that increases in rent are accompanied by falls in profit, whilst real wages remain stationary. With the development of the theory of rent, political economy for the first time reflects the rivalry felt by middle-class radicals towards the landed gentry and provides them with a justification for their economic assertion as the group most productive of wealth.

Not only are profits threatened by any increment in agricultural rent, but also they could diminish by any increase in wages. However a surplus of labour resulting from the constant growth of the population, restricts wages to subsistence level. Real wages will remain stationary unless population increase forces them below the subsistence level. Since such an increase is expected to continue 'the condition of the labourer will generally decline, and that of the landlord will always be improved',[13] as the demand for foodstuffs and the supply of labour increases. Since any increment in rent is a direct threat to profits, a growth in the wage-earning population is against the interests of manufacturers, as it swells the demand for foodstuffs. The maintenance of profit in the hands of the manufacturers is defended and indeed justified on the grounds that redistribution could not improve the condition of the wage labourer. Since the lot of the worker can only be improved by limiting the number of his children, manufacturers have been absolved of responsibility for the condition of their employees.[14]

This concern with population increase is paramount in the work of Malthus. In contrasting the geometric extension of the population with the arithmetic growth of means of subsistence, he considers such a discrepancy as the main obstacle to human progress. Since the largest families are commonly found among the labouring poor, this section of society can be held responsible for aggravating its own condition by increasing the supply of labour over the demand for it: the poor are themselves the cause of their own poverty. Like Ricardo, he is opposed to public assistance under the poor laws since state intervention cannot increase wealth.[15] An exception is made only for education, as an increase in rationality will be conducive to an understanding of the natural laws which make population limitation essential.

Unintentionally Ricardo and Malthus thus free other sections of society from any responsibility for the fate of the industrial worker. No institution or legislation could alter the natural laws whose operation regulates the positions of all sections of society.[16] The position of the poor could not be improved unless they themselves came to see the principles of such laws and to change their behaviour accordingly. Thus the only useful intervention on the part of the middle classes is to acquaint the poor with this knowledge and to further the spread of moral restraint.[17] Education is thus seen as the only positive contribution to alleviating the condition of the lower classes which is compatible with the general interest. This interest appears to Malthus to be served more faithfully by the middle class than by any other social group. Therefore it is not on grounds of justice that he advocates education, but for reasons of utility, since it will teach men to regulate their needs.

All classical economists emphasised the connection between social order and the free play of natural laws. Since the possibility of social conflict would be lessened by inculcating an understanding of economic laws, the increase of education was seen as contributing to social stability through the spread of enlightenment. A common denominator of Adam Smith and all his followers was the conviction that the diffusion of economic knowledge would automatically eliminate social conflict. Not only did this emphasis on social control serve the interests of the emerging middle class but also the writings of classical economists providing a justification for the claims of this group. Ricardo, in stressing the productive role of this section of society in relation to others, vindicated their claims for further industrialisation. Malthus, by formulating the law of population, exonerated this new class from all responsibilities for the poor. Classical economics thus gave the Utilitarians a justification both for the self-advancement of the middle classes and also the social control of other groups, through education. Thus before Utilitarian theories were elaborated, classical economics had demonstrated that the self-interest of the middle class was tantamount to the general interest and that the general interest would be harmed unless corrective educational measures were taken.

This class had therefore acquired the main source of legitimation for its assertion in the productive role assigned to it by classical economics. In addition, such tenets had the advantage of containing built-in justification of the constraints ultimately to be employed against other groups. This was to prove particularly important later as a basis upon which the educational assertion of the working class could be repelled. Finally, classical economics constituted a platform from which the domination of traditional groups in politics and education could be attacked.

The indispensability of education to secular ethics: Utilitarian philosophy

While classical economists had provided the entrepreneurial middle classes with a general justificatory theory based on their contribution to the general interest through productivity and had also stressed the need for educational domination to protect economic output, they had thus concentrated upon the first role of assertive ideology. The importance of Utilitarian philosophy in this connection is its contribution to the second role: that is, challenging the source of legitimation upon which the existing dominant group depends. The two major propositions underpinning religious domination over education were, firstly, that the church represented the supreme moral authority and therefore should – rather than any other social agency – assume the instruction of the young, and, secondly, that it was the most desirable force for training character. Their importance as sources of legitimation is underlined by the fact that the former was defended by Newman and the latter by Arnold, when later seeking to protect religious domination. Utilitarianism, probably less due to the intentions of its founders than to its impact as a body of thought, constituted an attack upon both. By separating ethics from religion, its very existence challenged the supreme moral authority of the church and led to a corresponding reduction in the universality of the religious source of legitimation. As Utilitarian ethics took the general good as their standard, it also advanced the claim of representing a more desirable influence over character. In other words, Utilitarianism operated as a challenge of secular ethics to religious morality. This is not of course to claim that the major Utilitarians framed their philosophy in opposition to religion or launched outspoken attacks upon it (on the contrary, Bentham and James Mill in particular were cautious not to advance overt agnosticism),[18] but merely that their standpoint was considered as an attack by religious leaders – and attack stimulated defence.

Since to classical economists the existence of natural order embodied a providential design, their system already incorporated implicit moral assumptions. From the divine origin of the laws regulating society, they derived the duty of individuals to conform to such laws. Those whose behaviour was unconducive to the maintenance of order were punished for avoidance of duty. Retribution was direct, since any interference with natural order was necessarily detrimental to the offender. As the divine will could only be good, any deviation from it was by definition less good and therefore constituted a punishment in itself – for example, population growth carried its own sanctions. Conversely, conformity brought its rewards: thus, refusing financial assistance to workers maximised profit and, by lessening the population growth, promoted the general interest and at the same time furthered the special interest of the middle class.

The embryonic nature of moral theory in classical economics was demonstrated by the lack of ethical prescriptions guiding individual behaviour. Such prescriptions were conceivable only because order could be perfected by individual behaviour. If natural order were truly natural, in other words perfect, a moral system would be precluded, since prescriptions are essential to ethics and superflous when all behaviour contributes to the ideal. It was only the notion of perfectibility which made it necessary to regulate behaviour and therefore to formulate an ethical system. To act in accordance with the natural law was held variously to depend upon either untutored intuition or educational conditioning. The outlining of an ethical system on this basis required a primary definition of the motivation by which the natural order was guaranteed. A motive providing the highest common denominator of individual behaviour was sought by the Utilitarians in the related spheres of pleasure and pain. Morality consisted in the application of the pleasure principle to society as a whole. Motivation was linked to morality, since the individual's happiness was associated with that of the collectivity and indeed conducive to it.

The tenet enunciated to guarantee maximum concordance between individual and general happiness was that morality consisted in promoting 'the greatest happiness of the greatest number'. This was not necessarily to say that the wishes of the majority always had to prevail over those of the minority, but rather that every person is of equal weight and the happiness of each individual is of equal value. The moral goal of the collectivity was not merely to promote the greatest amount of happiness, but to ensure as far as possible that the whole population would have a share in it. In order to implement this ideal, it was not essential to convince people that they should act according to the Utilitarian ethic, but it sufficed to engineer a correspendence between their desires and the maximisation of general happiness. Education was to accomplish this task by increasing rationality and therefore promoting the pursuit of enlightened self-interest. To promote rationalism was not to convert the majority to the Utilitarian ethic, but merely to acquaint them with their true interests, which may differ from the misrepresentations prevailing among the uneducated. Such instruction was not to counteract hedonism, but merely to inform it of the most advantageous individual goals, thereby channelling behaviour towards the general good. Thus, just as education was indispensable to increasing productivity, it was also essential to increasing morality, it therefore underpinned both the general economic interest and the general good.

However, behaviour could be consciously directed towards the general good and therefore be based upon the Utilitarian principle rather than the pleasure principle. Those whose decisions influence the general good directly, instead of contributing indirectly and unconsciously towards it as do the actions of common men, should receive a privileged instruction. A problem arises with this implicit distinction between the masses and the elite. If the legislators and those who shape public opinion act solely according to a Utilitarian ethic, instead of merely letting their behaviour coincide with it, they are presumably acting from some other motive, such as duty. Thus, while the elite are expected to derive pleasure from the maximisation of general happiness, the mass promotes the general good through the pursuit of individual happiness. The co-existence of these two distinct forms of motivation was paralleled by the two educational levels proposed, which bore a striking resemblance to those advanced on purely economic grounds.

Since a concordance between the interests of the mass and the duty of the elite was posited, leadership was necessarily assumed to be benevolent and enlightened. While enlightenment was to be the effect of education, the origin of benevolence was not elucidated. It was not explained if this attitude coincided with the individual interest of those who held it, though it was clearly specified as contributing to the general good. Thus the leaders both served and shaped the interests of society. The basic distinction between elite and mass led to a theory of social control, implemented by education. Since two levels of instruction were essential for the achievement of the general good, the educational system implied a social hierarchy, but the existing hierarchy was endorsed only in so far as the working class was concerned. Thus both classical economics and Utilitarian philosophy contained the preliminary draft of an educational blueprint in specifying roughly to whom instruction should be given and what it should constitute. However their main role was to claim the practical and moral advantages to be derived from an education freed from religious domination.

The educational blueprint: James Mill and Jeremy Bentham

As has been seen, there is a very particular sense in which the theories supporting middle-class educational assertion advocate it so as to gain authority over the instruction received by others. Therefore it is hardly surprising that when Bentham and Mill outline their specific blueprints for education and its relationships with other social institutions, one of their central concerns is combatting the assertion of the lower classes. To both, education should be integrated with the economy rather than with religion, but this implies two forms of schooling, one for the lower classes (to protect productivity and property) and another for the middle class.

The connection between Utilitarian philosophy and classical economics is provided by James Mill, who, following Ricardo, identifies the interest of the middle class with that of society as a whole. As all sections of society are not equally responsive to the demands of the general interest, Mill, like the classical economists, advocates education in order to engineer this complementarity and justifies it on moral grounds. 'The question, whether the people should be educated, is the same as the question whether they should be happy or miserable.'[19]

To Mill the practical problem of education hinges on two theoretical issues: the nature of the mind[20] and that of qualities conducive to happiness.[21] Thus the mechanics of instruction are derived from principles of associationist psychology and involve the creation of a connection between feelings of pleasure and events which are conducive to the general good. Conversely, feelings of pain should be related to anti-social activities. 'The grand object evidently is, to connect with each pain and pleasure those trains of ideas which, according to the order established among events, tend most effectually to increase the sum of pleasures upon the whole and diminish that of pains.'[22] Mill views education as a process of conditioning whereby positive attitudes are linked with the socially desirable and negative ones with those which are detrimental to general utility.

While associationist psychology is used to define teaching methods, the qualities instruction should promote in the individual are derived from the principle of utility. 'Two qualities, the intelligence which can always choose the best possible means, and the strength which over-comes the misguiding propensities, appear to be sufficient for the happiness of the individual himself, to the pursuit of which it cannot be doubted that he always has sufficient motives.'[23] However, since education is concerned also, and perhaps mainly, with the greatest happiness of the greatest number, the individual should be endowed with additional qualities which will contribute to this end. To dis-tinguish between the good of the individual and that of the group is thus to abandon explicitly the notion of a spontaneous identity of interests and to renounce implicitly any hope of a *spontaneous identifi-cation*. Therefore any identification between individual and general interests must be *artificial*. The means of implementing it is by instilling two additional characteristics through education – justice and generosity. 'To abstain from doing them (others) harm, receives the name of justice; to do positive good, receives that of generosity.'[24] The importance attached to these attributes is an aspect of the role accredited to education in the formation of character and ability.

In rejecting the influence of heredity upon achievement, except in cases of physical or mental abnormality, Mill endorses educational determinism.[25] 'This much, at any rate, is ascertained, that all the difference which exists or can ever be made to exist, between one *class* [Mill's italics] of men, and another, is wholly owing to education.'[26] Thus any differences in ability registered between social groups are merely indices of variations in the instruction received by their members. Two different conclusions could be derived from this postulate: either a single educational system reflecting the basic equality of ability and contributing to social equality, or a plurality of institutions corresponding to the division of labour in society and perpetuating a social hierarchy without necessarily confirming the existing one. Mill chooses the latter.

There are certain qualities, the possession of which is desirable in all classes. There are certain qualities, the possession of which is desirable in some, not in others. As far as those qualities extend which ought to be common to all, there ought to be a correspondent training for all. It is only in respect to those qualities which are not desirable in all that a difference in the mode of training is required.[27]

Hence education is subdivided into several categories: domestic, technical, social and political. While Mill assumes that the forms of education which instil desirable qualities should be common to all (domestic education at an early age,[28] social education later),[29] it is in the discussion of intellectual training (technical education) that the elitarian implications of utilitarianism become clear. While denying previous claims that the working class was incapable of mental excellence, nevertheless Mill's liberalism implicit in this view stops far short of advocating a common educational system.

As we strive for an equal degree of justice, an equal degree of temperance, an equal degree of veracity, in the poor as in the rich, so ought we to strive for an equal degree of intelligence, if there were not a preventing cause. It is absolutely necessary for the existence of the human race, that labour should be performed, that food should be produced and other things provided, which human welfare requires. A large proportion of mankind is required for this labour. Now, then, in regard to all this portion of mankind, that labours, only such a portion of time can by them be given to the acquisition of intelligence as can be abstracted from labour.[30]

Since the division of labour is seen as conducive to the general good, its perpetuation must not be endangered by the educational system. 'There are degrees, therefore, of intelligence, which must be reserved to those who are not obliged to labour.'[31]

Not only is the instruction proposed for the working class mainly ethical, but those elements of intellectual training which are to be given are restricted to the first years of life. Both the decision to impart this education and the short duration assigned to it, reflect Mill's endorsement of the profit motive. 'With a view to the productive powers of their very labour, it is desirable that the animal frame should not be devoted to it before a certain age, before it has approached the point of maturity.'[32] Therefore the provision of schooling conforms to liberal tenets without detracting from economic requirements. Social stability is guaranteed thereby and output remains unharmed. For higher classes different forms of tuition are outlined. While apprenticeships are considered an important type of technical training, a special form of education is reserved for 'that class of society who have wealth and time for the acquisition of the highest measures of intelligence'.[33] Such training will be given in colleges and universities, which are to be the sole preserve of this class.

The repulsion of other assertive groups. James Mill's concern for stability is reflected in his concentration upon the maintenance of the existing distribution of property. Any amelioration of the condition of the poor must spring from enlightenment, and not from any form of redistribution. The theories of early socialists, such as the attacks on property by Hodgskin, were dismissed as 'mad nonsense' since 'these opinions, if they were to spread, would be the subversion of civilised society; worse than the overwhelming deluge of Huns and Tartars'.[34] However Mill considered that the danger of revolt stimulated by such ideas would be easily overcome by appealing to the reason of the working man.

I should have little fear of the propagation among the common people of any doctrines hostile to property, because I have seldom met with a labouring man (and I have tried the experiment upon many of them) whom I could not make to see that the existence of property was not only good for the labouring man, but of infinitely more importance to the labourers as a class than to any other.[35]

Despite this belief, Mill feared the dissemination of popular literature and supported censorship. His main criticism of the popular press was aimed at the way in which it blamed the government for the low level of wages. Such a limitation on free speech is in direct contradiction with the emphasis on the rational character of property.

Social stability, characterised by the maintenance of existing property relationships, also dominates Mill's thought on representative democracy. This is to him the best form of government, since it loosens the connection between the monarchy and the aristocracy, and increases the political role of the middle class.

There can be no doubt that the middle rank, which gives to science, to art and to legislation itself, their most distinguished ornaments, and is a chief source of all that has exalted and refined human nature, is that portion of the community which, if the basis of representation were ever so far extended, the opinion would ultimately decide. Of the people beneath them, a vast majority would be sure to be guided by their advice and example.[36]

Therefore the interests of the middle class are considered identical with those of the whole community. Paradoxically, while expecting the example of this class to provide a general pattern of the political goals to be pursued, Mill nevertheless rejects universal enfranchisement on the grounds that the public may mistake its real interests. The inconsistency underlying the assumption that there is a spontaneous identity of interests in society and that they coincide with those of the middle class is criticised by Macaulay in connection with Mill's attitude to enfranchisement. If such an identity exists, there is no reason to refuse the vote to any section of society. If such an identity is not spontaneous, education provides a way of implementing it artificially, by demonstrating to people where their true interests lay. The establishment of universal education must therefore necessarily precede universal franchise.[37] Whilst basically hostile to state intervention, Mill justifies it in this field by stressing the importance of organised tuition to an understanding of the general good. His approach to politics and his conception of education reflect the basic difficulty inherent in the Physiocratic legacy, namely the contradiction resulting from a simultaneous belief in the natural order and in its perfectibility.

Education for the middle classes. While the philosophical assumptions underlying Mill's theory are derived from Bentham's ethical system, Bentham's only work on education, the *Chrestomathia*, was stimulated by Mill. These connections illustrate the fundamental unity of the early Utilitarian school as well as the importance they attached to educational considerations. It is he rather than Mill who provides the blueprint for the instruction to be received by the middle classes themselves. The very title of *Chrestomathia* '. . . for the extension of the new system of instruction to the higher branches of learning, for the use of the middling and higher ranks in life' (1816–17), indicates that Utilitarian education was designed solely for the middle class. This restrictiveness was justified by the productive role of this class, which makes the main contribution to the wealth of society as a whole. Moreover only this class has both the leisure and also the willingness to increase useful knowledge; while the working class do not possess the former, the aristocracy is not intellectually inclined, by tradition.

Again the educational provisions will be relevant to practical life, but in a completely different sense from the protective ethical instruction given to the lower orders. Tuition will be of direct and positive relevance to future occupational activities. The principle of utility is applied at three levels by Bentham in *Chrestomathia*. Firstly, the general goal of schooling is to implement the principles of utility in individual behaviour – a fundamental assumption derived from his wider philosophy. Secondly, the content of instruction is defined in relation to its social function as the inclusion of subjects is determined according to their relevance to active life. Thus all tuition is centred upon vocational training. Thirdly, teaching methods are derived from Utilitarian principles. Bentham drew up an 'encyclopaedic table' of the different branches of knowledge, presented 'In the order in which they are most advantageously taught'.[38] This order was dictated by the principles of utility and facility. The introduction of facility was to apply a theory of learning to a curriculum, to achieve the most speedy assimilation of useful knowledge.

As in James Mill, educational assertion is linked with political and justified by the productive role of the middle class in the economy. Productive in wealth and learning, the middle class is the mainstay of democratic government since it executes its main objective. Among the four ends of government listed by Bentham – subsistence, abundance, security and equality – abundance is the one upon which civilisation rests. Since all other ends are inferior to abundance, equality is subordinated to productivity. 'The institution of equality is chimerical; all that can be done is to reduce inequality.'[39] This view reflects Bentham's rejection of natural rights, and his complementary emphasis on rights as created by law, and justified by their social usefulness. Thus the right of property is legitimated by reference to the social utility of the wealth it produces, and not with regard to an abstract notion of individual freedom. In the economic field, Utilitarianism is purely descriptive, and therefore is prepared to outline existing property relationships without questioning their justice. However since legislation is necessarily prescriptive, harnessing law to utility merely aids the class described as most productive.

Utilitarian philosophy allied to classical economics epitomised and sought to legitimate the ambitions of the emergent middle class. In the search for domination over a social institution, the assertion of a group is inseparable from its attempts to control others. Such activities may take two forms: endeavours to restrict the existing privilege of the dominant group and to prevent any increase in the claims of other assertive groups. In this context, the approach of the middle class to education was double-edged, since control over the instruction of workers was a major motive for its own assertion. Ideally it sought to replace the amateur tradition of the secondary and higher education by useful instruction and to replace religious by economic indoctrination in the elementary schooling of the working class. In the first instance emphasis on a broader curriculum, more relevant to the needs of industrialisation, served to support the claim that the middle class was the most useful section of society. In the second desires to communicate classical economics to workers reflected a conviction that an understanding of its laws would protect property from attacks against it.

The continuous underlying contradiction in middle-class thought was that although such economic indoctrination was considered necessary to buttress private property, it would then reduce profit by withdrawing workers from production. This contradiction was implicit in classical economics where state intervention in education was viewed as potentially another undesirable form of social welfare unless kept within strict limits. State intervention by providing children with instruction for which their parents ought to be responsible, would free families from a potential check upon their extension.[40] These two postulates are only contradictory when considered in the context of middle-class goals. While social control requires the spread of education, population control demands that parental responsibilities should be maximised and unalleviated by state intervention. In the long term this contradiction is resolved if education can be assumed to promote enlightened self interest represented by voluntary family planning.

Despite the firm connections which both classical economics and Utilitarianism had made between economic advance and the education of the lower classes, it seems highly plausible that the simultaneous concern for such instruction to be minimalistic made more impression upon entrepreneurs desirous to increase short-term profits. The unwillingness of this section of the middle class to make use of the educational prerogatives accorded under the Factory Act probably undermined the success of middle-class assertion in primary education. This attitude led Engels to declare: 'so stupidly narrow-minded is the English bourgeoisie in its egotism, that it does not even take the trouble to impress upon the workers the morality of the day, which the bourgeoisie has patched together in its own interests for its own protection'.[41] Instead the energy of the majority of this group was channelled to aiding 'the efforts of those who are destined to stand forth as thinkers above the multitude'.[42] Since methods of devaluing the Anglican monopoly by means of substitution were considerably more expensive in secondary and higher education, their relative lack of success during this period is scarcely suprising. Increasingly the middle class, for its assertion at all educational levels, was to rely on state intervention which Utilitarians had unwillingly conceded as essential. In the second part of the nineteenth century the middle class came to rely on devaluation through legal restriction, that is through their own manipulation of the parliamentary machinery. 'After 1832 criticism was replaced by an instant demand for Parliamentary action to enforce reform on closed corporations outside the reach of normal pressures.'[43] The weakness of middle-class educational ideology lay in its imprecision as a plan of action due to the ambiguity attaching to state intervention. Ultimately the group as a whole had to accept in practice what the classical economists and the Utilitarians had only reluctantly acknowledged in theory – that education would only be integrated with the economy by political intervention.

WORKING CLASS EDUCATIONAL THOUGHT

Enlightened philosophy and education as a natural right

The influence of enlightened philosophy on the ideology of English working-class educational assertion parallels that of Physiocratic economics on middle-class ideology. The philosophers of late eighteenth-century France shared with economists a common concern for rationality and a similar commitment to the maximisation of human happiness. However, while the Physiocrats equated rationality with submission to immutable economic laws and happiness with the acceptance of the natural order, the pre-revolutionary moralists – following Rousseau – saw rationality as a natural attribute of man and its operation as perverted by artificial institutions. Hence happiness could only be achieved by freeing individuals from the constraints imposed upon them by a society in which inequalities were neither natural nor consequently rational.

In emphasising individual rationality as a source of natural rights and institutional irrationality (as a corollary of their artificiality), the pre-revolutionary moralists – Holbach and Helvetius in particular – differed radically from the other trend in enlightened thought, to which man was an unreasonable being enmeshed in a system whose operation he does not have to understand. To Voltaire trusting in the enlightened decisions of benevolent despots – while stressing the absurdity of individual action – or to the Physiocrats positing that the pursuit of individual interests automatically contributes to the general good, governmental institutions or the operation of economic laws embody the rationality existing in society. Although considerable oscillation between the two outlooks occurred, even within the works of one author (for example, Diderot), eighteenth-century enlightenment thought can be polarised into these two extremes – an emphasis on natural order and the rationality of institutions embodying it on the one hand, and concentration on natural rights and individual rationality on the other.

It is the latter view which provided the main tenets of working-class ideology. Firstly, it was fundamentally egalitarian in its rejection of social differences as artificial and its assumption of rationality as common to all individuals. Secondly, it was optimistic about the nature of men, distorted by divisive institutions and insufficient or misleading knowledge, but eminently perfectible by appeals to their reason: 'The unhappiness of mankind is due to its errors.'[44] Thirdly, it relied on the formative power of education to rectify the imperfections of society and develop the innate rationality of individuals – thereby ensuring both their virtue and their happiness. 'It is possible and indeed easy to change the mass of men, to direct their minds to given ends, to standardize popular feelings.'[45] While the pre-revolutionary moralists agreed with the Utilitarians both about the educability of man and about the acceptance of human happiness as a goal, they differed in the role assigned to education because they did not seek to maximise happiness merely within the context of existing institutions. The Utilitarians inherited from the Physiocrats the acknowledgement of economic laws as rational, and hence accepted existing property arrangements. Therefore they wished to teach conformity to the economic system and derived from the statement that it was founded upon natural laws arguments in support of the middle-class claims for its members and for control of working-class institutions. By contrast the pre-revolutionary moralists posited the free operation of education as a natural right and accepted no constraints upon it by political or economic institutions. Any limitation on the instruction given to individuals was seen as a source of artificial differentiation between them and an obstacle to their happiness. Thus the main themes of human perfectibility – rationality and the formative role of education – were interrelated and provided arguments against any educational inequality rooted in the existing social stratification.

For all their explicitness about egalitarian ends, the pre-revolutionary moralists were highly ambiguous about the means which could be used for implementing equality in education and rationality in society. They implied an enlightened despot who – as *deus ex machina* – would remove obstacles to educational freedom and limit excessive economic inequalities, thereby facilitating the transition to a system of stratification founded on educational differences, alone considered socially relevant and morally justified. Yet this reliance on reformist rather than revolutionary means sprang from a belief in the adaptability of irrational institutions to rational ends which contradicted the initial natural/artificial dichotomy, as well as a trust in rulers hardly compatible with the accompanying distrust of the mechanisms through which they rule. This underlying contradiction between the condemnation of government as artificial and the expectation that it would through education restore the natural rights of individuals, was avoided by the English radicals – Godwin in particular. Writing under the influence of French revolutionary action as well as pre-revolutionary thought, Godwin transmitted to the early English socialists – Hodgskin and Owen – his distrust of governmental intervention in education, as well as the main themes derived from enlightened philosophy. Hence the reliance on educational substitution, the form of action recommended by the ideology through which the Chartists legitimated working-class educational assertion.

However, another aspect of the contradiction between the reformist and the revolutionary implications of English philosophy remained unsolved until the formulation of Chartist educational policies. While the theory of natural rights and Godwin's corollary to it – their usurpation by government – provided an ideology of educational assertion through substitution and of political action, it was unspecific about the means by which political rights could be gained. Either they would follow the spread of instruction in the working class or they were a necessary prerequisite to it – depending upon the interpretation given to an ideology unexplicit about the priorities attributed to various natural rights. Thus the division in the Chartist Movement between the education and the force parties reflects an initial theoretical ambiguity about the prevalence of natural rights over institutional constraints either by natural (purely educational) or by artificial (political) means.

Godwin – education against political indoctrination

Both Godwin's optimism about human perfectibility and his egalitarianism derive from his conception of nature. Since to him men are born morally neutral, there is nothing in human nature which in itself precludes the possibility of moral improvement.[46] Furthermore, at birth, moral neutrality co-exists with intellectual equality and therefore inequalities between individuals are purely artificial. 'There is no particular mould for the construction of lords and they are born neither better nor worse than the poorest of their dependents.'[47] Thus Godwin endorses a theory of moral, intellectual and social formation, since 'children are a sort of raw material put into our hands, a ductile and yielding substance'.[48]

As all men are capable of equal achievement, social inequalities can be eliminated by education. Indeed Godwin considers that ability is determined by environment and views intellectual and moral perfectibility as parallel. He finds in 'a spirit of prying observation and incessant curiosity' the motivation to learn which is the common denominator of all men. Intellectual achievement depends on it and can be deliberately produced through education. Consequently no limitation is placed upon the intellectual potential of any normal individual and universal genius[49] could be developed. In later works, this opinion is qualified to reintroduce some genetic determination of aptitude. Such innate differences however are not construed as absolute, but are merely presented as inclinations towards achievement in distinct fields of endeavour. In other words, Godwin moves away from a general theory of intelligence to adopt a postulate of specific abilities. 'Putting idiots and extraordinary cases out of the question, every human creature is endowed with talents, which, if rightly directed, would show him to be apt, adroit, intelligent and acute, in the walk for which his organization especially fitted him.'[50]

All differences between men being due to environmental factors, Godwin assesses the relative weight of various influences to which artificial inequalities are due. None is considered either so pervasive or so powerful as that of the government, from which all institutions derive their authority. Educational institutions are no exception to this rule, since teachers are not exempt from the values imposed by the state. Government influence is held to be harmful in that it distorts rationality and corrupts morality. Two stages are involved in this process of corruption. Firstly, the government encourages vice by perpetuating errors which would have been short-lived if they had not received state support. Indeed error unavoidably leads to vice (as reason leads to virtue). Secondly, the human mind is capable of detecting error and does so most accurately when dealing with full information. Governments impede this natural mental activity, thus perverting the truth and precluding the practice of virtue. 'They (the government) poison our minds, before we can resist or so much as suspect their malignity.'[51]

These undesirable characteristics are common to all forms of government, since even the best interferes with the operation of reason, and thereby hampers virtue. Since no action can be virtuous without being based on the exercise of reason, governmental dictates cannot be productive of moral behaviour. Even useful reforms cannot prove beneficial unless they are fully understood and desired by the community. 'It is in vain that you heap upon me benefits that I neither understand nor desire. The faculty of understanding is an essential part of every human being and cannot with impunity be overlooked in any attempt to alter or meliorate his conditions.'[52] Thus reform cannot be imposed by enlightened rulers, but must be deserved by rational citizens. While Godwin's ideal is the abolition of government, he considers democracy as the least obnoxious form of rule.[53] A democracy comes closest to 'the uncontrolled exercise of private judgement'[54] which enables men to define the truth through the use of reason and to attain virtue through the exercise of benevolence. The common possession of reason which is the source of human equality is also the instrument of social progress. When moral perfection is achieved in society, namely when men are fully rational and repressive governments have disappeared, social evils – war, crime, poverty – will no longer exist. Nor will private property, since men will become aware that ownership is trusteeship on behalf of society as a whole.[55] As general happiness becomes the predominant concern of all, a redistribution will occur and previous inequalities founded on possession will be abolished. Thus 'the improvement of individuals and the melioration of political institutions are destined mutually to produce and reproduce each other'.[56]

Thus the double role imparted to education is to develop the latent rationality of individuals, not only in order that they fulfil their own mental potential, but to produce a more enlightened society. To cultivate individual aptitudes and disseminate knowledge is to ensure that moral excellence will coexist with intellectual eminence. 'The great triumph of man is in the power of education to improve his intellect, to sharpen his perceptions, and to regulate and modify his moral qualities.'[57] Godwin therefore sees education and government as competing for influence on human development. While tuition stimulates reason, the state perpetuates error. While education restores natural equality, government supports artificial distinctions. Therefore it is logical that Godwin should attack state intervention in the field of education, since it would only distort rational thinking, promote mental uniformity and restrict individual judgement. The greater the governmental influence in education, the more it would 'strengthen its hands and perpetuate its institutions'.[58] This would further immorality by enforcing the claims of a ruling group at the expense of other social strata and by propagating their values to the detriment of rational thought. From his belief in individual perfectibility and his fear of government as the main obstacle to it, Godwin derives his opposition to a state educational system and his criticism of contemporary grammar schools. In these institutions, he remarks that pupils' intellects are stereotyped and incapable of original thought. Such a schooling gives rise to an individual who 'is no longer a man, [but] the ghost of a departed man'.[59] While man cannot fulfil his potential unless he is freed from the artificial constraints imposed by government oppression, he does not measure the full extent of these limitations on his natural rights. This is as true of underprivileged classes as it is of individuals and instruction would reveal the full extent of collective deprivation. Thus, in England, the working class, whose labour resulted in industrial prosperity, has not participated in this well-being. Its educated members are consequently 'induced to regard the state of society as a state of war, an unjust combination, not for protecting every man in his rights and securing to him the means of existence, but for engrossing all its advantages to a few favoured individuals, and reserving for the portion of the rest want, dependence and misery'.[60] Hence the obstacles to, and the limits on working-class education are the outcome of a deliberate policy intended to delay the development of rationality in its midst. Since the state is the main instrument of this obscurantism, educational substitution alone can free the workers by enlightening them. Thus Godwin's views provide the working class with a double-edged weapon. His theory of individual perfectibility provides a basis for advocating social equality as natural, aspiring to educational equality and claiming political representation. His theory of government provides a basis for challenging the benevolence of rulers, the paternalism of the middle class and the fairness of institutions – both political and educational. Thus he contributed arguments in favour of a working-class policy of educational substitution – though the emphasis on its political desirability somewhat overshadows the lack of precision about its economic feasibility.

Hodgskin – education against economic indoctrination

While the theory of natural rights legitimated the workers' educational assertion on moral grounds, it failed to challenge the economic postulates which underpinned the ideology of middle-class control. Without a new approach to economic theory, working-class demands for universal franchise and attempts at educational substitution could be rejected as impractical, since they conflicted with the recognised requirements of the market economy. The general acceptance and wide propagation of classical economics conditioned a belief in the unchanging role of labour, the immutability of property and their inseparable counterpart, the existing system of social stratification. Thus the main pressures for enfranchisement and for educational reform were only exerted after an alternative to classical economics had been offered.

The theory of rent had been the issue upon which the middle-class producer had challenged the traditional economic superiority of the landowner, and at the same time asserted his own superiority over labour. It is on this central element of Ricardian economics that Thomas Hodgskin, the author of *Labour defended against the claims of Capital*, attacks the economic orthodoxy of the time. He claims that economists have confused civilisation, which is by definition artificial and distorted, with the state of nature and have therefore misrepresented natural laws. Thus there is no natural law of diminishing profits, but a myth of growing rents perpetuated by capitalists in order to keep wages fixed. Similarly capitalists overestimate the value of the intellectual work involved in management, taking advantage of the educational deficiencies of workers to under-assess manual work and give excessive remuneration to themselves. 'The manual labourers, oppressed by the capitalist, have never been paid highly enough, and even now are more disposed to estimate their own deserts rather by what they have hitherto received than by what they produce.'[61] The same convention is used to vindicate 'the incomes of those who live on profit and interest, and who have no just claim but custom to any share of the national produce'.[62] The system of stratification is based on historical accident rather than nature and reason. As the only true source of wealth is labour, which alone is really productive, the contribution of the capitalist is limited to technical competence and managerial skill, acquired through education. Therefore education is the most productive of activities, since it creates skilled labour.

It is not only in the economic, but also in the legal sphere that Hodgskin makes a fundamental distinction between the natural and the artificial. Any system of control based on standards other than natural rights is necessarily repressive. Like capitalist property, state power is derived from force and therefore is the product of historical accident. State legislation, when it ceases to record natural rights and attempts to create other rights, is at the service of vested interests and results in 'legal oppression'. This attack on the state mirrors Godwin's philosophy, as does the statement that legislation is always conservative since the legislator cannot foresee the future. History is not shaped by positive law, merely designed to protect power, but by social change, reflecting imperfectly the natural law and taking place in spite of governments.

The main purpose of Hodgskin's works was to propagate an understanding of natural law and of contemporary deviations from it. In his view, education should serve the same end. However, the biased instruction meted out by the middle class is a fundamental obstacle to the knowledge of the truth. In addition, it is designed to perpetuate inequalities, whereas education for the workers ought, by increasing skills, to reduce differences in income. Since this is a result which neither the employers, nor the state, their oppressive tool, are prepared to allow, a national educational system would be contrary to working-class interests, which only a policy of substitution can serve. By organising their own schooling, workers would prepare themselves for political action leading to the franchise and to further social change.

As the labourers acquire knowledge, the foundations of the social order will be dug up from the deep beds into which they were laid in times past, they will be curiously handled and closely examined, and they will not be restored unless they were originally laid in justice, and unless justice commands their preservation.[63]

Education is thus a prerequisite for the emancipation of the working class from artificial institutional constraints.

Owen – education for economic emancipation

Owen's educational proposals are rooted in the natural rights tradition,[64] whereas his economic postulates are reminiscent of Hodgskin's; thus he links enlightened radicalism with early socialism. Like Godwin, he rejects the genetic determination of ability and asserts to the contrary that differences between men, whether in intelligence or in morality, are due to dissimilar environments. 'Any character from the best to the worst, from the most ignorant to the most enlightened may be given to any community, even to the world at large, by applying certain means.'[65] Hence he endorses a completely formative view of education, which he considers to be an exact science.

The educational experiment at New Lanark developed into an attempt at social planning, after Owen realised that not only individual achievement depended on environment, but also educational institutions did not function in isolation. In the blueprints for his model villages and co-operative communities, he outlined systems – rejecting classical economics – in which the worker benefitted from the whole product of his labour. It was only in such semi-rural communities, in which there were no great differences of incomes and where cultural facilities were provided, that the formative power of education could be fully realised. 'The members of a community may by degrees be trained to live without idleness, without poverty, without crime, and without punishment; for each of these is the effect of error in the various systems prevalent throughout the world. They are all necessary consequences of ignorance.'[66] This belief in infinite human perfectibility was seen as the source of individual happiness and good government. 'It is only by education, rightly understood, that communities of men can ever be well governed, and by means of such education every object of human society will be attained with the least labour and the most satisfaction.'[67] In such a society, instruction would be made relevant to active life and the information provided would counteract the stupefaction induced in the working class by increasing job specialisation.

While the main tenets of Owen's system were hardly original,[68] he differed from any other proponent of formative education at the time, since his experiments attempted to vary the factors thought to determine ability. The success attributed to his endeavours can be largely accounted for by the low level of expectations concerning the ability of working-class children at the time. Though his experiment was conducted on a very small scale, it raised the question of the environmental change required in order to ensure the efficacy of educational provisions. To introduce such change at the national, and not merely at the local level, implied governmental intervention. Therefore political action was a corollary of educational substitution, if it were to go beyond the experimental utopian stage. This became the central tenet of Chartist educational policy.

The Chartists – education for political emancipation

While the People's Charter of 1838 was the crystallisation and to a large extent the repetition of successive pleas for parliamentary reform since the end of the eighteenth century,[69] it was original in emanating from a purely working-class movement. The fact that the members of the Working Men's Association had

strong traditions of constitutional action determined the method whereby they strove to effect the sweeping changes desired. That method was by attempting to secure control of parliament through the enactment of complete democracy. Chartism was, therefore, a class movement for economic and social ends by political means.[70]

Unlike their middle-class counterparts, the Utilitarians, who favoured industrialisation, they reacted against the Industrial Revolution as a source of social injustice. However, they resembled the Utilitarians in a belief that education was inextricably linked with a programme for social transformation. In pursuing social change, the Chartists endorsed enfranchisement as a key to political reform and universal education as an instrument of social equality. Dissensions within the movement centred upon the historical priority to be allocated to these two goals of its programme. The moderate elements thought that self-education would be rewarded by enfranchisement, whereas the more radical insisted that parliamentary reform was a necessary precursor of any democratisation.

William Lovett epitomises the moderate outlook, with its condemnation of violence and optimistic faith in the efficacy of enlightenment. 'Whatever is gained in England by force, by force must be sustained; but whatever springs from knowledge and justice will sustain itself.'[71] From Godwin he derives the view that men are fundamentally equal and that differences between them are due to education. 'All men are not gifted with great strength of body or powers of intellect, but all are so wisely and wonderfully endowed that all have capacities for becoming intelligent, moral and happy members of society.'[72] Thus, without accepting complete environmental determination of ability Lovett accepts a formative theory of education, defined as 'All those means which are used to develop the various faculties of mind and body, and so to train them, that the child shall become a healthy, intelligent, moral and useful member of society.'[73] Without the benefits conferred by instruction, the working class is condemned to intellectual apathy and may become prone to moral deviance. While 'most social evils have their origin in ignorance'[74] this state is perpetuated by 'one part of the community (who) feel it to be their interest to cultivate mere *power and wealth acquiring knowledge*, and . . . to prevent or retard the enlightenment of all.'[75] Thus Lovett rejects both the content of the education imparted by the middle class and the limitations imposed upon the schooling of the working class. He condemns the restrictiveness of the aristocracy and indoctrination by the bourgeoisie in claiming that

while a large portion of the hawks and owls of society were seeking to perpetuate that state of mental darkness most favourable to the securing of their prey, another portion, with more cunning, were for admitting a sufficient amount of mental glimmer to cause the multitude to walk quietly and contentedly in the paths they in their wisdom had prescribed for them.[76]

It is on these grounds that he repudiates as indoctrination the attempts to impart classical economics to workers through such agencies as the Society for the Diffusion of Useful Knowledge and exhorts the working class to create its own educational institutions. 'Be ours the task, then, to unite and instruct them; for be assured the good that is to be must be begun by ourselves.'[77]

Not only is education essential to the advance of the working class, but to the welfare of society as a whole.

Entertaining the notion that the wealth, happiness, and security of a country depend more on the general enlightenment, good conduct, skill, and industry of the many, than on the superior attainment of the few, I am for the education and development of all the powers God has given to all without reference to the class they belong to, or the station in life they may hereafter fill.[78]

Thus Lovett rejects the educational control exerted under the cover of charity and justifies the claims of the working class by reference both to individual rights and to the general good.

Poverty, inequality and political injustice, are involved in giving to one portion of society the blessings of education and leaving the other in ignorance; and, therefore, the working classes, who are in general the victims of this system of oppression and ignorance have just cause of complaint against all partial systems of education.[79]

Therefore a national educational system is advocated, but at the same time Lovett fears that state control would be tantamount to social control. 'The education you should aim at is not merely the old routine of reading, writing and arithmetic, or such mere technical knowledge as shall enable your children to become more efficient tools of production; but such as shall serve to prepare them to stand on a footing of equality with all others . . .'[80] Lovett distrusts the class bias inseparable from state education which he considers incompatible with equality and antipathetic to freedom: 'While we are anxious to see a general system of Education adopted, we have considerable doubts of

D

the propriety of yielding such an important duty as the education of our children to any government and the strongest abhorrence of giving any such power to *an irresponsible one*.'[81] Since the educational aims of the working class would not be implemented by any government, he advocates a policy of substitution. This would involve creating a system of infant, preparatory and high schools as well as normal schools for teachers, to be supported by rate aid. State assistance should be limited to the provision of funds for erecting schools. The tuition given would differ greatly from that considered advisable by the middle classes, in concentrating upon science and emphasising free discussion rather than indoctrination through rote learning. While such an education would be a preparation for the suffrage, it would not in itself be a guarantee of enfranchisement. Although he outlines a theory whereby education precedes democracy, Lovett does not designate a mechanism to bring about this transition. As the main political philosopher contributing to the People's Charter, Lovett was able to assert simultaneously universal franchise and general schooling. As a political reformer, he had to assign priorities: either the granting of the franchise could be viewed as a prerequisite of universal instruction, or alternatively mass education could be presented as a necessary condition of political participation. This choice would inevitably influence both political and educational working-class activities. Tawney epitomises Lovett's creed in claiming that 'the condition of any genuine democracy is education: to work for the creation of a national system of education is the first duty of reformers. It is one certain instrument of emancipation'.[82] Education would both emancipate the people from the sway of corrupt government and fit them for governmental responsibilities. Thus Lovett and his followers relied upon the diffusion of enlightenment leading to an automatic acknowledgement of political rights. Their rejection of violent policies split the Chartist Movement into two groups[83] reflecting the differences between the skilled workers in the south and the northern factory proletariat.[84] The leaders of the latter reversed the priorities established by Lovett. A major exponent of political activism, Julian Harney, demonstrates the divergence of views within the movement in claiming

we fully appreciate the advantages resulting from education, and we would earnestly wish to see the principles of a sound educational system widely disseminated; but we cannot but consider all the ideas of amelioration from this source alone, to be chimerical, perfectly illusory. Depend upon it, Fellow Democrats, that that which your enemies will not give to justice, they will not yield to moral persuasion. No, we

must act upon their fears, if we cannot act upon their sympathies. Nor can we subscribe to the notion that, under the present circumstances, the adoption of a sound
educational system, one, the principal feature of which shall be to teach the people
their rights, and not merely, as now, their duties, is practicable. Men, interested in
the continuance of the present robber-like system of society – the lordly aristocrat,
the moneyed vampire and the prostituted priest – in a word the enemies to the
rights, the liberties, and the happiness of millions, will pretendedly acquiesce in the
propriety of educating – of moralising the people; and it will ever be found that so
long as the people's political rights are withheld from them, any system of education
which meets with the acquiescence of their foes, will have for its object the perpetuation of the people's slavery.[85]

Thus, without minimising the importance of education, Harney
emphasises its inadequacy as a way of obtaining the franchise. Reliance
on direct action, including the use of violence, is justified by reference
to natural rights and confirmed by precedents of the French Revolution.[86] The advocates of persuasion or moral restraint are rejected as
not being truly representative of the working class. 'Those men were
well fed and therefore they relied on moral force; but let them labour
for one week, and be ill-fed and clothed, and it would soon convert
their moral force to physical force.'[87] Thus working-class thought, in
seeking to overthrow social control increasingly adopted a revolutionary
attitude culminating in Harney's support for the Communist Manifesto.[88] This excludes the possibility of co-operating with the middle
class to achieve common political aims, because the difference in
economic interests is considered insuperable. This divergence breeds
hostility between classes and leads to entrenchment rather than
reconciliation. By claiming that political rights cannot be secured by
merit, but only be won through force, Harney highlights the essential
weakness of Lovett's theory – its lack of precision about the transition
between education and enfranchisement. Far from preceding it,
'education will follow the suffrage as sure as day succeeds night'.[89]

Throughout the first half of the nineteenth century, English working-
class educational thought can continuously be distinguished from its
middle class counterpart by its debt to eighteenth-century French
political philosophy rather than to the political economy of that period.
This legacy, interpreted by Godwin and Paine, channelled this thought
into political action by emphasising the notion of natural rights and
showing how government had usurped them. However, such a
proclamation may be a political platform, but cannot provide a
blueprint for action. While the theory of natural rights represents a
common denominator, it is sufficiently unspecific to allow for wide

divergencies of interpretation, leading to a lack of uniformity in the sphere of political action. A common feature of all prevalent interpretations is the inclusion of education among natural rights and its inseparability from enfranchisement. However, while a philosophical system can assert the joint importance of both factors, a pressure group has to assign a priority to either of them. Only two logical permutations are possible – either gaining the vote would assure education or the spread of instruction would secure enfranchisement. These two possibilities contain the whole fund of variety of working-class action. Granting a priority to education entailed the optimistic view that natural rights were bound to be recognised once the people were sufficiently enlightened to deserve them. Incidentally this highlights a contradiction between the alleged inalienability of human rights and the formulation of conditions under which they can be properly exercised. A parallel can be drawn with the similar paradox in Utilitarian thought, also inherited from eighteenth-century sources, whereby the pursuit of self-interest was natural, and yet increased by enlightenment. Alternatively viewing enfranchisement as a prerequisite for educational reform implied a disbelief in the automatic operation of rights and a pessimistic acceptance of their complete alienation. Increasingly this political realism tended to prevail over the earlier idealism. The division within the Chartist Movement reflects this dichotomy.

6. The defensive ideologies of Anglican domination

When Anglican domination over secondary and higher education was challenged by both dissent and Utilitarianism, it became clear to many churchmen that the rather diffuse forms of traditional legitimation required reformulation in the defence of existing institutional relationships. Two factors appear to account for the absence of a well-defined philosophy of Anglican education at the beginning of the nineteenth century. Firstly, the circumstances which surrounded the formation of the church of England had necessitated its loose constitution for it to be acceptable to all its members. From the Reformation onwards, no well-defined authority structure emerged, capable of pronouncing on dogma or policy, and hence lasting subdivisions were perpetuated within the church. The Prayer Book and Articles constituting the only standard in Anglican doctrine, it became clear 'as time went on that these ambiguous formulas were less and less able to cover the vast area of controversy or to provide a firm decision between conflicting views'.[1] The diversity of theological interpretation encompassed by the church thus partially accounts for the diffuseness of the dominant group's source of legitimation in education. Second, and of equal importance, is the fact that until the late eighteenth century the integration of education with religion had been challenged by no major social group. Its unopposed domination rested partly on the absence of groups perceiving any advantage to be derived from controlling instruction and partly upon the relative efficiency with which the tuition provided by the church met the administrative and professional requirements of a pre-industrial society. Thus no assertive forces stimulated a consolidation of the tenets on which legitimacy was based and the Anglicans continued to rely on the felt appropriateness of the established church dispensing national instruction. This basically nationalistic justification for domination was underwritten by the state in the form of protective legal constraints.

The growth of the middle class and the tendency of its nineteenth-century philosophical exponents (whether secularists or dissenters) to reject the intellectual supremacy of established religion had two distinctive consequences. Major efforts were made to redefine and tighten-up the ideology legitimating Anglican domination. While these remained fundamentally traditionalistic in type, they became vastly more specific. Since the Utilitarians in particular had also sought to discredit the classical content of instruction given, its defence by Anglican thinkers provided scope for the introduction of some rational elements of legitimation through the church insisting on the practical advantages of liberal education. A direct consequence of such rethinking was an intensification of internal conflict within the church itself once the vague and nationalistic justification was examined more closely.

Not only did these attempts to redefine the relationships between the religious and the secular in the field of education involve a reappraisal of those between church and state, but other events were also making this indispensable. Middle-class enfranchisement indicated the state's tolerance of both secularism and dissent and the suppression of the Irish bishoprics showed how religious interests could be sacrificed to political expediency. The eighteenth century of church and king could not easily be translated into a nineteenth-century equivalent of church and state. It is not surprising then that the new sources of legitimation advanced in the field of education represented an attempt to specifically defend the domination of the church, not the continuation of an Anglican/aristocratic alliance in instruction. This period thus marked the emergence of the church, which as a group in its own right sought to retain educational domination.

While many distinctive educational philosophies were elaborated within the established church during this period, two major ones, those of Newman and Arnold will be dealt with in detail because of their importance as leaders of competing groups within the church and their subsequent educational influence. Their respective parties, the High and Broad Church, represented divergent theological trends, the former stressing the Catholic notion of apostolic succession, the latter emphasising the Protestant view of individual freedom for private scriptural interpretation. At the end of the eighteenth century the High Church was characterised by nationalistic Protestantism and its allegiance to the monarchy. It was socially exclusive and politically Tory rather than Whig. Its acceptance of episcopacy, sacraments and liturgy in the early

nineteenth century reflected traditional attitudes rather than a theological appraisal. Therefore its exclusiveness was founded on social
rather than dogmatic grounds. In contrast, the Broad Church stressed
comprehensiveness rather than exclusivity. They 'wished to exclude
no one who did not exclude themselves'[2] and interpreted Erastianism to
imply that the state by enforcing comprehensiveness was the final bond
of church unity. The fundamental issue to the Broad Churchmen was
to protect Anglicanism as a national church and to prevent its reduction
to a sect.

Both Newman and Arnold from these initial standpoints devised
distinctive educational philosophies which, despite their striking
differences, sought to defend Anglican educational domination against
the same two attacks levelled at it by the middle class. Thus both
defend the right of the established church to control national instruction and are equally concerned with justifying its classical content.
Both endeavour to show that this type of control over, and content of
instruction are related. Hence they seek to repulse secular assertion and
to firmly separate education from training. In doing so, they redefine
church-state relations in education and dissociate the aims of instruction from that of confirming the status of traditional elites. Their
approach to these two issues clearly indicates the extent to which the
church was on the defensive as a group in its own right, pursuing its
interests alone.

THE OXFORD MOVEMENT

The Oxford Movement can in no way be seen as representative of the
High Church, but as an important attempt to reform it. This reappraisal
was initially prompted by political events threatening the position of
the church and by the growth of secular rationalism and religious
latitudinarianism. The success of the July Revolution in France and
the disappearance of the divine right monarchy was seen as 'the
triumph of irreligion'. The passing of the First Reform Bill in England
two years later was interpreted as a parallel attack on the state, which
could only have undesirable repercussions on the church. The connection between enfranchisement and Utilitarianism made it not only
a political danger, but also a philosophical threat.

As a reaction to the suppression of ten Irish bishoprics on grounds
of political expediency, Keble preached the sermon on the church as
a legal constitutional element of government, which is the starting

point of the movement. He justified the militantly anti-Erastian views which were to characterise the whole of Tractarianism by reference to the church's pre-eminent position in the civil law from which the establishment derived its sanction. More importantly he asserted the derivation of the established church from apostolic succession. The latter argument implied that any attempt to deprive the church of power was tantamount to sacrilege.[3]

The views of the Oxford Movement were presented in the Tracts published between 1833 and 1839. They firstly emphasised the role of the church as providing an authoritative interpretation of revealed truths. 'They rested their faith upon a twofold revelation: upon the Bible, as the Church and the Councils of the Church alone knew how to interpret it, but still more certainly upon the existence and the authority of the Church itself.'[4] This authority was derived from the continuity of the apostolic church which the Reformation had obscured, but not destroyed. This succession was the second tenet of the movement and was complemented by the rejection of the evangelical view according to which scripture and men's unguided judgement of its contents sufficed for salvation. The indispensable contribution of the church to individual salvation constituted the third proposition in this logical sequence. Since sacraments, including the priesthood, were the ordained means of grace, perfection of character could not be achieved without them. Fourthly, to consider the church as the divine appointment in society is to view its prestige and power as unequalled by any other institution. Consequently the Tractarians rejected its subordination to the state and asserted its independence expressed by the right to formulate and ratify its own dogma. The fifth point was a corollary of the church's monopoly in interpreting scripture and conferring grace, namely religious education must prevail or society will cease to be Christian. Indeed it is the duty of the church to propagate the truth of which it is the sole repository and the obligation of the state to facilitate the performance of this mission. This postulate implied the exclusion of non-Anglicans from higher education to prevent the corruption of truth. Conversely, Anglican education implied the direct religious instruction and moral formation of pupils and students.

The conjunction of these five points presented in the Tracts summed up the definition given by the Oxford Movement of the historical and contemporary position of Anglicanism. This Tractarian charter constituted the programme which Newman called the *via media* and which his supporters endeavoured to introduce into the church.

*John Henry Newman: defence of the church's
authority over education*

The educational theories of Newman are those of a Catholic, yet as a
convert they are his first works. Not surprisingly then his writings
draw upon both epochs – from Oxford and from Rome. They constitute a theory of education, in so far as Newman seeks to integrate the
classical Oxonian definition of culture with the Catholic notion of the
church's intellectual authority. His educational theory thus attempts
to engineer a complementarity between two incompatible periods of
history. It wishes to affirm the Renaissance while condemning the
Reformation . . . to assert the intellectual role of the medieval church
while maintaining the secular role of the contemporary cultured
gentleman. In doing this it is intellectually progressive, while socially
conservative. As an educationalist, Newman is concerned with an
alliance between the classical ideal of mental independence and his
complete distrust of private judgement in religious matters. The
success of his theory stands or falls by the extent to which his educational system enables men to be intellectually free and yet remain
religious; by the extent to which it defends the authority of the church,
while reconciling it with classical instruction.

Distinctive of Newman's approach to education is his acceptance of
its secular character. Although religion and instruction, the clergyman
and the teacher, the church and the school may jointly endorse certain
values, co-operate within particular institutions and overlap in subject
matter, they are nevertheless distinct activities with different goals.
His educational theory attempts to define the spheres of influence and
boundaries between culture and religion. The fundamental distinction
made between them is contained in the denial that intellectual education can make a man better or more religious and his refusal to accept
this as the highest aim of instruction. To Newman the notion of
'religious education' is therefore a contradiction in terms, since it is
compounded of two entities without common denominator.

Since instruction is founded upon truths in the natural order, thus:
'Each science so interpreted remains a stranger to spiritual life.'[5] This
distinction between natural and supernatural not only delineates the
contents of the two fields but also precludes their possession of common
goals. Education 'implies an action upon our mental nature, and the
formation of a character',[6] which in its ideal form can be typified as the
gentleman. While the gentleman will possess characteristics of virtue,

he is nonetheless the product of civilisation, not of Christianity. 'Knowledge is one thing, virtue is another; good sense is not conscience, refinement is not humility, nor is largeness or justness of view faith.'[7]

Reason may join with revelation in condemning various moral evils through its inculcation of fastidiousness and good taste. However, since some sins are compatible with refinement, reason is not an infallible guide to morality. In addition, education can result in superiority and self-sufficiency which are directly opposed to religion. Thus reason may lead to truth, but never the whole truth, since it does not encompass revelation; reason may lead to virtue, but never to complete virtue, since it is amoral and lacks the means of grace to transform intentions into actions.

Since education, being secular, can only have secular results, it is not as a religious apologist that Newman can champion it; its extension might be thought immaterial or even antagonistic to the church. However to Newman, education, like health, is good in itself. 'Knowledge . . . is valuable for what its very presence in us does for us after the manner of a habit, even though it be turned to no further account, nor subserve any direct end.'[8] The form of instruction which best embodies this intrinsic goodness is the liberal education – 'the process of training by which the intellect, instead of being formed or sacrificed to some particular or accidental purpose, some specific trade or profession, or study or science, is disciplined for its own sake, for perception of its own proper object, and for its own highest culture, is called Liberal Education.'[9] Such instruction stands opposed to training and to trade as much as to social or religious utility. 'I consider Knowledge to have an end in itself . . . it is a real mistake to burden it with virtue or with religion as with the mechanical arts.'[10] It is his educational attitudes, then, which, as much as his religious convictions, cause Newman to condemn the principle of utility. No field is immune from its intrusion – theology which should be 'cultivated as a contemplation'[11] tends to limit its objectives to the training of clergy. Thus the inculcation of independent modes of thought and the development of good taste, the hallmarks of a gentleman, are placed in contradistinction to any form of professional training, even its highest product, the clergyman.

To assert the intrinsic goodness of education is not to deny that society and religion will be the beneficiaries of its extension. It is merely to claim that such advantages will be by-products of, rather than justifications for liberal instruction. Thus education may be useful to society without being utilitarian, and conducive to religion, while not religious.

The function of a university is the dispensing of liberal knowledge and the subsequent formation of the gentleman. By this ideal, Newman does not imply 'that antiquated variety of human nature and remnant of feudalism'[12] which originates from the aristocracy and, after university, is returned to it. Indeed, he encountered criticism for his dismissal of the Oxford 'gentlemen commoners', precisely because he considered good breeding insufficient in itself. These views do not make Newman liberal, but more extremely elitist than traditional aristocracy itself. While the upper classes could encompass the man of letters and the man of action, only the complete man satisfied Newman's ideal. His gentleman was not the product of English civilisation, but of classical culture. Thus while the characteristics of his ideal are to be 'acquired, where they are to be found, in high society',[13] liberal education transforms the aristocrat into the cultured man.

In defining a university as a *studium generale* or school of universal learning, Newman commits himself to the classical tradition. His purpose is to unite classicism and Catholicism, but the complementarity has to be engineered, as neither ideal automatically serves the other. The very authority of the church enforces this separation. Since it alone pronounces on faith and morals and since its clergy teaches dogma, educational institutions would engage in the illegitimate practice of private judgement, if they intervened in this sphere.

The role of theology in education. These problems are again restated when Newman considers the content of the university syllabus. The keynote to this argument is contained in his definition of a university as a school of universal learning. This being so, all disciplines contributing to the total fund of knowledge have a right to be represented. Man has three types of relationships which add to this store, relations with things, with other men and with God. To omit or suppress the information gained from any one of these would contravene the constitution of the *studium generale*. While criticisms have been brought against the universities for their religious exclusiveness, it is in fact the 'godless colleges' themselves who are guilty of such exclusivity through their opposition to theology. 'A University, I should lay down, by its very name professes to teach universal Knowledge: Theology is surely a branch of Knowledge: how then is it possible for it to profess all branches of Knowledge, and yet to exclude from the subjects of its teaching one which, to say the least, is as important and as large as any of them.'[14]

Three arguments are then adduced to substantiate the claim of theology to have a rightful place in education. For each of these Newman relies upon the single proposition that religious facts are of the same order as those produced by the natural sciences. Thus that 'Religious doctrine is Knowledge, in as full a sense as Newton's doctrine is Knowledge'[15] is the content of his first defence. The tendency to neglect or deny this proposition is a product of the Reformation. The Lutheran transformation of faith, from it being a statement based upon facts to one justified by feelings alone, is the origin of attacks on the academic relevance of theology – facts constitute a part of instruction as feelings cannot. To the Tractarians, however, 'Revelation itself may be viewed as one of the constituent parts of human Knowledge, considered as a whole, and its omission is the omission of one of those constituent parts.'[16] With their belief in the authority of the church to pronounce correctly on dogma, to believe in God contained 'a Theology in itself'.[17] Thus Newman's defence of theology rests completely on the authoritative character assigned to dogma by the Oxford Movement. Hence when he claims of a university which excludes theology that 'such an institution cannot be what it professes, if there be a God',[18] this statement becomes more easily comprehensible if one substitutes the word church for God.

Newman's second defence introduces the new premise that 'Its [theology's] omission from the list of recognised sciences is not only indefensible in itself, but prejudicial to all the rest.'[19] The inter-relationship between disciplines is so great that to speak of the auto-nomy of a subject is not only a mental abstraction, necessary for specialisation, but a dangerous one if it ignores the findings of other fields. The doctor concentrating on the physiological causes of disease would deny the influences of psychological factors, if traditional medicine was considered self-sufficient.

That revealed truth enters to a very large extent into the province of science, philo-sophy and literature, and that to put it on one side, in compliment to secular science, is simply, under the colour of a compliment, to do science a great damage. I do not say every science will be equally effected by the omission; pure mathematics will not suffer at all; chemistry will suffer less than politics, politics less than history, ethics or metaphysics.[20]

Thus Newman seeks to show that theology makes an indispensable contribution, though one varying in proportion, to the other disciplines. Even Newton's laws involve metaphysical assumptions, that natural conditions remain unchanging, and indeed are only laws rather than observations because of this presupposition. Hence the reply to those wishing to reject theology that 'When Newton can dispense with the metaphysician, then may you dispense with us.'[21] In stressing this connection between dogma and natural science, Newman is claiming that revelation can inform reason. While in his first defence of theology it was said to be factual, Newman now asserts that these facts are of the same kind as those in science. In other words he negates the existence of any barrier between the natural and the supernatural, if the knowledge of the one can supplement and develop that of the other.

The third defence represents a change of ground, since it is made from the point of view of theology itself, not other disciplines. To omit it from the university syllabus is to permit other sciences to usurp its place.

> If theology is not allowed to occupy its own territory, adjacent sciences, nay, sciences which are quite foreign to Theology, will take possession of it. And this occupation is proved to be a usurpation by this circumstance, that these foreign sciences will assume certain principles as true, and act upon them, which they have neither authority to lay down themselves, nor appeal to any other higher science to lay down for them.[22]

As example Newman cites the dictum of the political economist that 'easy circumstances make men virtuous'. This he claims is not the enunciation of a science, but the assertion of private judgement. Since it is a dogma that such individual freedom in religious interpretation is an unwarranted challenge to the authority of the church, this must be precluded by the presence of theology in education.

This final argument makes explicit a contradiction contained in the previous two – if theology is an essential and intrinsic part of the university syllabus, how can the gentleman remain a secular product of an instruction which is partly religious? There are two possible defences of this position. The first would state that dogma taught as liberal education *cannot* have a morally improving influence. Yet this proposition is impossible to Newman who maintains that the teachings of the church are the only authoritative form of moral guidance. If to follow this dogma does not result in improvement, then moral betterment itself is precluded, since this is its source. The second statement could assert that dogma taught at university *does not* lead to amelioration. Yet this would contradict the role Newman assigns to the tutor –

a moral influence which, if properly exercised will affect the student body. Thus, in his defence of theology within the university, Newman has in no way resolved the contradictions between classicism and Catholicism. He has not shown how men may be free yet obligated, he has only asserted that they should learn both science and theology, not how these should be digested. Indeed, in treating the truths of revelation as facts like any other, he has undermined one of the main sources of religious obligation – the claim that religious truths in being supernatural are mandatory.

In the foregoing discussion Newman had two contradictory aims, to establish theology on the same footing as other disciplines at university, and at the same time to protect it from their encroachment. In the second half of his *Idea of a University*, Newman retreats from his stance in defence of theology, gradually retracting his earlier views on the similarity of dogmatic and scientific facts. The starting-point is his assertion that science and religion can never be in conflict. 'If then, Theology be the philosophy of the supernatural world, and Science the Philosophy of the Natural, Theology and Science, whether in their respective ideas, or again in their own fields, on the whole are incommunicable, incapable of collision and needing, at most to be connected, never to be reconciled.'[23] The two are made even more distinct when Newman now states that 'Theology begins, as its name denotes, not with any sensible facts, phenomena or results, not with nature at all.'[24] Physics on the other hand keeps 'within the material system with which it began . . . with matter it began and with matter it will end, it will never trespass into the province of mind'.[25] The barriers between natural and supernatural have been re-erected. It is now impossible for theology to aid physics or for natural sciences to take over the domaine of dogma. Further distinctions are advanced to differentiate the two, science is deductive, religion inductive in method, and science progresses regularly, dogma sporadically. Furthermore, attempts to link the two such as Paley's 'natural Theology' – the search for evidence of Christianity – 'cannot be Christian in any true sense at all',[26] because science deals in laws and cannot brook their suspension by miracles. Religion and science now having been firmly separated, their relationship has to be redefined. While Newman's earlier position advanced intellectual freedom at the expense of reducing theology, his final stance reverses these priorities.

Newman's first defence of theology had sought to establish its position, primus inter pares; his second approach is to distinguish it from other sciences as 'architectonic' – that which best serves to decide the relations of other disciplines to the scheme of knowledge as a whole.[27] In reappraising the three sources of knowledge, man's relation to things, to man and to God, he decides 'that the last relation is the most fundamental of the three, and the second more important than the first'.[28] Thus the advantages of the humanities in the development of character and judgement are asserted over those of the natural sciences. At the same time 'Theology is the queen of sciences because of the transcendence of its object and because all other sciences in their different ways subserve it.'[29] Classicism is no longer in conflict with theology, but only because it has been defined as subservient.

The role of the church in education. If theology is superior, then it is insufficient merely to make pleas for its representation in a university, its dominance there has to be guaranteed. Since the church is the only authority on dogma, her presence in higher education becomes axiomatic. 'Where Theology is, there she must be; and if a University cannot fulfill its name and office without the recognition of Revealed truth, she must be there to see that it is a bona fide recognition, sincerely made and consistently acted upon.'[30] However, it is no longer the mere presence of dogma that the church will protect, exercising its authority to maintain doctrinal purity, but its position in relation to other subjects. 'Hence a direct and active jurisdiction of the Church over it [liberal education] and in it is necessary, lest it should become the rival of the Church within the community at large in those theological matters which to the Church are exclusively committed.'[31] Thus to Newman it is now 'not sufficient security that for the Catholicity of a University, even that the whole of Catholic Theology should be proposed in it, unless the Church breathes her own pure and unearthly spirit into it, and fashions and moulds its organisation, and watches over its teachings, and knits together its pupils, and superintends its actions'.[32]

In assigning this role to the church it would seem that Newman was relinquishing his secular notions of education and finally admitting that the function of instruction was the promotion of morality. However, he still maintains the bifurcation between tuition and religion. The fact that the church guarantees the 'integrity' of the university does not mean that 'its main characters are changed by this incorporation: it still has the office of intellectual education: but that the Church steadies it in the performance of that office'.[33] None of the discourses show how this interplay would operate in practice. Supervision without intervention, authority without interference and dominance without domination are statements of theory lacking blueprints for their application. Their vagueness is indicative of Newman's failure to relate intellectual freedom to religious obligation. Since a formula for their reconciliation could not be found, this must be done imperatively within the university by the church's assertion of her supreme authority.

Yet it is this very belief that the church is the sole legitimate arbiter of religious matters which prevents the solution of this problem. Thomas Arnold, concerned with the same issue, had only to assume that education must be religious, to deduce that it must lead to individual improvement and by corollary the moral advancement of society. The greater the approximation to perfection, the more do church and state become identical for they are composed of the same individuals. To Newman the first postulate of religious education is unacceptable, since it endorses private judgement on religious matters. The teacher is given the role that only the clergyman defined by canon law may exercise. As Newman saw clearly, the logical conclusion to Arnold's argument was a diminution in the authority of the church, represented in his support for ecumenicalism – the lowest common denominator of dogma which free-thinking individuals were willing to accept. If, as to Newman, the teaching of the church is divinely inspired, there can be no private judgement and therefore no question of averages. If the gentleman and the Christian could not become the same individual, it is the church's duty to prevent them from being unacquainted. Modern Rome must assert itself over ancient Rome. While the *Idea of a University* remains a Catholic document, it provided an intellectual justification to the Anglican church to defend its position in higher education and fight against the development of a state system.

THE BROAD CHURCH PARTY

The main opposition to the Oxford Movement within the Anglican church came from clergymen and educationalists perpetuating the latitudinarian tradition. Although they never published collectively, or attempted a public proclamation of their common views, they shared a comprehensive doctrine. Fundamental to this unanimity was the assumption that it was not the church, but the example of Christ which was supremely important in religion. From example being more important than dogma they deduced that the role of clergy was only one of edification, and not one of mediation. In so far as a direct personal relationship between the divinity and the believer was the focal point of their religious life, the church could only promote this relationship, but not be a partner in it. Thus to the Broad Church Party a maximal role pertains to the individual and a minimal one to the church.

Three important consequences follow from this initial premise. In concentrating upon the exemplary rather than dogmatic element of Christianity, they highlighted the scriptural tradition rather than subsequent doctrinal developments of organised religion. This importance attached to the Bible as the common fund of all Christian creeds led Broad Church members to minimise the distinction between church and dissent. The logical implication of this standpoint was that instead of justifying doctrinal division within the church, and between church and sect, they sought to advance ecumenicalism.

While the Oxford Movement was consistently anti-Erastian, wishing to establish the independence of the church from state intervention, the Broad Church Party did not wish for any separation between the religious and the civil society. State patronage would preserve the doctrinal comprehensiveness which the Thirty-nine Articles were intended to instate. While secular arbitration thus maintained a balance within the church, religious instruction guaranteed cohesion in society. Citizenship was viewed as a corollary of Christian virtues and religious practices as conducive to social integration and political stability. Therefore, since the diffusion of religious values could only be advantageous to society as well as to the individual, education ought not to be secular. From the point of view of religion, a civil education would be unjustifiable; from that of society it would be unsound. Thus the true Liberal education must be religious rather than only including religious instruction.

Thus whereas the main issue which confronted Newman – reconciling intellectual freedom with religious obligation – arose from defining education as good in itself, there was no problem for the Broad Church Party, who rejected this definition. To them education could be useful, as professional training, but this was not to say that it was good. In so far as tuition can only contribute towards the good, or promote moral improvement, by incorporating religion, it can only be justified on the grounds of its religious content – if such legitimation is to be other than utilitarian. Since the formation of character is the main end, it follows logically that the secondary school represents a particularly important stage in the process of higher education.

Thomas Arnold: defence of the church's moral influence in education

To Arnold religion is an integrative force. By increasing virtue in individuals, it automatically promotes order in society. As the only source of individual morality and the main component of social order, it cannot be left out of education. While Arnold's social ideal is derived directly from his religious convictions, his educational views are founded upon the related notions of ecumenicalism and citizenship. The contrast with Newman and the opposition between Broad Church-manship and Tractarianism are illustrated by the connection he established between the religious and the secular, and the unity of church and state.

Religious philosophy – ecumenicalism. The central point to a discussion of any of Arnold's work is his belief in the exemplary aspect of Christianity. 'Arnold stood four-square on the life and example of Jesus Christ. This is the one thing about which he would not argue at all, at least in his maturer years. All the problems raised by class structure, politics, the Church, the State, were resolved about his ideal.'[34] Therefore to him revealed truth is restricted to the scriptures and could not be supplemented by 'official' interpretation. The only additional authority he accepts in religious life is the personal judge-ment of the faithful, guided by conscience, not clergy. Private judge-ment is not seen as binding over other individuals, but only as an expression of the equality between Christians before God. True relig-ion is protestant since it is egalitarian and consequently Arnold can only accept an ecclesiatical hierarchy as an administrative institution, not as a scale of religious authority.

This concentration on the scriptures and on Christ's example minimised the importance of church membership in religion. 'Dr. Arnold's view of the Church was very simple. He divided the world into Christians and non-Christians. Christians were all who professed to believe in Christ as a divine person, and to worship Him and the brotherhood – the "Societas" of Christians – was all that was meant by the Church in the New Testament.'[35] Differences between denominations are thus matters of tradition rather than fundamental divisions. 'This meant that, apart from the paraphernalia of Church government, there was very little separating the Established Church from Presbyterians, Methodists of all types, Independents, Baptists, Moravians. It left only the Quakers, Roman Catholics and Unitarians.'[36] Since church and dissent are agreed on doctrinal essentials, the Anglican establishment ought to sponsor tolerance and initiate reconciliation. In fact, the only objection Arnold holds against dissent is that 'it has prevented the nation from feeling the full benefits of its national Establishment, and now bids fair to deprive us of them altogether. Dissent, indeed, when it becomes general, makes the Establishment cease to be national'.[37] Thus all the elements of Arnold's ecumenicalism are inextricably related to nationalism.

Arnold's ecumenicalism is an attempt to integrate all denominations within a common system of morality. It is complemented by an attempt to promote an identity between religious morality and secular philosophy. The embodiment of this unity will be the church-state – the most extreme expression of Arnold's ecumenicalism. Thus from Coleridge[38] he inherits religious tolerance personified by a 'clerisy not exclusively teachers of theology, but leaders and helpers in all that concerned the intellectual interest and the social life of the people'.[39] He supplements and extends it with a broader notion of church–state interaction, which acknowledges their identity of purpose in promoting human happiness. However

religious society aims at it truly and really, because it has obtained a complete knowledge of it. Impart then to civil society the knowledge of religious society and the objects of both will be not only in intention but in fact the same. In other words, religious society is only civil society fully enlightened; the State in its highest perfection becomes the Church.[40]

The church–state is the ideal towards which all Arnold's reforms are directed and to which all social institutions should be subordinated. The state church is a mere instrument for the implementation of this ideal.

In order to achieve this end, the Anglican church should become truly national – in other words, democratic. In criticising it for reflecting the social hierarchy, Arnold claims that 'our Church bears, and has ever borne, the marks of her birth. The child of royal and aristocratic selfishness and unprincipled tyranny, she has never dared to speak boldly to the great, but has contented herself with lecturing the poor.'[41] While the Oxford Movement advocated an increased separation between clergy and congregation, Arnold supports popular election of ministers and growing secular control in church administration.

Social philosophy – citizenship. As a social philosopher, Arnold outlines a plan for social integration which parallels his religious ecumenicalism. Like Christianity, citizenship is reduced to the lowest common denominator of all groups in the nation. Thus his ecumenicalism minimises differences between denominations, in an attempt to unite Anglicans and dissenters, and his theory of citizenship minimises differences between classes, in order to unite the enfranchised and the unenfranchised. However, the object of ecumenicalism is to bring about attitudinal change by transcending dogmatic differences, whereas the goal of citizenship requires social change to overcome class differences. The latter is more complex, since it involves not only changes in attitude towards stratification, but changes in the social hierarchy itself. Moreover, the common denominator on which ecumenicalism is based is a fund of scriptural belief already shared by the denominations which Arnold wishes to draw together. In society the common denominator uniting citizens cannot be said to exist until political participation has been extended to all classes.

It is in order to promote citizenship throughout society that Arnold supports the claims of the middle class in their desire for enfranchisement. Thus, in a letter to the *Sheffield Courant*, he writes: 'We are all aware of the growing power of the middling classes of society, and we know that the Reform Bill will at once increase this power and consolidate it.'[42] While supporting this move towards greater equality, he is not inclined towards egalitarianism. In all spheres, Arnold advocates that measure of equality which is indispensible for political participation without involving any perturbation in the social hierarchy. The limiting clause on any sort of egalitarianism being that it must not disturb the social order, seen as divinely appointed

Our business is to raise all and lower none. Equality is the dream of a madman, or the passion of a fiend. Extreme inequality, or high comfort and civilisation in some, coexisting with deep misery and degradation in others, is no less also a folly and a sin. But an equality in which some have all the enjoyments of civilised life, and none are without its comforts, where some have all the treasures of knowledge, and none are sunk in ignorance – that is a social system in harmony with the order of God's creation in the natural world.[43]

The counterpart of the privileges enjoyed by the upper class is the responsibility incumbent upon it for the aid and instruction of its social inferiors. Arnold looks only to the aristocracy for social reform. He deplores that this group is badly equipped for such a task, 'an evil which is as much to be regretted on the one side as on the other, and which is quite as mischievous to the minds and tempers of the rich as it is to the bodily condition of the poor'.[44] He condemns the established church for its lack of enlightenment in instructing the aristocracy in its social responsibilities and deplores 'those evils by the insolence and want of sympathy too frequently shown by the children of the wealthier classes towards the lower orders'.[45] Political reform should be granted from above rather than wrenched from below by violent means. Therefore Chartism, unionisation and all forms of popular association are opposed to social stability and to the English political tradition. For despite his criticisms of the contemporary upper class, Arnold believes nevertheless that

the great amount of liberty and good government enjoyed in England is the security of the aristocracy; there are no such pressing and flagrant evils existing as to force men's attentions from their own domestic concerns, and make them cast off their natural ties of respect or of fear for their richer or nobler neighbours.[46]

The overriding social duty of each group is the maintenance of social order, yet at the same time the higher strata should work constantly for peaceful social change. Arnold 'wanted the results of revolution without any of its violence – namely the production of maximum reform in minimum time without the truncation of the social system'.[47]

In order to reconcile the measure of political change required with the continuation of social stability, Arnold formulates proposals of reform based on compromise. The main one is franchise reform which has the advantage of extending citizenship within a stable parliamentary context. Therefore he supported the First Reform Bill while at the same time he advocated that its provisions should cover agricultural and industrial workers as well as the middle class. In drawing constant analogies with the slave system in ancient Rome, he claims that depriving this group of political rights 'was the readiest way of solving the problem, how to ensure the happiness of civil society – shut out from society those whom it is most difficult to render happy'.[48] He condemns his own society for giving to the industrial worker only the material prerogatives of a slave, without the political rights of a citizen. In considering means for endowing this group with citizenship, Arnold rejects the old formula of redistributing property. Not only are there insuperable practical difficulties in applying such a policy, but the masses are in his opinion psychologically antipathetic to this solution – 'having no property of their own, they hate property'.[49] As alternatives, he considers emigration – which is a fragmentary solution at best – and, above all, education.

Education, Christianity and citizenship. The desire for peaceful political change is connected in Arnold's thought with an optimistic belief in progress. He sees a natural evolution from the slave–master relationship to that between employer and employee, and expects it to culminate in relations between fellow-citizens. This end must be furthered by parliamentary reform, but enfranchisement will only guarantee rights – education is necessary to inculcate the duties of citizenship. Immediately before the passing of the First Reform Bill, he writes: 'I am earnestly desirous that the people should grow jointly in power and true knowledge; but at the same time I should regard their power as the worst of evils if true knowledge were not to accompany it.'[50] This approach is in the mainstream of the formative view of education, but whereas this view refers usually to intellectual development, Arnold is mainly concerned with moulding character. The main aspect of character formation is instruction in one's social duties; to the lower and middle classes – a responsible use of the vote should be taught, to the aristocracy – a moral use of leadership. Thus political progress allied to social stability can only be secured if the aims of citizenship are defined by Christianity and inculcated by education.

All the educational ideals propounded by Arnold are underpinned by the two concepts of Christianity and citizenship – his religious and social philosophies. Education is never envisaged as an end in itself, its justification is religious and its outcome is social. However, religion is both an end and a means in the process of schooling – since tuition will produce Christians and Christianity will shape citizens. Thus the mutual relationship between religion and citizenship is dependent upon education which, by making Christians, will produce citizens. 'The idea of a Christian School, again, was to him the natural result, so to speak, of the very idea of a school in itself; exactly as the idea of a Christian state seemed to him to be involved in the very idea of a State itself.'[51] Thus all forms of instruction, for all types of students, must be fundamentally religious. This is not merely to say that religious teaching must be given in all schools. Indeed 'he who thinks that to provide schools is to provide education, or that to provide schools where the Bible and Catechism are taught is to provide religious education, will undoubtedly be disappointed when he sees the fruit of his work'.[52] Thus Arnold's ideal for the educational system, illustrated by his policy in Rugby, was 'not based upon religion, but was itself religious'.[53]

While a Christian education does not necessarily imply the teaching of theology, there are compelling arguments for including it in the curriculum. The main reason for this inclusion is the same as that advanced by Newman: other disciplines would unavoidably suffer if it were left out. A purely secular curriculum 'would be very possible if Christianity consisted really in a set of theoretical truths as many seem to fancy; but it is not possible, in as much as it claims to be the paramount arbiter of all our moral judgments'.[54] Certain scientific disciplines may be able to dispense with any dependence on theology, but 'once you get off from the purely natural ground of physical science, philology, and pure logic – at the moment, in short, on which you enter upon any moral subject – whether Moral Philosophy or History – you must either be a Christian or an Antichristian, for you touch upon the ground of Christianity'.[55] In exempting the natural sciences from any connection with theology, Arnold appears more moderate than Newman. Furthermore he is prepared to dispense with compulsory theological teaching in higher education under certain conditions. 'Nor does it follow, so far as I can see, that University College must have a Professor of Theology, because we expect its members to have a knowledge of the elements of Christianity.'[56] The exclusion of theology, wholly unacceptable to Newman, would only be deplorable to Arnold. They share the view that it would be morally undesirable for the students. However, Newman holds that it would be damaging to the authority of the church, since other disciplines would usurp the field of theological truths. This argument is alien to Arnold's conception of the nature and origin of theology, which is entirely derived from the scriptures and which may be interpreted by private judgement. Therefore in advocating the teaching of theology, Arnold is not defending church authority, but supporting a good influence over human character. Hence in his dispute with University College, Arnold's withdrawal from it was less motivated by the absence of theology in its curriculum, than by the lack of Christians on its staff. Arnold formulates the syllogism that all teaching of moral subjects involves Christianity, to teach such subjects without Christianity is to be Antichristian, University College teaches subjects in this way and is therefore Antichristian.

'A degree in Arts', he contended, 'ought to certify that the holder had received a complete and liberal education; and a liberal education without the Scriptures must, in any Christian country, be a contradiction in terms.'[57] The intellectual content of instruction is considered as less important than its moral impact on character.

It may be said generally that Arnold's conception of a school was that it should be first of all a place for the formation of character, and next a place for learning and study, as a means for the attainment of this higher end. Discipline and guidance were in his view still more prominently the business of a schoolmaster than the imparting of knowledge. Thus Arnold subordinates mere knowledge, which is termed professional training, to the true formative education, which is termed liberal. The humanities, and particularly the study of the classics, are the most formative subjects, when taught in a Christian perspective. It may well be doubted whether he would ever have regarded any acquaintance with the material forces of nature as good substitutes for the intellectual culture derived from classical studies, or as equal to them in disciplinal value.[58]

Rather than have his son pre-occupied with science, Arnold 'would gladly have him think that the sun went round the earth, and that the stars were so many spangles set in the bright blue firmament. Surely the only thing needful for a Christian and a gentleman to study is Christian and moral and political philosophy'.[59]

The common feature of all types of education, regardless of the class for which they are designed, is the predominance of religion, as a means of perfecting character. 'The management of boys has all the interest of a great game of chess with living creatures for pawns and pieces, and your adversary in plain English the devil, who truly plays a tough game and is very hard to beat.'[60] However, in spite of acknowledging the formative power of instruction, Arnold wishes to apply it differently to the various social classes in order to adapt them to their dissimilar roles in society. This discrimination is indicative of the importance attached to social control in his philosophy.

It is in order to dispense a religious education to the working class that Arnold joined the Society for the Diffusion of Useful Knowledge, hoping to publish articles 'Cobbett-like in style, but Christian in spirit'.[61] His breach with this society was due to its concentration on purely secular knowledge: 'I never wanted articles on religious subjects half so much as articles on common subjects written with a decidedly Christian tone.'[62] The same view prevailed in his approach to lectures in mechanics' institutes, which he envisaged mainly as a preparation for citizenship. Therefore he overlooked the material or commercial advantages to be gained from adult education.

Hence he dwells much on the need of such studies as philosophy, languages, and logic, as helping to foster a love of truth, and to qualify the student to think more soundly and accurately about any of the subjects in which he might become interested, especially those which concerned most nearly the duties of the citizen and the formation of right opinions about the past and future.[63]

While wishing to prepare the workers for enfranchisement and train them for political participation, Arnold does not intend to equip them with the practical skills required for climbing the social ladder.

The need for training in citizenship was even more imperative for the middle class, since it had been granted the franchise. It seemed to Arnold that 'the education of the middling classes at this time is a question of the greatest national importance'.[64] He deplores that it should be left to private initiative rather than organised by the Anglican Church:

The schools for the higher classes are, as it is well known, almost universally conducted by the clergy; and the clergy, too, have the superintendence of the parochial schools for the poorer classes. But between these two extremes there is a great multitude of what are called English, or commercial schools, at which a large proportion of the sons of farmers and of tradesmen receive their education.[65]

Arnold does not doubt the adequacy of the professional training given in these institutions – again he is relatively unconcerned about the teaching of special skills. His interest is in the integrated rather than the open society.

I have little doubt that boys will be sufficiently taught all that they require for their particular calling: and scientific knowledge is so generally valued, and confers a power so immediate, that I think its diffusion may safely be reckoned on. This, however, has nothing to do with the knowledge which the Reform Bill calls for.[66]

It is in the general interest to fit the middle class to exercise its new-found rights and therefore the state should organise appropriate educational institutions:

the interference of government seems to me indispensible, in order to create a national and systematic course of proceeding, instead of the mere feeble efforts of individuals; to provide for the middling classes something analogous to the advantages afforded to the richer classes by our great Public Schools and Universities.[67]

Thus, the preparation of the middle class for its political role does not involve their participation in the educational establishments of the aristocracy. Their political function may be important, but their social position is not such as to fit them for leadership.

Arnold envisages therefore the expansion of education for all citizens, but not the creation of an articulated educational system. Each part is seen as discrete, reflecting the separation between social classes. As the aristocracy is given the role of political and social leadership, so its educational institutions are privileged establishments. Their curriculum is centred on the classics, which provide the best intellectual formation for political responsibilities, as well as the best preparation for university entrance. Their organisation as boarding schools is most suited to the inculcation of Christian discipline, providing the best moral formation for these responsibilities. Between these two features of public schools, there is no doubt that Arnold values the second most. By stressing individual responsibility, he wants to make his pupils true Christians rather than nominal churchmen. By making social responsibility a part of Christian duty, he wants to turn a leisure class into political leaders.

While Arnold's plans do not result in an articulated educational system, they are nevertheless integrated by his key notion of citizenship. In his attempts to make the aristocracy more useful and the middle class more polished, he expresses that degree of social change which is sanctioned by his religious philosophy, without deviating from the degree of social stability required by his social philosophy. Fundamental to his social philosophy was the maintenance of classes in society, fundamental to his religious philosophy was the extension of citizenship to all classes. Since class differentiation implies relations of superiority and subordination, this basic inequality contradicts the postulated equality of citizenship. To Arnold, education is the agent which should engineer the complementarity between the rights of citizenship and the duties of class. It can be said to succeed in so far as all its products are citizens, and to fail to the extent that it reproduces the category of senior citizens. This failure of Christian equality is a victory for the conservative social structure of nineteenth-century England. Like all theories placing a high premium upon social order, Arnold's ideal of Christian citizenship fails to be egalitarian, as does his proposed secondary education.

Throughout the 1830s the conflict between the High and Broad Church Parties grew, each seeking to impose itself as representative of Anglican opinion. Arnold denounced the Tractarians as the 'Oxford Malignants', while Newman criticised the 'spiritual pride' of liberalism. As Newman's intellectual influence spread throughout the colleges, many of Arnold's best pupils were entering them from Rugby. By 1841, after repeated attacks on Tract 90 by the Broad Church Party, Newman conceded that 'they have beaten me in a fair field'.[68] His conversion to Rome in 1845 consolidated the victory in public opinion. While the blueprint contained in the *via media* and the ideal of liberal education were transmitted by Pusey to the Anglo-Catholic Party, the influence of the anti-Erastian defence of Anglican domination was over. The concept of liberal education continued to gain support within the colleges, but it became completely dissociated from the doctrinal authority of the church over instruction. This authority which Newman had derived from placing the church in the historical continuity of apostolic succession represented the weakness of his traditional source of legitimation as he acknowledged himself in conversation –

In the confident days of the via media he meant by it (by Catholic) the doctrine of the early universal church, before . . . the growth of Roman error. But already he had begun to see that the appeal to antiquity was a doubtful criterion. In what sense were the councils of Nicea, Constantinople, Ephesus and Chalcedon true councils, in which the Council of Trent (AD 1545–63) was not a true council also? His idea of Catholic truth was now hardly to be distinguished from the pure Roman doctrine defined at Trent.[69]

During the forties, the Broad Church consolidated its position – Arnold gained the chair of modern history at Oxford and with the support of Jowett, Stanley, Tait and Lyell had a strong internal pressure group for reform as well as representing the majority Anglican view on education. Since it was not the authority of the church but its moral influence for social good which Arnold defended, the Broad Church was willing to support any measures which would enable this influence to be extended. Their version of Erastianism involved considerable change in church–state relationships, in such a way as to enable the church to be identified with the nation rather than the aristocracy, but this certainly did not preclude the use of state machinery to this end. The pressing need to bring the middle classes to citizenship and dissenters into the national ecumenical church, through education, made its use imperative, if university reform were to be accomplished. With the support given by the Broad Church to the university commissions, this led to the paradoxical situation in which 'even though the protagonists of reform were themselves in orders, the struggle to introduce changes necessarily took on an anti-clerical character; and this was enhanced by the fact that the changes desired could only be brought about by breaking down the semi-ecclesiastical character of the colleges and the hold of the Church hierarchy over the University.'[70]

The paradox was only an apparent one for those committed to the view that to sacrifice control was to increase the sphere of influence of the church. As Arnold had willingly participated in the early stages of London University, despite its secular authority structure, believing that education could still be Christian, so his party offered up the universities to secular reform. It was an attempt by allying with dissent to fight off secularisation and by encouraging the upper middle classes to weaken social radicalism. Despite opposition from the colleges and tutors at Oxford and Cambridge many of whom in the Tractarian tradition correctly diagnosed that control over education and influence over its content are closely related, the commissions (with their strong Broad Church membership) succeeded in bringing about reform. The principle of state intervention into higher education was established and shortly afterwards extended to secondary establishments. Arnold and his followers had supported such intervention as the first step towards establishing the church-state; in fact they had contributed to the destruction of the educational domination of the state church.

7. Change in French primary education

Under the *ancien régime* primary education was a semi-integrated institution only articulated with the Roman Catholic church. While some secular fee-paying establishments existed, schools provided by the church constituted the vast majority. This clerical domination was founded upon an almost complete *monopoly* of material facilities and teaching staff. In the eighteenth century this monopoly was practically unchallenged, since schemes for state intervention at primary level remained theoretical. As in all cases when this social institution is semi-autonomous, the main means of *constraint* available were educational. However, religion provided an additional symbolic form of constraint. Thus the church used the curricula for religious indoctrination, thereby strengthening its own position and propagating faith rather than literacy. This *ideology*, in so far as it incorporated the concept of station in life, legitimated the *status quo* and could therefore be construed as serving the interests of social stability. Since the clergy was a privileged estate, like the nobility, this socially conservative content of education was only to be expected. Therefore, this instruction was of necessity distrusted by the bourgeoisie, who wanted the state to train useful citizens rather than the church to indoctrinate loyal Catholics. Philosophers and Parliamentarians were agreed in this condemnation of the clergy – an attitude shared by the growingly anti-clerical bourgeoisie.

The Revolution, led by the bourgeoisie, constituted a successful political challenge to the privileged orders, and subsequently an educational challenge to clerical domination over primary education. However, since education was a semi-integrated institution, depriving the clergy of those rights associated with its previous legal position in the state did not automatically destroy its position of educational domination. While the confiscation of church property curtailed its pre-revolutionary monopoly of educational facilities, this did not prevent it from continuing to be the only agency with a body of experienced primary-school teachers at its disposal. Political persecution during the Terror precluded clerics from teaching and thereby from using the remaining element of their monopoly.

Revolutionary educational blueprints, partly incorporated into legislation, represented the assertion of the bourgeoisie in this sphere and its attempt to integrate primary education to the state. As an assertive group, the bourgeoisie possessed a secular *ideology*, derived from the philosophy of the Enlightenment, and the most effective *bargaining power* (synonymous here with the possession of political power), as displayed in its successful conduct of revolutionary operations and its complete control of successive parliamentary Assemblies. Through this control of legislation, the bourgeoisie could engage in activities *instrumental* to devaluing the educational monopoly of the clergy. The discussion of blueprints and, in some cases, their adoption by the Assemblies showed a continuing will to replace the former network of religious primary schools by state establishments, staffed by secular teachers and propagating republican citizenship. However, the fact that legislation remained largely theoretical witnessed to an inadequacy of personnel and of funds to pay them. Therefore the revolutionary legislators had been able to destroy the previous integration of primary education with the church, but unable to replace it by an integration with the state. Thus the instrumental activities of the bourgeoisie had merely restricted the clerical monopoly of educational facilities, but not substituted for it.

Under the successful revolutionary regimes, the church had been debarred from dispensing primary education, while the state had proved incapable of doing so. Napoleon's decision to restore the teaching orders to their former position reflected a realistic assessment of educational priorities in relation to state needs and resources. The overt endorsement of a policy of social control for the lower orders made it possible to dispense with the lip-service which revolutionary Assemblies had paid to egalitarianism and to concentrate on secondary instruction for an elite. Leaving primary schooling to the clergy implied the official endorsement of a double standard – reason being the preserve of the bourgeoisie and faith the guarantee of popular passivity. This recognition by Napoleon that the imperial state was financially unable to integrate primary education necessarily allowed the recovery of its eighteenth-century monopoly by the church. The regrets he expressed towards the end of his reign for not having devised a system of primary-teacher training indicated Napoleon's ultimate discontent with the endurance of clerical domination over this level of instruction. The experiments made at the time with the Lancastrian method and continued under the Restoration represented anti-clerical attempts which benefited from a measure of state support. They corresponded to an emerging policy of substitution rather than mere restriction of the clergy's monopoly.

This policy of substitution was officially endorsed by the July Monarchy on grounds of anti-clerical ideology and economic needs. Not only had development made the training of operatives, clerks and administrators essential to productivity and state efficiency, it had produced the wealth required for financing school buildings and teachers' salaries. Therefore popular instruction became an investment for the bourgeoisie and a state responsibility. Although the church retained its own private schools, the bourgeoisie had finally succeeded in supplanting clerical domination by creating a network of state primary schools and teacher-training establishments throughout the country. While religious schools remained competitive at the local level, it is characteristic of its subordinate position that the church increasingly turned to the state for educational subsidies. Integration had thus been achieved under bourgeois government and the educationally dominant bourgeoisie could promote its own ideology in primary schools. It had replaced the church as the group endowed with educational control over the people. This position, justified on theoretical grounds in the writings of the Doctrinaires and Destutt de Tracy, and upheld on politico-economic grounds by Cousin and Guizot, was not yet challenged by organised working-class educational assertion. However, an assertive ideology was being crystallised by the precursors of socialism, from Lamennais to Proudhon, although they had no mass following before the Revolution of 1848. Thus the first half of the nineteenth century corresponded to successful bourgeois assertion in primary education.

THE PRE-REVOLUTIONARY PERIOD

Under the *ancien régime*, primary schools were organised by the church and intended to propagate religion. While not universal in intake and unevenly distributed throughout the country, their network was more widespread than its Anglican counterpart in eighteenth-century

England. Indeed the impact of the Reformation had acted as a spur on the Catholic church, persuading it that religious conformity should be taught rather than assumed. Catholic control over primary education was ensured by the church's virtual monopoly over the training and certification of teachers. While there was some diversity in financing as well as organisation,[1] the common feature of existing schools was their emphasis on religion at the expense of other subjects. However, some elementary instruction in literacy and numeracy was dispensed in those establishments and this met with criticisms as a source of popular restlessness and discontent.[2] 'The people should be guided and not instructed; they do not deserve to be so.'[3] The Parliamentarians, and La Chalotais in particular, echoed this condemnation of elementary education, which they saw as socially disruptive, economically wasteful and politically harmful, since it increased the power of the church in the state. Primary schools were criticised more for their religious bias than for the low level of the tuition given.

In the eighteenth century economic change, resulting in growing urbanisation, increased the proportion of the town-dwelling proletariat, less amenable to control by virtue of its greater concentration and its receptiveness to new ideas produced by the bourgeoisie. It is from this section of the people that the Revolution of 1789 recruited its troops, although most revolutionary leaders were of bourgeois origin. While popular participation in the revolutionary movement ensured success, it was in the streets of Paris rather than in the political Assemblies that the bourgeoisie required or welcomed this support. The lack of communication and solidarity between urban and rural workers prevented the constitution of a Fourth Estate or the development of any truly popular ideology. Hence the revolutionary role of the people should be viewed as collaboration in bourgeois political action. It was not until 1848 that the elements required for independent popular action began to appear and even then the Revolution depended on bourgeois leadership.

Ideas originating in, and disseminated by the bourgeoisie provided the justification of the Revolution of 1789. To imbue the people with this new ideology was essential in order to perpetuate the revolutionary alliance and to ensure popular allegiance to the new regime. This was interpreted as education for citizenship though it could be construed as indoctrination for compliance. Such a purpose could only be achieved by eradicating religious influence and replacing it by a secular system of instruction, reflecting and propagating republican ideology. It was thus a logical outcome of revolutionary doctrine and a necessary consequence of political expediency to devise a secular educational system, controlled if not actually monopolised by the state.

REVOLUTIONARY PLANS FOR PRIMARY SCHOOLS

A concern for elementary education was thus an inseparable part of successive attempts by various revolutionary Assemblies to promote national unification and to replace religious teaching by secular enlightenment. The extent to which each Assembly made provision for schools was a function of the legislators' awareness that popular support was needed for the survival of the regime.

The members of the Constituante Assembly, with their bourgeois outlook, had little concern for popular education. Under the influence of Condorcet, the Legislative Assembly was better disposed towards it; but, absorbed by other problems, harrassed by the war, the second Revolutionary Assembly neglected primary education. It is only with the Convention that one enters the phase of concrete achievements . . . It is to (its members) that one owes the affirmation of the main principles, these dominating ideas which were to rule Republican educational policy during a century: the right of children to be educated – equality of educational opportunity – the duty of the State to organize primary instruction as a secular and gratuitous public service – the duty of families to guarantee school attendance – the use of French as the teaching language.[4]

Consecutive plans submitted to those Assemblies reflect the shifting priority assigned to elementary education. The table below illustrates the main aspects of revolutionary policy in this sphere and accentuates the consistency of the demands made for universal literacy and secular morality, whilst revealing a margin of uncertainty about the methods most likely to achieve these ends.

The common characteristic of revolutionary plans was a concentration on individual rights which state action should implement but never curb. The extent to which the state is relied upon to ensure the implementation of freedom and equality in the educational sphere is a function of the growing awareness of legislators that individual initiative alone could not eradicate traditional social and religious biases. Hence after the plan of Mirabeau[5] which only endorsed a fee-paying and voluntary primary school, all the blueprints that followed recognised that gratuitous schooling was essential if no child was to escape its influence.[6] This insistence was prompted by a desire to increase the appeal of state education and supersede the pre-revolutionary religious charity schools. The emphasis on natural rights in educational planning

E

MAIN EDUCATIONAL PLANS PRESENTED TO REVOLUTIONARY ASSEMBLIES	Primary education						
	Gratuity	Compulsory attendance	State monopoly	Secular morality	Vocational	Female equality	Universal provision
Mirabeau	×	×	×	√	×	×	√
Talleyrand	√	√	×	√	×	√	√
Condorcet	√	×	×	√	×	√	√
Romme/Lanthenas	√	×	×	√	×	√	√
Lakanal/Sieyès/Daunou	√	×	×	√	×	√	√
Lepelletier	√	√	√	√	√	√	√

had two related implications. Firstly, a total absence of the vocational principle which was viewed as a form of social determinism. Thus schools were intended to inform citizens, not to train for vocations. Secondly, since no theory of natural rights can justify discrimination between the sexes, the education of girls received equal attention and this unprecedented defence of parity was endorsed in each plan after Mirabeau's. The extent to which each blueprint relied on compulsory school attendance to implement its ends depended on the extent to which it could countenance state intervention on behalf of equality involving a limitation on the freedom to accept or reject educational opportunities. Others, more realistically, recognised that equality of opportunity – inseparable from liberty – could never become established unless parental prejudice against instruction were disregarded.[7]

The most complete expression of this tendency can be found in the plan of Lepelletier who carried egalitarian postulates to their extreme conclusions, thereby sacrificing individual liberty. 'I ask you to decree that between the ages of 5 and 12 for boys and until 11 for girls, all children without distinction or exception will be brought up in common at the expense of the state and that all, in the sacred name of equality, will receive the same uniform, food, instruction and care.'[8] This communal education away from family influences was to be centred on manual labour and on the elementary reading and writing skills which all citizens would require in later life. It was intended to favour the most deprived sections of the population by giving equal advantages to all at primary level and allowing none to assert their latent intellectual superiority, since no definite provisions were made for higher instruction. Equality had been pursued to its extreme conclusion – that of the lowest common denominator.

The revolutions of the last 3 years were all to the advantage of other classes of citizens, hardly at all to that of the most needful, the proletariat, whose only property is work . . . Equality between citizens has been restored, but they lack instruction and education; they carry all the weight of citizenship; are they made truly fit for the honours to which any citizen can aspire?[9]

This concern for the people corresponds to the most militant phase of Jacobinism and its acceptance by the Convention resulted in the adoption of a short-lived law (13 August 1793–19 October 1793) which created communal, but not compulsory primary education. Such a concession to an egalitarian ideal, granted at a time when the Republic was threatened on its frontiers and when the ruling Assembly was divided, and its prompt withdrawal illustrate the half-hearted nature of bourgeois commitment to popular education.

Even during this most 'revolutionary' phase of the Revolution, the willingness to countenance ambitious educational plans far outran the determination to apply them. 'If one adds to national fêtes and to elementary books a constant concern for the elimination of local dialects and universalisation of the French language, one has in a nutshell almost all the educational ideas of Robespierre's contemporaries and friends.'[10] The double aim of educational policy at the time was to achieve social levelling and national integration, although there was no definite consensus about the means to be used. After the fall of Robespierre, national unanimity mattered more than the abolition of social distinctions. There was thus a redefinition of ends and no greater measure of agreement about means. This uncertainty is indicated by the frequency with which educational legislation was changed between 1793 and 1795.[11] Successive laws were too short-lived to shape a new system and truly replace the former religious approach to elementary instruction. Difficulties in securing adequate teachers and lack of funds increased the effects of this legislative instability. Under the Directorate, the fundamental concern was one of national integration, particularly in eradicating local dialects. The hightide of egalitarianism had been reached and the main political issue appeared to be the provision of secondary education for an emerging elite rather than the universalisation of primary schooling for the people.

NAPOLEON'S NEGLECT OF PRIMARY INSTRUCTION

Thus Bonaparte's educational policy, with its neglect of primary schools, merely reinforced an existing trend. It was a logical corollary of his disregard for popular participation in government and for parity of individual prestige in society. To him neither efficiency in the state nor stability in society could be served by treating unequals equally. The acceptance of social inequality as a source of educational discrimination which had been tacitly admitted under the Directorate was officially encouraged under the Consulate and legally acknowledged under the Empire. 'Napoleon no more acknowledged the right of each citizen to receive primary education than he later accepted the right of each citizen to elect rulers.'[12] Abandoning an educational philosophy based on individual rights for one which he framed in relation to state needs, Napoleon relegated primary education to the lowest priority in his policy. As the inculcation of useful skills was to be the supreme end of instruction and as the state only required small numbers of trained individuals, any extension of training to the masses would be economically wasteful and socially dangerous. The minimal amount of knowledge they required could be imparted to them in fee-paying or charitable schools. The state need not create primary establishments, but could content itself with controlling the loyalty of teachers. Initially reluctant to restore the church to its pre-revolutionary educational position since he distrusted its support for his regime, Napoleon made provision for the training of primary teachers within special forms at the *lycée*. However, this plan was never executed, although the main religious order engaged in instruction at this level, the Frères des Écoles Chrétiennes, were refused the official right to teach.[13] This unwillingness to authorise teaching orders corresponds to the early stage of the Imperial University in which the state was to be responsible for the overall organisation of education and the certification of all teachers. As this task proved too onerous, economies could most easily be justified at the level considered least important, since primary instruction was a luxury for the people rather than a necessity for the state. Therefore the Imperial University came to rely on the services of the brothers and the idea of training secular teachers was forgotten. Nor did this trend merely reflect financial expediency, since it coincided with the use of religion for social control which was increasingly characteristic of the Imperial regime.

Under this regime, the Brothers remained what they had been before and their subordination to the University was nothing but nominal . . . It appeared that the main goal of primary instruction was as before to instruct the people in the Catholic religion: hence the favour with which the Brothers were viewed.[14]

The state left elementary schooling to the church,[15] insisting only that it should not extend beyond the rudiments of reading, writing and arithmetic – under the decree of 1811, inspectors were to verify that, apart from religious knowledge, no other subjects were taught.

Although the First Consul repudiated the materialistic theories of Condorcet and Lakanal, decreeing that popular education would again be based on religion,[16] Napoleon never truly trusted the clergy and attempted to control it through the Imperial University. While the role of the church at primary level gradually increased, it never recovered its former monopoly. In fact, at the end of his reign, Napoleon was seeking alternatives and regretting clerical entrenchment in primary schools. During the Hundred Days in 1815 Carnot outlined a plan for the reorganisation of elementary education and suggested the universalisation of the Lancastrian method on the English pattern.[17] Under the Restoration there was violent Catholic resentment of the Lancastrian schools which totalled 1,300 in 1820 and appeared a new supply of the scarce resource – teachers – thus further threatening the remaining element of religious monopoly. These schools received some official support, since the Restoration had inherited an ambiguous attitude to the predominance of the clergy in elementary education. While Catholicism was acknowledged as a national religion, the clergy as a social group was neither trusted by the liberals nor fully accepted by the administrative personnel of the Imperial (by then Royal) University.

THE INTERLUDE OF THE RESTORATION

The increased interest in primary education evidenced during the Restoration was prompted by political and economic considerations alike. Elementary schools were looked to by the liberals to reinforce constitutionalism and by the monarchists to inculcate dynastic loyalty. Anti-clericalism predominated among the former, but was not absent among the latter who had inherited the eighteenth-century distrust of religious orders. On the other hand, the pace of modernisation was increasing and there was a new need for a section of the people to assume more sophisticated commercial or administrative roles, and to be trained accordingly. This was one of the main arguments advanced in support of Lancastrian schools. 'Popular morality and the preservation of the social order are not the only reasons which call for popular education.'[18] This climate of opinion prompted the Ordinance of 1816 which made primary school attendance compulsory (without however foreseeing any punishments for absenteeism) and organised the teaching profession under the academic supervision of the university and the moral control of the local mayor and the parish priest.[19] 'The ordinance of 1816, very important in spite of its gaps, particularly in relation to women's education and to the financing of school expenditures . . . truly ensured the take over of primary education by the University.'[20] In spite of the difficulties involved in applying this legislation, particularly the distrust of the university by the local authorities and the frequent inimity between mayor and priest, this was a landmark in the expansion of primary schooling.

Primary schooling was greatly stimulated during the first years of the Restoration. The important groups in the nation, the Church, the Liberals, the State, under the guise of the University, work to this end. While the moderate royalists and the University, who dream that their educational activities will ensure a reconciliation of the old and the new France, fail, at least the rivalry of the three powers results in considerable progress.[21]

In subsequent years, the legislation fluctuated between concessions to the church and their withdrawal in favour of secular influences, reflecting the political vicissitudes of the clerical and the liberal parties.[22] (Throughout this period utilitarian preoccupations precluded any interest in primary schooling for girls, which remained the preserve of the church.) However, a Catholic monopoly over the whole of primary education was not considered desirable because in a church–state alliance neither party fully trusted the other. The main Catholic objections to a subordination of the church to secular ends were voiced by Lamennais at the time, while the ultra-royalists preference for a state-sponsored school were expressed in the last educational ordinance passed before the July Revolution. This Ordinance of 14 February 1830 made the creation of primary schools compulsory for local authorities and provided for state and university contributions towards their cost and for the organisation of the teaching profession.[23] While political events prevented the application of this legislation, its enactment marked an official recognition of state responsibilities in this field and a departure from the policy of relinquishing it to the church whose domination had prevailed, albeit in half-hearted forms, since the beginning of the nineteenth century, as a full policy of substitution had proved impossible at this level.

BOURGEOIS DOMINATION UNDER THE JULY MONARCHY

The July Revolution consolidated bourgeois domination. The bourgeois victory in 1830 permanently abolished the notion of divine right to rule and undermined the traditional, if uneasy, church–state alliance. The growing economic importance of this class and its political supremacy signalled the success of its assertion against the church by finally enabling the bourgeoisie to substitute for, rather than merely restrict the religious monopoly of teachers. The ideas which legitimated both the economic structure and the political regime of the July Monarchy were predominantly utilitarian. They incorporated the criticisms addressed in Parliament to the Restoration government by the Doctrinaire Party which had constantly challenged the divine right of kings as a source of royal authority and attacked the privileged position of the clergy as being irrational in theory and dangerous in practice. The very enunciation of this programme underlined the weakness of the philosophy on which the Restoration was founded and hastened its decline. The July Revolution, fought in the streets of Paris as a popular insurrection, was led by the bourgeoisie and concluded to its advantage by the establishment of a regime fully dedicated to its interests. Thus the aristocracy had been replaced as a political elite by the bourgeoisie and a monarch of Divine right by a bourgeois king. Goals of economic prosperity and secular rationalism replaced traditional values of inherited social prestige and religious orthodoxy. While popular support had been essential for the success of bourgeois action and for the proclamation of the July Monarchy, this had been but a temporary alliance. It had revived the unity of the Third Estate to which the Revolution had owed its triumphs, but necessarily resulted in frustrating again popular aspirations when the bourgeoisie was firmly in power.[24] A parallel could be drawn with the English alliance between middle class and working class on the eve of the First Reform Bill. In both cases, the victory of Utilitarianism over traditionalism could not have been achieved without the aid of the people, but brought them no gain, only the replacement of one form of social control by another.

The parallel with England can be continued in so far as there was in both countries a departure from the traditionalistic methods of educational social control based on the assumption that the less instruction was given to the people, the less dangerous they would prove to social stability. 'The conservative bourgeois thought that an educated populace are rebels and that serene ignorance was the best safeguard of their privileges.'[25] The traditional bourgeois fear of elementary education as a source of social unrest – which had prevailed since the final phase of the Revolution – gradually gave way before the employers awareness that commerce, administration and emerging industry required trained personnel. Hence the diffusion of primary schooling appeared as a concomitant of economic and urban development. The corollary of this utilitarian approach to education was that the state should direct curricula in accordance with 'the needs of society' rather than the aspirations of individuals.

Society ought to intervene in education and to shape it in its own image, so that there should be a reciprocity of exchanges between education and society; otherwise society sows with its own hands unrest, discontent, rebellion. From this viewpoint, which is the correct one, the right to teach is neither a natural right of the individual nor a private industry; it is a public duty.[26]

Thus there is an unchanging right of the state to adapt education to the changing needs of society. However, the educational structure inherited by the July Monarchy was ill adapted both in its form and in its content to the inculcation of the skills required. The main inadequacy was the gap between an exceedingly elementary primary school and an exceedingly classical secondary.

That which worried Cousin most was the lack of agreement between State education and the spirit of modern society. On the one hand, he saw the world moving more and more towards industry, commerce, agriculture and the applied sciences; he understood many fathers to desire an industrial profession of their children and to demand to this effect special studies; at the same time, he was aware that education provided by the *Université* did not correspond to this need; literature was its only object; there was no vocational instruction.[27]

The main gap of the existing educational system was thus between the classicism of the elite and the mere literacy of the people. The nature of secondary and higher education made it irrelevant to practical life, while that of primary schooling made it insufficient. Indeed educational institutions at all levels had been designed to fulfil political rather than economic or administrative goals. Since the Revolution, the goal of primary schooling had been to produce citizens or subjects loyal to successive regimes, submissive and literate. That of higher institutions had been to produce an elite useful to the state in administrative or professional capacities. This dichotomy was adequate in a predominantly rural country, it broke down with the increasing complexity of the division of labour. Possible solutions ranged from a diversification of secondary education, which would have democratised its intake and broadened its curricula, to an extension of primary. The social bias of the July Monarchy made it obvious which alternative would prevail. The conception of secondary and higher education as the preserve of the bourgeoisie remained unchanged. 'A crowd of children coming up to learn in the secondary school that which they neither need nor want, because they could not find elsewhere what they needed and wanted'[28] was Guizot's justification for diversifying primary instruction rather than making secondary more generally available.

Thus the creation of *primaire supérieur* as an extension of primary schooling by the law of 28.6.1833[29] introduced the degree of expansion in popular education which the evolution of the occupational structure demanded and a stable society could accommodate. As Guizot wrote,

Primary instruction enables the lower classes of society to increase their output, to improve their living standards and thus to create new sources of wealth for the State . . . The less enlightened the multitude, the more amenable it is to being misled and subverted . . . Even if this were not proved by the whole of history, our deplorable revolution would suffice to convince us of it.[30]

The fact that this educational legislation was inspired both by the requirements of economic growth and by those of social control is made more explicit in the writings of Cousin, on whose comparative investigations the reform was based.[31]

Cousin thought that there were three disadvantages to bad secondary education: that of not giving the petty bourgeois the education they needed; that of giving to those incapable of it an education which they could not understand and which would only inspire them with pride without increasing their earning power; finally, that of debasing literary studies in secondary schools, standards which could be bettered if these studies were reserved exclusively to an elite. Not to give to the masses anything more than that instruction which is strictly necessary, but to give it liberally to all; to give to the middle classes a positive and practical instruction; not to teach them anything but useful subjects; on the contrary, to advance as far as possible mental culture in the schools reserved to the high classes and to the intellects composing the elites; such was his blueprint.[32]

This sums up the main arguments in favour of a sharp distinction between primary and secondary schooling – namely that the people should be given vocational training and that secondary classical education should remain exclusive. It shows the main way in which the new dominant group in primary education used legal constraints derived from the political nature of its monopoly to advance its own members and to control those of other groups.

8. Change in French secondary and higher education

Under the *ancien régime*, secondary and higher education was – like primary – a semi-integrated institution, articulated only with the Catholic church. While secondary establishments were the preserve of religious orders, the universities were also clerical and retained their medieval collegiate structure. The domination of the church over those levels of education was founded upon the same factors as in primary. Its *monopoly* of material facilities and teaching staff was complemented by the educational *constraints* available in a semi-integrated institution, as well as the symbolic forms of control derived from religion. The *ideology* was religious, socially elitarian and politically conservative. The first assault on this domination was aimed at the predominance of Jesuits in secondary schools and was conducted by the Parliaments, whose intervention in education was prompted by nationalism and Gallicanism. Although many establishments disappeared after the expulsion of the order, the principle of religious secondary instruction endured until the Revolution. Of the three elements of the church's educational monopoly, the ideology was challenged first by the blueprints of the Parliamentarians. These plans expressed the philosophy of the Enlightenment which was gaining ground among the bourgeoisie and weakening religious affiliations. While in the short term such ideas appeared to coincide with the interests of the monarchy, they were in essence incompatible with it, endorsing as they did achievement rather than ascription, and political representation rather than royal prerogative.

It was by reference to this nationalist and secularist *ideology* that the revolutionary bourgeoisie condemned the educational domination of the church. Hence revolutionary policy was aimed not only at depriving the clergy of the elements on which domination was founded, but also at substituting alternative secular establishments. This educational assertion of the bourgeoisie was based upon its *instrumental* activities in the successive revolutionary Assemblies which by closing clerical schools and universities devalued the monopoly of educational facilities to their possessor. The passing of such legislation was made possible by the *bargaining power* consisting in bourgeois control over legislative bodies, the machinery of government and public opinion. However, the need for popular support within the Third Estate both restricted the full use of this power and diluted the supportive ideology. The meritocratic elements of this philosophy could not be fully implemented while restrained by the egalitarianism of revolutionary slogans. This position is best illustrated by Sieyès, whose educational philosophy was tempered by political compromise.

On the other hand, the instrumental activities aimed at substitution for the monopoly of the church were curtailed by financial difficulties and an insufficient supply of teaching staff. Thus the *écoles centrales* planned as a national network were in fact few and scattered, while higher education never went beyond the setting up of isolated and often short-lived institutions. Therefore, as in primary education, the church's monopoly of teaching staff was an obstacle to successful educational assertion by the revolutionary bourgeoisie. While the clergy could be debarred from teaching, its replacement by secular staff required financial resources, administrative provisions and training facilities which did not exist until Napoleon came to power.

Under the rule of Napoleon, educational policy was no longer geared to securing popular allegiance. With the advent of strong government, the main concern ceased to be for equality and the demands of specialisation were no longer sacrificed to egalitarianism. However, liberty was subordinated to the exigencies of state efficiency. Napoleon's policy served the educational interests of the bourgeoisie from among which the future elite was to be recruited. Thus it was 1802 rather than 1789 which marked the advent of bourgeois educational domination and its dissociation from revolutionary claims for equality of educational opportunity, which had limited instrumental activities but had been necessary to strengthen bargaining power. The humanistic ideology expressed by Condorcet was replaced by a narrower form of justification emphasising utility at the expense of individual rights. Napoleon was the main exponent of this approach which permeated the institutions devised under his reign and which survived his fall. The Imperial educational system improved the social position of the bourgeoisie by conferring upon its members alone the educational qualifications which gave entry to the civil service and the professions. It was thus under the Empire that the bourgeoisie ceased to be an assertive group and became educationally dominant, since the institution of the Imperial University deprived the church of its pre-revolutionary monopoly.

The church continued to give a strong ideological challenge to this domination – advocating traditional values at the expense of utility. However, the Restoration was the return of a dynasty, not the rehabilitation of the pre-revolutionary elite or of aristocratic ideals. Therefore it could not undermine the position acquired by the bourgeoisie and the only advantage the church derived from the patronage of the royal government was an increased share in a state educational system. When, under the July Monarchy, this patronage could no longer be relied upon, the transitory threat which the Catholic religion had represented for bourgeois utilitarianism lost its acuity, The monarchy was no longer one of divine right and, owing its existence to bourgeois support, merely treated the church as a useful device of social control over the people without appealing to religion for its own legitimation. This policy paved the way to an alliance between the social conservatism of the bourgeoisie and the intellectual conservatism of the Catholic church.

Under the Imperial University, which outlived the Empire, secondary and higher education was integrated to the state and therefore the educationally dominant group was identical with the politically dominant group. Actual bourgeois domination over both spheres was formally recognised in 1830, when the divine right of kings was replaced by the political representation of the propertied class. Under the July Monarchy this new ruling class had a *monopoly* of legislative control over educational policy and administrative control over educational facilities. Its means of *constraint*, directly derived from those monopolies, were both legal and educational. The supportive *ideology* justified both the existence of a secular system and the domination of the bourgeoisie by reference to the needs of economic development.

THE PRE-REVOLUTIONARY PERIOD

In the eighteenth century, secondary and higher education were entirely dominated by religious orders and were still regulated by statutes passed in 1598 under Henry IV, which remained in force until the Revolution. Under the *ancien régime*, no clear distinction was drawn between secondary and higher establishments. The faculty of

arts, while part of the university, merely provided the initial qualification required for admission into any of the other three faculties. Thus
in Paris an arts degree was a prerequisite for professional specialisation: '[The students] followed the courses in the Faculty of Arts: once
they had obtained the degree of Master of Arts, they registered with the
so-called higher Faculties, theology, law, medicine, there to pursue
professional studies.'[1] University studies had thus evolved towards a
vocationalism which contradicted the initial intentions of college
founders to provide a free general instruction for the deserving poor.
Not only were the faculties of arts secondary enclaves in universities,
the *grands collèges* or *collèges de plein exercice*[2] overlapped with them and
further blurred the demarcation between secondary and higher studies.

While several prototypes of post-primary education, either provided
in *collèges*[3] by the clergy and by religious orders – Jesuit, Oratorian,
Josephite, Barnabite and Doctrinarian – or in universities, co-existed in
the first half of the eighteenth century, it was the Jesuit model which
tended to prevail. It was characterised by a concentration on Catholic
doctrine and literary classicism; the former led to religious conformity,
the latter to the intellectual homogeneity of the ruling elite. Within this
limited range of subjects, a scholastic approach prevailed. Conservatism was reinforced by the authoritarianism pervading the boarding
establishments run by the Jesuits and the overriding aim to produce a
stereotyped Christian classical scholar. The use of Latin as a teaching
medium was conducive to both these ends,[4] but was an enduring
obstacle to the introduction of new subjects in the curricula. 'There is
no possible choice between courses in various subject matters. A single
one-way road is open to all types of intelligence. The homogeneity
which is the result desired is at the same time the precondition of this
result.'[5]

However, it was not merely the classicism inherent in the organisation of Jesuit institutions, but also the privileged social origin of their
intake which enhanced their conservatism. The *collèges* tended to produce pupils equipped for the duties corresponding to their station in
life. The *esprit de corps* engendered by a traditionalist education, more
concerned with furthering group homogeneity than with fostering
individual talents, was designed for status differentiation within a
completely stable social structure. It was equally unresponsive to the
pressures of social change and the challenges of intellectual progress.
While many criticisms were levelled at the quality of the instruction
given by the Jesuits, the main reason for their expulsion from France in

1762 was the antagonism inspired by their submission to the papacy – which disqualified them from providing an education acceptable to the state.

Criticisms were not addressed to teaching methods tested by experience, but to a religious corporation which was at the same time an international power . . . The Jesuits had been expelled. They were the victims of a secular movement engulfing all catholic countries during the 18th century. They were condemned for having defended the Church and for having intended to produce above all in their colleges 'a devotion to the Pope' . . . They did not teach their young pupils the democratic spirit of the old monarchy and the origin of aristocratic privileges. Their pupils knew how the Roman Senate was run; they were unacquainted with the States General and its procedure.[6]

The rejection of this Jesuit ideal towards the middle of the eighteenth century corresponds to an upsurge of cultural, political and secular nationalism expressed in the writings of the Parliamentarians. This attitude was sufficiently widespread at the time to unify diverse groups while the provincial Parliaments saw the expulsion of the Jesuit Order as a means of secularising French life, they were supported by other religious interests antagonistic to papal claims. 'Jansenists, Gallicans, Encyclopaedists, Parliamentarians wished to rid the religious colleges of their Roman influence.'[7] While this campaign was prompted by political considerations, it coincided with the diffusion of academic disciplines stimulated by the Enlightenment and previously ignored in the traditional educational institutions. 'One can view the condemnation of the Jesuits in 1762 as the first act of the educational revolution which aimed to replace Graeco-Roman humanism by scientific humanism.'[8]

The type of instruction provided by the Jesuits had been widely criticised, but had at least offered a nation-wide network of establishments whose suppression left a major gap. Aware of this, the Parliaments invited projects for the reorganisation of studies at all levels, the universities having come under attack for being equally outmoded as the *collèges*. While this appeal enhanced the popularity of the Parliamentarians, it did not yield practical results, though it produced blueprints, such as La Chalotais', which had lasting influence. While all the plans produced in this interim period concentrated on nationalism, secularism and utilitarianism, none of them was actually applied and therefore education remained in religious hands. The main beneficiary of the Jesuit expulsion was not in fact the state, but the Order of the Oratorians. Its system of instruction, in which French was the main teaching language and the scientific subjects played a greater role, predominated at the end of the *ancien régime*. While its curricula corresponded closely to bourgeois needs as set out by the Parliamentarians, the religious character of the order precluded its full acceptance by secularists.

On the eve of the Revolution, higher degrees were granted by twenty-two universities, usually composed of four faculties (law, medicine, arts and theology) and by specialised institutions, such as the Écoles des Mines, du Génie, des Ponts et Chaussées and the medical schools. However, the intellectual life of the time was centred around the learned societies and local academies which were free from traditionalism, classicism and clericalism. The stimulus given by the Enlightenment to mathematical thinking and scientific research meant that the formal tuition in universities represented a diminishing proportion of the intellectual pursuits valued and new knowledge during the eighteenth century. 'Thus the university stagnated. A gap widened between it and society. The old routine continued in the collèges. Education was inadequate, equipment was deficient. Everywhere the trend was towards the nationalisation of education and the abolition of the monopoly of corporations.'[9]

The privileged position of the clergy in the educational system reflected and served the interests of social control. While the bourgeoisie were never formally excluded from secondary establishments, not only was the syllabus unrelated to their demands for modernisation, but also educational qualifications were insufficient to guarantee social promotion or even suitable employment.

The colleges burst with students. Each year instructed, ambitious and intelligent young men graduated from them. But their legitimate ambition came up against almost unscaleable obstacles; money, titles . . . The Army, high positions in the Church, judicial offices were the prerogative of the rich and noble families . . . The Ancien Régime had educated its students well; it had not offered its graduates positions commensurate with their worth.[10]

Thus education contributed to discontent, although it had been designed to further conformity.

REVOLUTIONARY PLANS FOR SECONDARY AND HIGHER EDUCATION

The growing political strength of the bourgeoisie was based on a double alliance – with the nobility of the robe in the last years of the *ancien régime* and with non-bourgeois members of the Third Estate in the revolutionary period. While the former were bourgeois by origin but endowed with legal privileges under the monarchy, the latter differed from the bourgeoisie by their economic and educational positions, but legally belonged to the same estate. For all these differences, the bourgeoisie and the people were equally deprived of political privilege. Therefore in 1789 their claims were expressed jointly – the political identity of the Third Estate concealed its social diversity. After the Revolution, not only did the bourgeoisie receive full legal and political recognition, but also its ideology became that of the republican state and this group was sufficiently powerful to preserve its position throughout the political vicissitudes of the post-revolutionary period.

However, this strong position was only achieved by the bourgeoisie thanks to its alliance with other members of the Third Estate. The three revolutionary Assemblies – Constituante, Législative and Convention – attempted in vain to design a common denominator for the whole of the Third Estate. In education as in politics, because of the diversity of interests involved, this search was bound to be prolonged and ultimately unsatisfactory. The two spheres were interrelated – politics could not provide a stable context for the framing of legislation and education could not fulfil its role of political socialisation. During the revolutionary period, educational legislation was more concerned with seeking to reconcile the two elements within the Third Estate than with any more positive goals. Parliamentary debate dealt with the relative merits of social solidarity through minimal instruction and educational selectivity leading to the production of an elite. In other words, the criterion against which education was assessed was political rather than economic.

Because of the controversial relationship between education and politics, this was a period of debate rather than achievement. The constant need to placate the non-bourgeois members of the Third Estate delayed the enactment of an educational legislation consistent with bourgeois interests. Consequently secondary and higher education were neglected over a comparatively long period, since state intervention in this sphere was considered as elitarian. Initially the Constituante reflected a climate of bourgeois optimism and the educational programmes of the time ranged from elementary to higher institutions without showing undue concern for complete equality, but with overwhelming emphasis on individual liberty. It is these features which characterise the two main plans produced under the Constituante –

those of Mirabeau and Talleyrand. Mirabeau's blueprint, published posthumously, stressed individual freedom as a means of fostering well-being in society. 'In a well organised society, everything prompts men to cultivate their natural talents: without any outside intervention education will be good; it will be all the better for independence among teachers and emulation among pupils.'[11] This involved two main repercussions, the payment of fees and minimal state intervention. These principles are equally valid for both secondary and higher education, to be dispensed respectively by the *collèges de littérature* at *département* level[12] and by the Lycée National[13] in the capital. While specialisation was not catered for at either level, the needs of the professions were to be met by vocational schools training directly for them.[14] Classicism still prevailed in this plan as it was to in the plan of Talleyrand, presented to the Constituante Assembly in September 1791. While very similar to Mirabeau's proposals, particularly in avoiding a state monopoly of instruction, this blueprint already displayed a willingness to accept some limitations on freedom in education for the sake of equality. He delineated the same levels of secondary and higher education, but within this framework provided scholarships for the most able pupils from poor families (and made some provision for the instruction of women at secondary level, in non co-educational institutions).[15]

The Législative disregarded these reports neither of which was ever publicly discussed. Its Committee for Public Instruction, seeking for a more egalitarian formula, entrusted Condorcet with the preparation of a new report which was presented to the Assembly in 1792. This plan, with its five degrees of instruction[16] endeavoured to reconcile the dual requirements of freedom and equality. In its insistence on selection by merit for secondary and higher education and its provision of scholarships for both these levels, it sought to implement equality of opportunity. The compromise embodied in this plan consisted in stressing egalitarianism at primary level and meritocracy above it. The political prosecution of Condorcet for his Girondin allegiance, and the fall of the Gironde Party itself at the hands of the Jacobins meant that these proposals were never discussed. The domination of the Jacobins at the end of the Législative, implied a more egalitarian bias in an attempt to re-establish popular support.

Under the Convention national integration was the main political and therefore educational target. Liberty was subordinated and equality was used to this end. Significantly the two educational plans elaborated at the time by Lakanal in conjunction with Sieyès and Daunou, and by Lepelletier restricted themselves to primary instruction. It was felt that the state should limit its efforts to the provision of a minimum common education for all. Hence it was explicitly admitted that the maintenance of equality between men required the lowest possible educational denominator.

> We do not need academics; we need men who are free and worthy of the name . . . let no one believe that the attainment of freedom was due to the sciences and the arts. The opposite is proved by the fact that it was not won by intellectuals. Look at the sans-culottes, look at the patriots! Are they intellectuals? Look at members of the Academy, makers of speeches, full of erudition; I ask you are they patriots.[17]

A distrust of secondary and higher education as elitarian marked all blueprints presented to the Committee of Public Instruction until the fall of Robespierre.[18] It had been a period in which educational ideology appealed to all members of the Third Estate, and not to bourgeois interests alone, in order to retain the bargaining power achieved – which would have been weakened by popular defection.

From then on the dangers of this policy became increasingly apparent. Since the lack of legislative provision for secondary and higher education had not excluded public demand for it, there was a growing fear that private initiative would take an unfair advantage of this situation, by training an elite unresponsive to national interests and

MAIN EDUCATIONAL PLANS PRESENTED TO REVOLUTIONARY ASSEMBLIES	Secondary education								Higher education								
	Gratuity	Compulsory attendance	Selection by merit	State monopoly	Secular morality	Vocationalism	Classicism	Female equality	Gratuity	Compulsory attendance	Selection by merit	State monopoly	Secular morality	Vocationalism	Classicism	Female equality	
Mirabeau	×	×	×	×	√	×	√	×	√	×	√	×	√	×	×	×	Constituante
Talleyrand	×	×	√	×	√	×	√	×	×	×	√	×	√	×	×	×	
Condorcet	√	×	√	×	√	×	×	√	√	×	√	×	√	×	×	√	Législative
Romme/ Lanthenas	No secondary schools								No higher establishments								
Lakanal/ Sieyès/ Daunou	No secondary schools								No higher establishments								Convention
Lepelletier	Proposals unspecified above								Primary level								

republican ideology. The end of the Terror made it possible to voice this concern. Under the chairmanship of Lakanal the Committee of Public Instruction framed legislation extending state responsibility to secondary education by the creation of *écoles centrales*. Thus in its last phase the Convention introduced a new type of institution in response to bourgeois pressures. Their structure was to reflect many aspects of previously abandoned plans. The extent to which Lakanal's schools mirrored earlier suggestions, incorporating features from most revolutionary blueprints, is illustrated by the table above.

THE REPUBLICAN 'ÉCOLES CENTRALES'

Founded in 1795,[19] the *écoles centrales* embodied some aspects of the plans drawn up by Mirabeau, Talleyrand and above all by Condorcet. Initially there was to be one such school per 300,000 inhabitants, but this ratio was later reduced.[20] The schools were to be subsidised from public funds while a portion of the teachers' salaries was contributed by the pupils. They catered for the group included between twelve and eighteen years of age approximately, drawing from among the most able primary-school children. However, the preference given to merit was to some extent limited by the families' ability to pay and therefore it was the children of the bourgeoisie who predominated. The content of the curriculum tended to be encyclopaedic and departed from the former concentration on classical learning. For two centuries the *collège* tradition had supported and maintained an emphasis on classical humanism, while scientific humanism was overshadowed. Reversing the trend, the *écoles centrales* were founded on scientific humanism, while they relegated classical humanism to the background.[21] Not only was the bias predominantly scientific, there was also a multiplicity of optional courses available. Pupils were to select areas of study according to their interests and abilities rather than being cast in the same mould. 'Education ought to offer a variety of subjects to the children, so that each one can select that which nature meant him to cultivate.'[22] The range of choice between subject matters was only limited by a broad division into three sections corresponding to three age-groups: from 12 to 14, the emphasis was on drawing, natural history and classical languages; from 14 to 16, on mathematics, physics, and chemistry; from 16 to 18, on grammar, literature, history and law. Within these sections, tuition was given by lectures to the whole age-group. Discipline in the classroom was replaced by a reliance on self-control rather than authority. Together with the concentration on scientific subjects, the cult of reason permeating the whole system is reminiscent of Condorcet's plan. The major implication of this rationalism was the teaching of secular morality which took the place of religion. 'In the curricula of the old *collèges*, religion was the dominating and fructifying subject matter; in those of the *écoles centrales*, the focal point was provided by law . . . by the cult of reason.'[23] Rationality was construed as the basis of citizenship and enlightenment as an aid to democratic politics. This attitude was exemplified by the republican slogans, such as 'Ignorance gave rise to despotism. The sciences and the arts will protect liberty.'[24]

The *écoles centrales* covered both secondary and higher education. In fact one of their defects was an exclusive use of those teaching methods best suited to more mature students and requiring use of too much intellectual discipline from young pupils. Another was the lack of connection between their academic curricula and the requirements of practical life.

Écoles centrales were neither colleges nor faculties. They shared features of both. At twelve years of age pupils were already students. They chose their course according either to its appeal or its usefulness to them. They were often amateurs left to their own devices . . . For them the courses were too quick and too abstract.[25]

However, it was not so much the educational deficiencies as the political origins of these schools which led to their abolition . . . 'It would have been easy to remedy the faults of the écoles centrales but it was no longer timely to do so.'[26]

The two principles upon which the *écoles centrales* had been founded, were the individual rights to liberty and equality from which both the form and the content of the instruction given had been derived. At the beginning of the Consulate in 1800 these very principles were considered as the cause and blamed for the consequences of the Terror. Governmental instability, social disorder and administrative inefficiency were attributed to the revolutionary concentration on individual rights which had deprived the state of any power to direct society. The Consulate then marked a return to the acceptance of the state's right to relate education to general needs rather than to individual rights and thus a change in the assertive ideology. The educational ideal of the Parliamentarians seemed better suited to the requirements of a government seeking to restore social order than any reform of institutions based on revolutionary ideology. Hence the schools were officially abolished in 1802. 'The consular government preferred to break with the system of écoles centrales and to restore, under the name of lycées, the former collèges.'[27] However, the period following this abolition was one of debate about the goals and means of instruction rather than of advancing assertion through an active policy of substitution.[28] After this time of reappraisal the only revolutionary establishments to survive were those which the Convention had created to train specialists in those skills deemed essential.[29]

In the field of secondary and higher education the Revolution left behind it . . . as its main achievements, schools for public servants (Polytechnique), special schools and *écoles centrales*; as plans, Condorcet's blueprint, pruned, and simplified and the proposed creation of several literary and scientific conservatories. The Consulate rejected these projects and achievements, it destroyed those which the Revolution would have probably retained, the écoles centrales, and maintained and developed those which it certainly intended to replace, the special schools.[30]

The result of this debate was the law of 11 Floréal Year X (1.5.1802), based on the twelfth successive draft submitted to the Council of State,[31] which represented the first step towards state monopoly over secondary education. It instituted selection by merit for entry into the *lycées* whose curricula were initially biased towards science, but emphasised classical languages after 1808. Already under the Consulate their organisation was modelled on military discipline – which was to increase over time. This was a complete departure from the loose structure of the *écoles centrales*, although some elements of their syllabus were retained during this transition period. 'The Consulate suppressed that which was over-abundant in Condorcet's plan. The intention was not to abolish the teaching of science, but in giving it its due, not to neglect classical studies. Thus the literary teaching of pre-revolutionary collèges confronted the scientific teaching of the écoles centrales.'[32] The legislation passed during the Empire increased this deviation from the educational patterns of the revolutionary period: from 1808 onwards there was a constant growth of classicism, a re-introduction of religious teaching and an attempt to relate instruction to state needs rather than individual inclinations. This vocational bias prevailed also in higher education, since the range of training dispensed in specialised establishments reflected governmental concern for professional efficiency.

THE IMPERIAL UNIVERSITY

The continuity between the educational policy of the Consulate and that of the Empire witnessed to Napoleon's enduring wish to use instruction as a means towards greater efficiency in the state. He commissioned investigations of foreign universities which could serve as models for France and in 1806 he instigated the legislation creating the Imperial University. This institution was intended to embody the monopoly of the state over secondary and higher education. By centralising educational administration and nationalising the teaching profession,[33] the Imperial regime established a unitary structure with powers of control over private schools. Initially this control was largely theoretical, but the legislation of 1808 provided the positive and negative sanctions needed to make it effective. From this date onwards no schools could function without the authorisation of the university, no one could teach without a qualification delivered by it and no other institution could deliver valid diplomas. In fact it was a degree-granting rather than a teaching body[34] whose main function was to issue certificates of aptitude to enter either state employment or establishment of specialised training. The role of the *baccalauréat* epitomised administrative control over the testing of merit and constituted a demarcation line between secondary and higher education. It also symbolised the social bias of the system towards the bourgeoisie.

The organisation of the Imperial University deprived the Catholic church of its former domination in pre-revolutionary universities. While Napoleon was prepared to rely on religion as an instrument of social control and while the Imperial catechism was designed to this end, the teaching profession was secular. However as a concession to the church and in an attempt to secure its co-operation for the new university – of which seminaries and religious schools were a part – the first *grand maître*, Fontanes, was chosen for this post on the grounds of his Catholic allegiance. This compromise initially favoured the private sector in education and strengthened the position of the clergy, since Fontanes did not actually attempt to enforce the state monopoly. Distrusting the royalist leanings of clerical teachers, Napoleon ordered an enquiry into the progress made by the educational system to be conducted in 1810. 'Although this investigation was inadequate, it convinced Napoleon of the urgent necessity of defending lycées and collèges against the competition of private establishments, especially religious ones.'[35] As a result, new decrees were passed in 1811 in order to turn the monopoly into a reality. Not more than one religious school was allowed in each *département* and none in towns where *lycées* existed already. Limitations were placed on those whose activities were sanctioned by the university,[36] while the property of all others was confiscated by the state. This reform reduced by half the number of pupils in religious secondary schools and stimulated free thought in state establishments.

However, until 1811 the monopoly of the Imperial University remained largely theoretical. It entailed merely the duty of private schools to make payments to the state and the right of the university authorities to inspect them. Even the decrees of 1811 failed to fully implement a monopoly because of the partiality the *grand maître* continued to show towards religious schools. 'Therefore the monopoly never existed in the sense that the University was never alone in giving instruction, as it had been intended to be.'[37]

THE UNIVERSITY AFTER THE EMPIRE

It was precisely the fact that Napoleon's educational design was not fulfilled under his reign which enabled the university to secure some allies among the political right and to survive the fall of the Empire. While it was initially abolished on 17 February 1815, it was re-created during the Hundred Days and re-organised by an Ordinance of 15 August of the same year.[38] The second Restoration spared the university and conserved most of its administrative structure, merely suppressing some faculties.[39] The clergy played a greater role in the Royal University than it had in the Imperial,[40] those educational establishments which had a purely secular tradition – such as the École Normale for the training of secondary-school teachers – being suppressed or redesigned.[41] Throughout the Restoration clerical influence in the university grew, but the principle of state monopoly remained unaltered in spite of the attacks which it attracted from the supporters of educational freedom. By an apparent contradiction both the defenders of secularism, affronted by ecclesiastical infiltration in education, and the protagonists of religious schools which they wished to exempt from state control, were allied in this campaign. Indeed the writings of Lamennais initially expressed the latter trend, but showed a growing awareness of the common points underlying opposition – on whatever grounds – to a state educational system.

The July Monarchy did not instigate any major educational reforms at this level. The anti-clericalism which marked the Revolution of 1830 and the liberalism which led to the re-opening of École Normale were subordinated to the requirements of social control, well served by the existing university structure. Expediency rather than ideology justified the maintenance of religion in secondary schools, although it was no longer considered as the basis of education or as a source of loyalty to the regime. Furthermore the Bourgeois Monarchy, while accepting that Catholicism was the religion of the majority, endorsed utilitarianism as its own philosophy. This attitude marked a return to the Imperial policy of using the clergy to enforce political conformity – though neither regime could rely on its unqualified allegiance. In both cases this policy was inseparable from a concern for training a highly qualified elite wholly devoted to the state and therefore imbued with secularist leanings. Thus the 1830s were marked by an increase in secondary education, where a greater number of scientific subjects were added to the curricula. The form of the state educational system remained unaltered in spite of these variations in content. The abolition of the state monopoly continued to be a controversial political issue throughout the period and successive attempts at introducing educational freedom[42] failed in a context of ministerial instability.

9. Assertive French educational ideologies

The educational domination of the church was challenged at the end of the *ancien régime* both on grounds of rationalist philosophy and of nationalist policy. Not only was the religious content of secondary and higher education incompatible with the secularist demands of the enlightened intellectual elite, the control of the religious orders over educational establishments was construed as a political threat. The distrust of interference from Rome which had underpinned the Gallicanism[1] of the monarchy prompted the philosophers and the Parliamentarians' attacks on the Jesuits.[2] Their campaign was success-ful precisely because of this coincidence between traditional anti-Ultramontanism and new bourgeois anti-clericalism.

While ideology and expediency intermingled in the denunciation of teaching orders at post-primary level – and in pleas for a rationalist education, less classical and more utilitarian than in the past, the approach to primary schooling was wholly dictated by practical considerations. It was expedient that the instruction given to the majority in a predominantly rural and agrarian society should be minimal. It was equally indifferent to the economically and education-ally privileged bourgeois section of the Third Estate as it was to the legally privileged aristocracy that the people should be enlightened – and equally important to both that it should accept the concept of station in life. Thus the social usefulness of religion as a legitimation of existing stratification was recognised by the philosophers, who simultaneously rejected it for the elite and advocated it for the rest of the population. This educational double standard – exemplified by Voltaire's acceptance of religious instruction for the populace and his restriction of rationalism to the bourgeoisie – was a common feature of enlightened philosophy. It was spelt out in Diderot's blueprint for an educational system submitted to Catherine II, but never implemented in Russia.[3] His proposals largely coincide with those put forward by Parliamentarians, when the twelve French regional Parliaments,[4] exceeding their initial functions as judiciary courts, assumed the role of political assemblies and addressed petitions to the king on issues of national interest, educational as well as financial and administrative. This concordance between the views of Diderot as an exponent of enlightened ideals and of the Parliaments as self-styled spokesmen for the enlightened elite, witnesses to the wide diffusion of a selective secularism, which would not extend to popular institution. The corollary was that the state should control the educational activities of the clergy and restrict them to the sphere in which religion would legitimate social stability to the exclusion of that in which it would harm intellectual development. This reliance on the state – equally comprehensible in the case of Diderot, trusting in the benevolence of enlightened despots, and actually writing for one, and in that of the Parliamentarians, enmeshed in the authoritarian tradition of the French monarchy – is the major feature of the challenge to religious domination over education. In the secondary and higher courses, it is governmental intervention which is expected to uphold rationalism, reduce classicism and support the claims of the rising bourgeoisie. In primary schools, religious instruction is to be continued by governmental permission and the clergy is thus to serve secular ends by dispensing it.

Diderot – education and enlightened despotism

Two major assumptions underpin these proposed reforms: that the state is the agency which will promote rationality by dislodging the church from its position of educational domination, and that the bourgeoisie is the group most susceptible of rational thought in eighteenth-century society. Like other philosophers of the time, Diderot – having discounted the aristocracy as a potential source of reform – wrote 'Not for the crowd who will not be able to understand for a long time, but for those who can instruct the crowd, give it laws and form its morality.'[5] He consistently assumed the need for an elite to maximise happiness in society by promoting rationality in politics as in economics.[6]

The elitist implications of Diderot's philosophy are clear in his discussion of religion. He echoes other enlightened philosophers in denouncing graft in the church, corruption in the priesthood and falsity in theology. One by one, all his philosophical postulates are used to condemn Catholicism and religion in general. To begin with, theology is defined as the science of illusion and therefore as anti-rational. Hence the selection of its precepts is only governed by the self-interest of its priests who alone benefit from the prejudices disseminated by the church. 'Interest gave rise to priests, priests to prejudices, prejudices to wars, and wars will continue so long as there are prejudices, prejudices so long as there are priests, and priests so long as there are advantages in being one.'[7] Thus his third and related attack is that the presence of clergy in society destroys the happiness, as well as the rationality of its members. Furthermore, no church is ever content with spiritual power alone, but each will seek to extend its political influence in the state; witness the use of the confessional as a means of bringing monarchs to their knees. 'The priest, good or bad, is always an undependable subject, a being strung between heaven and earth . . . In league either with the people against the sovereign or with the sovereign against the people.'[8] Diderot sees history as the record of an alliance between religion and despotism – royal or popular – for purposes of social control. Thus Jesuits: 'To the people they preached blind submission to kings; papal infallibility until masters of one, they made themselves masters of all.'[9] It is from this subordination to the clergy that he wishes to free society – beginning by the elite. The rejection of religion will thus pave the way to the diffusion of rationality. The state alone can achieve this by officially depriving the priesthood of any political prerogatives and of economic independence. 'While it is difficult to dispense with priests wherever a religion exists, it is easy to keep them quiet, if they are remunerated by the State and threatened upon the slightest misdemeanour to be dismissed from their posts, deprived of their functions and of their fees, and reduced to penury.'[10]

Subordinated to secular authorities, it will no longer be an impediment to enlightenment. Religion, like thought, should be harnessed to the requirements of the state which should be identified with the general happiness: 'The sovereign must keep the priests up one sleeve and the man of letters up the other. These are two preachers who ought to be under his control.'[11]

The ultimate success of this anti-clerical policy would be represented by the separation between ethics and religion. A secular morality founded on reason and aimed at happiness would replace the religious morality founded on revelation (interpreted as superstition) and aimed at salvation (interpreted as submission). New ethics were to become a branch of natural science: 'Philosophy should be founded on physiology, natural history, medicine . . .'[12] The acceptance of this naturalistic ethical system would be initially limited to the most enlightened class in society. At this stage, religion would not disappear, but would be reduced to a subordinate position in the state. Ultimately it would be restricted to deism which consists of a single theological postulate – the existence of God – without implying any ethical postulates.[13] While hoping for the eventual enlightenment of society as a whole, Diderot cannot visualise the immediate decline of religion among the people as opposed to the elite. Since he does not foresee the secularisation of the masses, nor the disappearance of the church, he looks to the state for restraining the clergy.[14] This erastianism would provide the ruling class with an instrument of social control and the government with an instrument of political control over the people.

While preaching had been used by the church to disseminate dogma, the state should use the school to propagate rationality. As the agencies of the church had sought to mould the faithful, so national education would serve to raise citizens. It is only by taking over the educational role traditionally assumed by the clergy that the state can begin to instil the duties of citizenship in society. 'Diderot did not conceive public instruction as anything other than the exclusive privilege, the monopoly of the State.'[15] This transfer of authority has been likened to the pattern of the *Kulturkampf*[16] – involving a secularisation of culture and a domestication of religion. However, to imbue citizens with secular morality is not the only objective of Diderot's educational plan for Russia, embodying his ideal. State monopoly over instruction should not only lead to the diffusion of rationality, but also provide the skills deemed useful to society. In so far as education is equated with training, its content must fulfil the requirements of utility by lending itself to immediate application in the professional sphere.

Therefore an important aspect of state monopoly over instruction is the control over subjects taught, classified in order of decreasing utility. Such a vocational approach is contrasted by Diderot with the exaggerated classicism of existing curricula in religious establishments. He rejects the imparting of useless knowledge, 'wonderful knowledge which becomes perfectly useless',[17] characteristic of French education in his time. His objection to concentrating on the classics is that they are unrelated to the needs of most occupations in society: 'The ancient tongues are only useful now to some specific sectors of society.'[18] In fact only the least useful occupations – the priesthood, literature and erudition – require a knowledge of such subjects.[19] 'The science of words, i.e. the study of languages, has had its day. It should be replaced by the science of things, the study of quantities, forces and laws, and of natural objects.'[20] In his scheme, while primary education is limited to the three Rs and elementary ethics, secondary commences with mathematics, leads on to the experimental sciences and only includes the study of languages in its last two years.[21] Hence every characteristic of education, from the syllabus to the intake of schools is governed by the single principle of utility.

For the state to reap the maximum benefits from vocational training with the minimum investment, some element of selection according to ability must be taken into account. Therefore in Diderot's three-layer system with elementary instruction common to all, 'gymnasia' for the trades and the minor professions, and university for the occupations which require higher learning, movement between these stages is on the grounds of merit. The state should provide scholarships for the outstanding poor and establish schools in each town, to which parents would be obliged to send their children.[22] Instruction is therefore compulsory and cheap, if not free.[23] While no attempts are to be made to equalise opportunities, every appearance of merit will be harnessed and directed to an appropriate occupation. It is significant that there is no recognition of environmental influences on achievement: egalitarianism is of little importance to Diderot's considerations of utility. The mechanism proposed to assess merit and later to assign posts is the competitive examination: 'I would like all posts in an empire, including the most important, to be filled by competitive examination.'[24] Thus Diderot advocates the formation of a new elite which will differ from the existing aristocracy by virtue of its qualifications rather than its powers.

This emphasis on recruitment by merit seems to imply – in the content of Diderot's educational plan – the notion of a ladder, with free movement from elementary to higher institutions. The formal provisions outlined would seem to warrant this assumption. However, the way in which the primary stage is designed shows that the system is intended for a static rather than a mobile population. Indeed apart from literacy and elementary arithmetic it incorporates a political and ethical catechism[25] for the formation of the lower social orders in the duties of citizenship. This level of instruction is construed as the only guaranteed minimum and passage to the next is envisaged as a privilege for the very exceptional rather than a right conferred on all pupils endowed with the necessary ability.[26] Furthermore, Diderot's designation of university students as *savants* sets the intellectual elite apart from the mass. Since education is not to be gratuitous and scholarships will be the exception rather than the rule, the propertied class is clearly going to be privileged. One can identify in this plan the embryonic notion of social position determining educational opportunity which was to be taken up and extended in the Imperial University.

Two postulates were central both to Diderot's Russian and Napoleon's Imperial University: rationalism and *étatism*. They were interrelated in that reason was to be used to serve the state and the state was committed to the diffusion of rationality. Two consequences followed from this: knowledge should be useful rather than abstract and training should be vocational rather than theoretical. In addition, the sway of religion over the population should be used by the government for purposes of social control and the power of the clergy over the state should be broken. Both religion and education should be subordinated to the requirements of the state and, while their aims are mutually exclusive, their functions should be complementary. The intellectual elite emerging from competitive examinations should subscribe to secular ethics alone, while the mass whose instruction was restricted to the primary level could take refuge in faith, provided a subservient clergy did not challenge the primary duties of citizenship.

One of the most remarkable characteristics of his pedagogical system is that one already finds in it, clearly expressed, two of the fundamental concepts which were later to direct Napoleon I in the organization of the educational system and the relationships between Church and State: the subordination of priests to civil power; the control of studies confirmed exclusively to the State . . . His Russian system resembles point by point, and forty years before the event, the imperial system of 1808.[27]

The Parliamentarians – education and Gallican nationalism

Several plans for educational reform were presented to regional Parliaments in the second half of the eighteenth century, all of them imbued with secularism and the desire to replace the educational domination of the church by state control. The main exponents of this approach were President Rolland d'Erceville of the Paris Parliament and Caradeuc de la Chalotais of the Parliament of Brittany.[28] Both were anti-clerical, endorsing the freedom of the Gallican church and condemning the Jesuits. Both sought to foster a state education system, nationalistic in that the formation of citizens, the teaching of secular morality and the use of the mother tongue would be its main attributes. Both used the criterion of utility to define the form and content of schooling. Neither accepted egalitarianism as a feature of a state system or as a corollary of utility.

The Parliamentarians share a debt to the philosophy of Enlightenment. They accept the formative power of education and see the diffusion of rationality as the goal of tuition; to spread instruction is to lessen prejudice and to increase morality. It is for this reason that both authors question the fitness of religious orders as educators. 'I will not enter here into the difficulties of knowing whether religious membership [of an order] is compatible with the duties education imposes, and if a monk, necessarily governed by a particular rule, and who – experience shows – is in general more attached to his Order than to his country, can be chosen to give to citizens a national education.'[29] Thus not only does the tuition given by such an order conflict with the requirements of rationality in stressing faith at its expense, it also undermines patriotism in placing religion above citizenship. 'The servitude of the mind is more repugnant than that of the body.'[30] Moreover the intellectual level of the order is low and it has proved singularly unsuccessful in producing men of distinction in either science or literature. 'They have had more than fifty thousand professors of philosophy without one philosopher of distinction.'[31] Accused of neglecting their role in education, the Jesuits are condemned both for curbing the intellectual development of individuals and for endangering society by failing to train responsible citizens.

As exponents of Gallicanism, the Parliamentarians challenge religious orders rather than the church itself. While they want Catholicism to be national rather than Roman, they envisage ethics as separated from religion. Thus 'La Chalotais is a determined Gallican . . . He is otherwise sincerely religious. But he wants a national religion which does not subordinate the interests of the country to a foreign power. He wishes above all that the Church, keeping for itself the teaching of "divine truths", relinquishes to the State the teaching of morality and the direction of studies which are purely human.'[32] To this end both he and Rolland protest against the monopoly the orders held over the teaching profession. La Chalotais asks: 'How had one been able to think that men unattached to the State, who are accustomed to place a monk above the heads of State, their Order above the country, their Institute and its Statutes above the laws, would be capable of bringing up and instructing the youth of a kingdom.'[33] Not only is such instruction unfavourable to citizenship, it is also unjust to parents who are deprived of the right to influence the formation of their children. 'It seems that to have children constitutes an exclusion from bringing them up.'[34] For all these reasons, the two Parliamentarians advocate a purely secular teaching profession. Thus in Rolland's blueprint, 'Masters will be citizens, they will be dependent only on the State.'[35] The protests of the philosophers and the pressures of the Parliamentarians culminated in the expulsion of Jesuits from France in 1762. The other teaching orders were considered less undesirable, because less directly linked with Rome and less hostile to scientific progress.

This measure of success achieved by parliamentary influence indicates that educational plans emanating from these institutions must not be considered as purely theoretical. The departure of the Jesuits left a gap which only an overall reform could duly fill. Hence discussions intended to define the form and content of education were directly aimed at a change of policy. State intervention in this field already appeared as unavoidable. It was the purpose of Rolland and La Chalotais – as it had been that of Diderot in a more abstract framework – not only to describe the content of such a reform, but to justify it. The legitimation of a state educational system takes precedence in both plans over the concrete proposals about institutions and curricula. The kernel of the arguments used in support of such a system is contained in the title of La Chalotais's proposals (*Essai d'Éducation nationale*). This is in fact the first time that the word 'national' had been used in connection with education in France, although elements of this approach appeared in Diderot's work. 'I claim for the Nation an education which depends upon nothing but the State, because it belongs to it in essence; because the Nation has an inalienable and imprescriptible right to educate its members; because in the end the children of the State must be brought up by members of the State.'[36] Thus the common features of Parliamentarian projects is to turn education into a purely secular activity organised and supervised by the state, whose right of control is asserted against the prerogatives of the church.[37] This argument which does not take into account the rights of individuals illustrates how close the Parliamentarians are to the formulation of a social control theory.

The main task assigned to a national educational system is to train citizens. 'As education should prepare citizens for the State, it is clear that it must be in accordance with its constitution and its laws; it would be deeply at fault if it contradicted them.'[38] Since education is defined as training for citizenship, it should only be given to future citizens, to the exclusion of foreigners, and should only be imparted by citizens, to the exclusion of those religious orders which rejected the sovereignty of the state. Thus the duty of the state is to control education and the duty of education is to serve the state. By forming citizens educational institutions will fulfil their mission. Such tuition will have a double purpose: it will dispel the prejudice born from ignorance, and detrimental to a rational government, while at the same time it will inculcate actual skills useful to the community. 'The more ignorant the people, the readier they are to be dominated by their own prejudices or by charlatans of all kinds who threaten . . . on the one hand Religion and the State . . . will gain faithful servants and on the other Science will not run the risk of losing talent which a basic instruction would have revealed and enabled to be recognized.'[39] La Chalotais shares the view of Rolland that it is the needs of the state which should shape the goals of education. 'This is why he proposes an education of the State, by the State and for the State.'[40]

This emphasis on the supreme importance of the state is inseparable from a nationalistic bias. It has all the characteristics of the theories which place society above its members and the nation above the individual. Educational organisation, the teaching profession and the content of curricula alike are to be devised in the light of a nationalistic ideology, implying a quest for administrative uniformity and political independence. The first of these targets can be achieved by centralisation, subordinating all establishments to a common control and the provinces to the mandates of the capital. To this end, Rolland first advocates the predominance of Paris over provincial universities.

To turn Paris into the centre and the fountainhead of public education, to establish lines of dependence and communication between the Universities located in the Provinces and that of the Capital, and to give to the latter over all others, if not an absolute authority, which might constrain education, at least a habitual influence which serves for support and encouragement.[41]

Secondly, he suggests the creation of administrative bodies (*bureaux de correspondance*) in each university town in order to inspect secondary establishments (*collèges*) within its jurisdiction. The control of universities over existing schools is to be guaranteed by the introduction of this inspectorate and all institutions would fit into an educational pyramid, with the University of Paris at its apex. Both Parliamentarians insist on the state system being unique. Previously the Jesuit colleges had possessed the right to grant degress to their students and even the power of conferring degrees in the University of Paris was vested until the Revolution in a chancellor endowed with this prerogative by the Pope. The Parliamentarians demand a secular monopoly in this respect. Such a centralised secular system corresponds closely to the main features of the Imperial University.[42] Not only do the Parliamentarians advocate a unitary system of control over education, they also wish to unify the actual content of the tuition given. They propose the standardisation of curricula, the certification of teachers and the identity of teaching aids throughout the country. The unification of all educational institutions will minimise regional differences while maximising the diffusion of enlightenment.

Thus everything will be linked in the system of public education, enlightenment, until now nearly always concentrated in big towns, will spread to the villages, the country-dweller and those whom Providence gave the highest station in life will all receive the instruction suited to them, and as in the human body the heart is the centre which pumps the blood to animate all parts of the body, the Kingdom will receive from the Capital the energy it needs and the same principle of life will extend to the most remote Provinces.[43]

Thus the power of the state and the diffusion of rationality are inextricably linked: the state propagating reason as it asserts its authority against that of the church and rationality in turn reinforcing secularism. Two inter-related consequences follow: on the one hand, the teaching profession should be secularised and brought under state control. On the other, rationalistic ethics should be promoted at the expense of religious morality. Thus La Chalotais desires that a secular code of behaviour be propagated in all schools, a position which is only tenable for one who dissociates morality from faith. 'Pagans separated ethics from religion: it can be done now too.'[44] 'I have spoken of Ethics which precede all positive, divine and human laws; the teaching of divine laws concerns the Church, but the teaching of Ethics belongs to the State and has always done so: it existed before Revelation and therefore is not dependent upon Revelation.'[45] It is significant that the Parliamentarians see no contradiction between emphasising the operation of individual reason and advocating the propagation of a state ideology. While the one would lead to a diversity of private judgements, the other would favour a uniformity of beliefs. An initial rationalism intended to emancipate the individual from prejudice turns into an authoritarian nationalism which defines the state as the embodiment of reason in society. The state is no longer a means to an end – namely to the propagation of enlightenment. It has become an end in itself.

A concomitant of nationalism in the blueprints of the Parliamentarians is the condemnation of classicism, to be replaced by a greater use of the mother tongue. 'If it is not necessary to proscribe Latin, it is equally irrational to give it pride of place in our education.'[46] Therefore French should be taught more thoroughly and to La Chalotais should serve as the main teaching medium, whereas Rolland is content with parity between the mother tongue and the classical languages. Similarly national history should predominate over that of antiquity: 'The young men who attend the Colleges know the name of all the Roman Consuls and are ignorant of those of our kings.'[47] Thus the Parliamentarians wish to reshape the syllabus, demoting classicism from its traditional pre-eminence and introducing studies such as national literature, regional geography and modern history.

However, it is not only on nationalistic grounds that the teachings of existing establishments are criticised. They are also attacked as unrelated to the needs of the community. Both Rolland and La Chalotais differentiate between the training of loyal citizens and the formation of useful servants for the state. While these targets are in no way contradictory, they are not implicit in one another. In fact one of the main criticisms addressed to the existing system of classical education is its inapplicability to active life.

Are public Schools destined only to produce clergymen, judges, physicians and men of letters? Are soldiers, sailors, tradesmen, artists unworthy of the attention of the Government, and because Literature cannot maintain itself without classical studies, should these studies be the sole preoccupation of an instructed and enlightened people?[48]

Instead of tradition, the criterion of utility should determine the content of schooling, since its purpose is vocational: 'to successfully fill the different occupations in the State'.[49] While admitting that education has the power to increase enlightenment in the population, nevertheless the Parliamentarians believe that it should only be given in conjunction with vocational training. 'Everybody in the State must have some religion, a morality and knowledge related to their occupation; reading and writing which are the keys to all other knowledge must therefore be universally spread . . . The peasant who has received a kind of schooling is all the more aware and skilful.'[50] La Chalotais also agrees that instruction should be given because it is conducive to greater occupational proficiency and only in so far as it is so. The two goals which the Parliamentarians assign to education, namely the furthering of citizenship and the inculcation of skills, are reconciled in their blueprints by the juxtaposition of a common elementary instruction and a differentiated further training. The former is intended to spread secular morality and the basic knowledge required from all members of society, mainly literacy. The latter will constitute a branching system whose various segments correspond to various levels of professional specialisation. 'The part of Education which is concerned with morality would be common to all; only instruction (in other subjects) would vary; public education would then be truly important; it would offer to all social groups and all minds the knowledge which they needed; no talent would be lost for Society.'[51]

The main feature of vocational training as advanced by the Parliamentarians is that manifest ability should be channelled rather than latent ability detected. The amount of tuition given should be determined by considerations of national interest rather than of distributive justice. While egalitarianism would require a concern for individual potential, state efficiency merely postulates that obvious talent should not be wasted. Nationalism need never imply equality of opportunity unless the state requires more trained personnel than is currently produced. However, in a situation where no such shortage is apparent, the state has nothing to gain by tapping latent intellectual potential. In fact the Parliamentarians claim that more people are being educated than the country can use. 'Thus it is more advantageous for the State that there be few *Collèges* but that they should be good and that they provide a full course of studies, rather than to have many of a mediocre standard. It is better to have fewer students provided they are better educated; and they will be more easily taught, if they are fewer in number.'[52] This contrast between quality and quantity corresponds to the requirements of a predominantly agricultural society whose government could only employ a small trained elite. The educational system must therefore be highly selective, to serve national needs rather than to fulfil individual aspirations. Social mobility through education is thus the exception rather than the rule; it is only permitted when the state finds it useful, but never represents an ideal in itself.

In addition, the Parliamentarians are not complete genetic determinists, but adopt the much more modern position that both nature and environment contribute to achievement. 'Nature makes some difference between men (one cannot doubt it), perhaps education makes more.'[53] Nevertheless while La Chalotais is doubtful about forming intelligence by tuition, he is completely convinced about the possibility of forming character by teaching ethics. State education can make all men into dutiful citizens, it neither should nor could attempt to make them all learned. Thus moral instruction should be universal, whereas academic education should be selective. The generality of the former and the limitation of the latter are equally dictated by national interest.

The well-being of society would not be achieved if the instruction given to the majority went beyond the requirements of their station in life defined by their occupation. 'The goal of society requires that the knowledge of the people should not go beyond their occupations. Any man who looks beyond his dismal trade will never practice it with courage and patience.'[54] Since neither Parliamentarian considers that the state needs a large number of educated people, it is clear that selection will play a large part in education though not obvious along which lines it will operate. The system envisaged by the Parliamentarians could be meritocratic and need not imply social conservatism. However, like the English Utilitarians, they do not challenge or even examine the legitimacy of the class structure with which they are faced. Like James Mill, they assume that a large proportion of the population must labour in the interest of society as a whole. Their implicit theory of social control emerges as education is increasingly related to occupation rather than merit. Hence vocation is less determined by intellectual ability than education by occupational ranking.

The full elitarian implications of the system are revealed by the fact that higher education is to be reserved for a numerically limited and socially restrictive group. It is characteristic of the agreement between philosophers and Parliamentarians on this point that Voltaire congratulated La Chalotais for excluding the people from the *collèges* – 'I thank you for proscribing studies for the peasantry.'[55] Not only are the common people to be banned from higher education on the grounds of national utility, the interest of the state also requires the limitation of their numbers in secondary establishments and the restriction of elementary instruction to mere essentials. 'Working class parents, tempted by the cheap or gratuitous education offered, send their children to secondary schools, and in consequence there is a shortage of entrants into the manual trades, while the recruitment of the navy also proves difficult – a serious matter in view of the wars with England. Even elementary education is overdone.'[56] This exaggerated diffusion of learning, unrelated to national needs, has been allowed by the church, but should not be perpetuated in a state system. 'The Brothers of the Christian Doctrine, called "Ignorantins" . . . teach reading and writing to people who ought to learn nothing beyond how to use a plane or a file, but who are no longer willing to do so.'[57]

Thus the Parliamentarians advocate a double standard of education – elementary to control the people, secondary and higher to further the bourgeoisie. In this they are fully in accord with the philosophers of the Enlightenment, even Rousseau, for all his Republican leanings – 'The poor have no need of education. It is shaped by their situation. They can have no other.'[58] However, in their nationalistic justification for such restriction, they are mainly indebted to Diderot, whom they acknowledge as a source of inspiration. In fact, an anonymous pamphlet entitled *De l'éducation publique* was bound together with the first edition of La Chalotais's scheme, which it strongly resembles. 'Its authorship has been attributed to various contemporary litterateurs; but we shall probably be right in ascribing it to Diderot.'[59] The main theme of Utilitarian secular education was thus directly transmitted from enlightened thinkers to pre-revolutionary planners.

The pre-revolutionary planners – from Diderot designing an educational system for Russia to the Parliamentarians urging reforms in France – were imbued with and expressed a secularist nationalism which was later used to legitimate the educational assertion of the bourgeoisie, after the Revolution had destroyed the structure of estates and their legal privileges. It was only when the bourgeoisie had emerged from among the non-privileged as the politically leading, as well as the most prosperous and most enlightened section of the Third Estate, that this assertion occurred in the context of Napoleon's Imperial University. However the ideology by reference to which it was legitimated predated the Revolution and it is in the blueprints of La Chalotais and Rolland that its clearest formulation can be found. Their writings fulfil three of the functions associated with assertive ideologies: they provide a criticism of the challenged dominant group (in this case, the Catholic church); a justification of the claims formulated against this domination by a competing group, the bourgeoisie; and, lastly, a set of concrete proposals for educational change.

REVOLUTIONARY ASSERTIVE IDEOLOGIES

The educational ideology advanced by Condorcet and Sieyès differs from that of the Parliamentarians by considering instruction a right of the people, not a useful instrument for social control. A major part of Condorcet's writings are devoted to attacking the interested aims of the clergy in dominating education, on the original grounds that this is contrary to free thought. Because this attack is based on natural rights rather than political expediency Condorcet condemns the Parliamentarian formula of religious instruction under state control and advocates complete secularisation in education and the separation of church from state. Thus he sought not only to undermine the dominant group but also refused to see as legitimate any continuation of the church's activities in the field of education, either in the long or short term. The Parliamentarians could sanction it on grounds of utility and expediency, but to Condorcet indoctrination was incompatible with liberty. Such views were influential under the revolutionary Assemblies when the church monopoly had been totally restricted but incompletely replaced – if the secular powers could not supply instruction then the country had better go without it than recall the teaching orders as a stop-gap.

Secondly, Condorcet attacks the major goal of the Parliamentarians of merely wishing to replace the church by the state in education. Diderot, Helvétius and La Chalotais had only seen the practical utility which the state could derive through controlling education and viewed its distribution as regulated by political needs. Both the secular indoctrination and restricted distribution explicit in this ideology, were in Condorcet's view as hostile to natural rights as the religious system had been. Thus he reverses the Parliamentarians' priorities and advocates education as a duty of the state towards citizens, not a right through whose exercise it can control them. While he acknowledges that only the state can provide a national educational system, his fear of it being manipulated by the political elite makes him define this intervention as minimal. The state as paymaster – *l'état comme caissier* – represented the degree of integration with the political structure necessary to assure the universality of education while protecting pupils from indoctrination.

Universal education as advocated by Condorcet and Sieyès would restore natural rights by destroying artificial social inequalities, defined by the former as those of wealth, occupation and instruction, and by the latter as summarised by the existence of privileged estates. While both advocate a political system of representative democracy, they also accept that 'a constitution which establishes political equality will neither be durable nor desirable if it permits the existence of social institutions favourable to inequality'.[60] Thus democracy depends upon the spread of enlightenment and in its turn only a democratic government acknowledging natural rights will tackle artificial social inequalities. It is from this association between democracy and education that the legitimation of revolutionary assertion springs. While the group held responsible for bringing about the two is left vague by Condorcet, it was Sieyès's main contribution to revolutionary ideology to relate this struggle to the contemporary system of social stratification and show how political and educational reform could only come through the united action of the Third Estate.

Both Condorcet and Sieyès worked out complete blueprints for future educational systems which were submitted to different revolutionary Assemblies. Each represents a similar attempt to devise institutional arrangements which are compatible with both liberty and equality. The solution they gave to this problem was identical. If equality (defined as independence from others, not social uniformity) is to be ensured then universal primary instruction must be the first priority. It must be sufficiently practical for daily life and sufficiently general for citizenship. Sieyès considers that if national resources are limited they must be concentrated on primary to the detriment of other levels of instruction, in other words the exact opposite to what would occur if state needs were the criterion of distribution. Supposing sufficient resources, the requirements of liberty demand the establishment of secondary and higher education for those with ability to proceed. Ultimately Condorcet and Sieyès advocate a meritocracy but one in which, because of universal elementary instruction for independence, the political elite of a democracy would not replicate the privileged estates.

Condorcet – education and emancipation from prejudice

Condorcet resembles most eighteenth-century philosophers in positing a state of nature in which human rights are rooted. He uses it both philosophically and sociologically – in other words, to delineate individual rights and to account for social development. From it are derived the three postulates about human nature which underpin the whole of his political and educational thought. The basic concept from which all others are deduced is that of man as reasonable being. 'The main element of Condorcet's social philosophy is the idea of man in general or, to use his terminology, of man considered only as "a sensate being, capable of reasoning and of acquiring moral ideas".'[61] Rationality is thus the first postulate; it is a characteristic which enables man to apprehend the truth without resorting to faith. 'By reason one may also mean the truths which the human mind can attain naturally without being helped by religious revelation.'[62] The second and related postulate is that a rational being has rights which are truly natural, since they originate in human nature itself. 'The preservation of these rights is the sole object of the grouping of men in a political society.'[63] Political activities in society consist in protecting and extending such rights, 'to guarantee the conservation of these rights with the utmost equality and to the greatest extent'.[64] The third postulate, inseparable from the others, is that of a natural equality between men, based on their common rationality and justifying the exercise of their rights. 'The natural equality of men, the first basis of their rights is the foundation of all true morality.'[65] However, equality is used by Condorcet as an axiomatic rather than descriptive term. It is intended to stress a basic similarity rather than a superficial likeness. 'Beneath the idiosyncrasies and accidents of their physical make-up, of their customs, of their ideas, of their morals, of their history, all men at the bottom of their mental and moral nature are identical.'[66] Thus men may differ in culture, but share a common nature; it is this nature which is identical, not themselves who are equal. Hence natural equality to Condorcet has a specific philosophical meaning, it does not imply equality on every criterion. He freely admits the existence of considerable differences between men, 'established by nature and consisting in differences of age, health, of physical strength and of qualities of mind or of body'.[67]

As society developed, artificial inequalities were produced and tended to negate the rights of men derived from their common nature. The agency held responsible for this evolution is the legal-metaphysical class. While primitive men had the simplest form of deism as their religion, the priesthood had extended this belief into a set of superstitions which ensured their own power. Similarly the simple code of behaviour prevailing in early communities had been transformed by professional lawyers for their own ends. 'They formed codes which were complicated, obscure, written in a style unintelligible for anybody but themselves.'[68] These groups had perpetuated errors and prejudices which had acted as obstacles to progress and barriers between men. 'Almost everywhere two classes have exercised control over the people, from which instruction alone could preserve them, these are the lawyers and the priests; the former have a hold over their conscience, and the latter over their business.'[69]

Human progress has been restricted by tendentious religious teachings, as each epoch has been the scene of a struggle between superstition and reason. Therefore religion and progress are antithetic. Hence the struggle against clericalism since the end of the middle ages.

At the beginning of the 15th century, all Europe, steeped in ignorance, suffered under the yoke of the aristocracy and of clerical tyranny; and since then, progress towards liberty has, in each nation, followed that of enlightenment with such regularity as to indicate between these two facts a necessary association, founded on the enduring laws of nature.[70]

Conversely progress is only gained by the increase of rationality – the less enlightened the members of a society are, the more easily they can be dominated by ambitious groups pursuing their own interests at the expense of the general good. 'Any society which is not enlightened by philosophers is misled by charlatans.'[71] Therefore to spread enlightenment is to ensure progress, since an increase in rationality necessarily leads to a corresponding development in morality. An obvious corollary of this position is that Condorcet sees no connection between ethics and religion.

The influence of the legal–clerical class on social development has given rise to three main categories of artificial inequalities. These are inequalities of wealth, of occupation and of education.[72] Fundamental to Condorcet's philosophy is the firm belief that the state must not only respect the natural rights of men, but also ensure their operation in society by eliminating such inequalities. This does not mean that he wishes to eradicate natural differences between men, 'but there are inequalities which are quite artificial, which result from social organization or from the grouping of men in society; and it is these inequalities which the State is in duty bound to prosecute and destroy'.[73] It is only in this that justice can prevail and society progress.

Reviewing the role of education in history, Condorcet claims that 'inequality of instruction is one of the main sources of tyranny'[74] and thus the most influential of artificial inequalities. In the past, one class had dominated another by having sole access to knowledge. Priests, professionals and warriors have in their turn ruled society through the possession of scarce knowledge. 'There will therefore be a real distinction which laws will be unable to destroy and which, by separating the enlightened and the unenlightened, will turn enlightenment into a means of power for some rather than of happiness for all.'[75] Therefore instruction must be made universal to diminish artificial inequalities, which in Condorcet's time are primarily represented by class differences. 'The son of the rich will not belong to the same class as the son of the poor if no public institution brings them closer by instruction.'[76] Without education spreading reason throughout society, good government is precluded since it is by reason, not by legislation that one can 'conserve good laws, a wise administration and a truly liberal constitution'.[77]

The functioning of democracy is thus held to depend directly upon the educational level of the people – democracy cannot exist where man's natural rights to liberty and equality are not recognised, and the recognition of these rights can only be ensured by the diffusion of reason. 'Here the art of bringing up children appeared closely related to the art of governing men.'[78] Thus his educational philosophy underpins his political thought – the function of instruction being the training of citizens for democracy. Without such training democracy cannot exist. It is for these reasons that Condorcet claims: 'Society owes to the people a popular instruction.'[79] Universal education underpins both free trade in economics and popular sovereignty in politics, since they equally depend on the operation of reason.

The connection made between government and education was common to all thinkers of the eighteenth century. What distinguishes Condorcet is that instead of seeing education as an instrument of social control, he views it as a prerequisite for democracy. 'What was most essential to human progress was therefore, not to enlighten the ruler but to enlighten people.'[80] It is a duty not a right of state. The people must not be educated to conform to the requirements of an elite. Instead they must through education regain the rationality perverted by religious and secular prejudice and reclaim the natural rights distorted by artificial inequalities. Education then is given the sole task of stimulating reason and must be exclusive of indoctrination. To indoctrinate is always to inculcate some prejudice and therefore to hinder the operation of rationality. Condorcet's idea of liberty which dictates that politics should be democratic makes it equally necessary that education should be non-doctrinaire. 'No public power should have authority or even credit for preventing the teaching of theories contrary to its particular policy or its temporary interests.'[81] For these reasons the first part of his educational philosophy is concerned with establishing freedom of thought. Since to him instruction and indoctrination are antithetic, because one furthers reason and liberty while the other limits them, the educational system should not be used to spread the ideology of the state or of the church.

Against indoctrination in education. The influence of the clergy over education would be as dangerous as that of the state. To teach religion would be to limit freedom of thought and give an unwarranted advantage to certain opinions – 'would give to particular dogmas an advantage contrary to freedom of thought'.[82] Moreover, social inequalities would be strengthened and the privileged position of the clergy confirmed. 'Furthermore he establishes that all religions are made, shaped and invented by men, owing on the one hand, to popular ignorance, and, on the other, to the self-interest of priests.'[83] To Condorcet, not only is religion purely human, it corresponds to the lowest aspects of human nature, since it furthers irrationalism, conservatism and immorality. 'Theological ethics seem dangerous to him not only because they consider religion as the source of behavioural motivation, but also because priests who in reality are only men, have taken upon themselves the right to dictate, judge and teach duties.'[84]

Therefore morality must be secular if it is not to result in unreason and inequalities. 'Ethics are viewed as independent from religion and metaphysics, and are made to depend on the analysis of Man's moral character.'[85] Since Condorcet believes in the fundamental unity of human nature, he is convinced of the existence of moral laws divorced from religion, and yet non-utilitarian. These laws need not be modified by circumstances of time and space. 'A distinction should be made between local mores and those which are universal'.[86] It is only general secular ethics of this type which must be taught in schools, since the only party who would benefit from religious teaching would be the clergy. Condorcet thus differs from the other enlightened philosophers, Diderot and Voltaire in particular, in claiming that religious education has no social utility. 'Condorcet was the one who had most sense of the future, and he felt that the separation of the Church and State meant the rule of Liberty.'[87] Education was the vital social institution in which this separation should occur.

It is because to Condorcet the natural rights of man are inseparable from rationality that freedom from state indoctrination in instruction is essential: 'In a way the independence of instruction is part of the rights of man.'[88] This means that the government has no right to impose any views on the population and should not attempt to spread the political attitudes favourable to the maintenance of its power.

May the example of England become a lesson for other peoples; a superstitious respect for the constitution or for certain laws to which one is invited to attribute national prosperity, a servile cult for certain tenets made sacred by the interest of the rich and powerful classes are there made part of education, there these are maintained for all who aspire to fortune or power, there these have become a kind of political religion which makes almost impossible any progress towards the improvement of the constitution and the laws.[89]

The implication is not that the state should become a spectator in education, but rather that it has the duty to present all ideas to the pupils and allow them a free choice. Thus 'The constitution of each nation must only be taught as a fact . . . the goal of instruction is not to make men admire a ready-made legislation, but to make them capable of assessing and correcting it.'[90] An educational system intended to perpetuate traditional attitudes or existing institutions is therefore illegitimate since it hampers freedom of thought. 'The duty of the State is to arm against error which is always a public evil . . . but it does not have the right to decide where truth or error lies.'[91] Therefore instruction should not inculcate values, it should restrict itself to facts – and the opinions of teachers about facts should be clearly separated from them. Even the subjects which are most difficult to approach objectively should be presented as rationally and as factually as possible.

Any attempt at constituting a state monopoly in education is opposed by Condorcet, he rejects as unjustifiable the submission of the teaching profession to governmental control as this would endanger the objectivity of instruction. Since he also dismisses the members of religious orders as equally incapable of objectivity, he therefore advocates a body of independent teachers, 'the idea to make the teaching body into a kind of State within the State, an independent power, a fourth estate, free from any outside authority, governing and administrating itself, while the State intervenes only as paymaster to remunerate services which it neither regulates nor controls'.[92] However, teachers should not be grouped in a corporation pursuing its own ends, but should be democratically elected on a regional basis. They should form a learned society rather than a union of teachers, *société savante*, not *corps enseignant*. This condemnation of a teaching monopoly is merely a special case of a wider dislike of educational cartels.

State domination over the educational system is both unjustifiable in theory and undesirable in practice, since it will necessarily tend to limit freedom of thought as did religious education. Condorcet supports the diversity of educational institutions because he relies on private schools to compensate for the ideological bias inevitably instilled in the population by state education. Such private schools 'have the means of correcting the vices of public instruction, of compensating for its imperfection'.[93] Indeed any state monopoly would give governments too great a temptation to use instruction for their own ends. 'Monopoly places a very powerful and therefore dangerous weapon in the hands of the State; it is safer to destroy it in advance, so that no government, no party can make use of it. Condorcet seems to have foreseen the Napoleonic University.'[94]

While it is, therefore, the duty of society to ensure that all its members will be educated, it is not the right of the state to design this education in order to produce a specific type of citizen. All a government should do is to ensure that a network of schools exist all over the country without deciding what they should teach or who the pupils should be. 'This great task should be accomplished by the State who will extend its benefits to all, including the poor.'[95] Hence Condorcet rejects the Parliamentarians' ideal of an educational system geared to the requirements of the state. In terms of his philosophy education and indoctrination are completely antithetic. The state may have the power to mould instruction, but it is never justified in doing so. 'The public powers should not take upon themselves the right to choose the philosophical, moral and political principles which ought to be inculcated in citizens.'[96] Indeed an education planned by the state to further citizenship would be unegalitarian, whereas instruction conducive to enlightenment rather than training would necessarily highlight social solidarity and undermine class divisions. 'By becoming aware of his rights and his duties, man learns that he is worth as much as any other man and rapidly acquires the notion of "equality", he understands that social inequalities are injust and can be abolished.'[97]

A blueprint for education based on natural rights. Consequently the role imparted by Condorcet to education is not one of social control, since instruction must be aimed at the restoration to man of his natural liberty. By this he does not imply that all men can be made equal, but only that artificial social distinctions would be obliterated by enlightenment. Hence he recognises that instruction would never eradicate all natural differences, and might even increase them by developing latent aptitudes. 'It is impossible for even an egalitarian instruction not to increase the superiority of those whom nature has endowed with a better constitution.'[98] This is because innate differences in ability will lead to a differential rate of learning. 'All people are not born with equal abilities, and if all are taught by the same methods during the same number of years, they will not learn the same things.'[99] Convinced that aptitudes are unequal, Condorcet does not believe that equality of opportunity would lead to complete levelling in society. Thus he differs from the view held by Helvétius that all differences existing between men are due to education. Instead any idea of complete equality is dismissed as utopian. 'A complete equality between minds is chimerical; but if public instruction is general and widespread; if it covers the sum total of knowledge, then this inequality is to the advantage of humanity which profits by the works of men of genius.'[100] Therefore equality is not synonymous with uniformity, but consists in giving independence to each individual. The aim of education is not to level, but to liberate. Universal instruction alone would eliminate dependence on others, 'this state of servile dependence where man, prey of the charlatan who wishes to seduce him, cannot defend his own interests and is obliged to deliver himself blindly to guides whom he cannot judge or choose'.[101] By ending such dependence, it will have promoted true equality. 'He firmly believed that to make each man independent of others is to make each man the equal of all.'[102] Equality is then defined as independence rather than identity. By this Condorcet means making people self-reliant in mental, moral and material spheres. The mind of people would be freed from prejudice and from errors inculcated by indoctrination. Morality would be guided by reason rather than dictated by religion. Finally if all were sufficiently instructed to possess some skills, none would be wholly at the mercy of an employer. In equating the furthering of independence with the eradication of artificial inequalities, Condorcet firmly links liberty with equality. 'In his view they were but two different aspects of a single reality. He is firmly convinced that all measures serving the cause of the former contribute to the victory of the latter.'[103]

It is on these grounds that Condorcet advocates universal primary education. A common elementary instruction would restore the natural equality which social life had disrupted. It would give to all citizens the minimum knowledge required to maintain their independence. Not only would such a system guarantee equality, it would also accelerate progress which proceeds more rapidly when the talent distributed throughout society is given a chance to develop. Moreover the justification of universal education is not sought in relation to intellectual progress, but to social justice. Spreading enlightenment is the only legitimate way of ensuring social order without education degenerating into an instrument of social control. Elementary instruction is therefore so important to society that money should be no obstacle to securing it. Condorcet wishes to create 'a form of instruction which does not allow any talent to escape undetected and which offers to it all the help reserved until now to the children of the rich'.[104]

To Condorcet the enlightenment of the upper class will not endure if 'the poor are condemned to stupidity'. When it spreads, not when it concentrates, does enlightenment increase.[105] It is both a right for the individual to acquire an education, and a duty for society to provide one. 'Nobody is entitled to remain ignorant, even if he wishes to do so: instruction should be compulsory.'[106] Since education is primarily designed for individual development and only secondly for progress in society, its character should not be predominantly vocational. Hence elementary schools should not be influenced by considerations of utility, but should be aimed at emancipating individuals from ignorance.

It is important for public prosperity to give to children of the poor classes, who are the most numerous, the possibility of developing their talents; this is a method not only of providing the country with more citizens able to serve it, science with more men capable of advancing it, but moreover of diminishing the inequality founded on difference of wealth, of bringing closer the classes which this difference tends to draw apart.[107]

Thus elementary instruction is intended to ensure equality between individuals and will do so by giving each man independence – which is synonymous with restoring his liberty.

Once all men have been made independent by elementary education, it will not matter to them that some are given a higher instruction. 'What does it matter to the man who does not depend on others that they be better educated than he?'[108] Thus so long as all have sufficient information to find suitable employment for their talents and to cope with the problems of daily life, the provision of advanced learning for some does not conflict with Condorcet's definition of equality. The man who knows the arithmetic rules necessary in daily life is not dependent on the academic who possesses to a higher degree the knowledge of mathematics.'[109]

Condorcet sees equality and liberty as in no way contradictory, but completely complementary. In his educational blueprint instruction is defined as being truly egalitarian if it fulfils three conditions. Firstly, if it gives all citizens a common background of knowledge. Secondly, if all have a special technical training to prepare them for the occupation related to their aptitudes. Thirdly, if all are enabled to acquire all the learning commensurate with their level of ability. The final requirement, far from leading to educational uniformity, would result directly in a meritocracy. This is a corollary of accepting differences in natural ability and defining equality as the exercise of freedom. The requirements of innate aptitude and demonstrated effort which determine the passage from one degree of instruction to the next are fully meritocratic and yet are justified by reference to equality. 'Indeed one ought not to prefer only those who have demonstrated ability, but those who can be seen to have added effort to it'.[110] Condorcet is fully aware of the repercussions such a system would have. He realises that it would result in inequalities, but these would be justified since they would be natural rather than artificial. 'In seeking to teach more to those who have less ability and talent, far from reducing the effects of this inequality, one does nothing but increase them.'[111] He accepts as natural the fact that the least gifted will occupy the lower posts in society. However, the allocation of jobs according to ability and taste does not preclude the unskilled from making useful contributions in practical life. In addition, Condorcet stresses that the unequal diffusion of instruction in society need not be a permanent phenomenon. As more people receive higher education, national productivity will rise and a more prosperous country can in turn afford to educate more of its citizens. Thus the intake of higher education will increase in the long run.

However, Condorcet values liberty more than equality, since the latter is dependent upon the former. Indeed unless men are independent of others, their relations cannot be egalitarian. To achieve independence is synonymous with being free. Therefore liberty is a prerequisite for equality. On the other hand, if equality were to be considered synonymous with complete identity between individuals, and if state policies were designed accordingly, this would deny a fundamental aspect of liberty – the freedom to realise one's potential and correspondingly to be different from others. This freedom is more important to Condorcet than the requirements of strict equality. It is for this reason that equality is given a minimal definition and liberty a maximal one. Hence Condorcet can advocate meritocracy in education as the expression of individual freedom. Unlike most meritocratic theorists, he does not tend towards elitism precisely because his educational structure is founded upon the egalitarian assumption that elementary instruction will make the people too independent to be manipulated by an elite.

As an educational ideology, the ideas advanced by Condorcet represented an abstract and philosophical condemnation of certain institutional arrangements. In terms of the functions of ideology for educational assertion, he largely concentrated on the latter three. On the basis of his theory of natural rights he condemned the dominant Catholic group, challenging the ideology and the self-interest it seeks to legitimate. Secondly, he perceptively challenged the right of any group controlling the political machinery to merely replace the church by the state in instruction – thus seeking to discredit the assertive ideology of the Parliamentarians designed to advance the bourgeoisie rather than the nation. Finally Condorcet provided a blueprint for new institutional arrangements in which education would both advance and protect natural rights. This plan foresaw the integration of education to the state in terms of financing but distinguished this from integration to the political structure since it could not use instruction for indoctrination and would not possess an educational monopoly. However, this philosophy did not legitimate the assertion of any particular social group or relate the problem of educational reform to social conflict. It was the writings of Sieyès which related the natural rights approach to education to the assertion of the Third Estate as a whole.

Sieyès – education and emancipation from privilege

The difference in their social origins accounts for the dissimilarity of the educational ideologies advanced by Condorcet and Sieyès. His aristocratic origins prevented Condorcet from expressing or even fully realising the claims of the Third Estate. The Revolution appeared to him as an opportunity for complete social change rather than a confrontation of competing interest groups – his commitment to it was on behalf of mankind, not in support of the demands made by any one estate. This dispassionate approach prevented him from gaining acceptance in any of the main revolutionary groups or from influencing legislation and eventually led to his death. On the other hand, Sieyès belonged to the Third Estate by origin and by choice.[112] From the beginning of his career he actively engaged in politics and the whole of his literary output took the form of political pamphlets, not philosophical treatises. In his writings, he was an exponent of the rights of the Third Estate; in his political activity, he was one of its main leaders. Thus his conceptions of liberty and equality are informed by the perspectives of class struggle. Perhaps the main common denominator uniting their thoughts was that every social institution should be adapted to the imperatives of individual freedom. To both, while liberty enables natural inequalities between individuals to flourish, it is incompatible with artificial inequalities. Therefore differences in ability are recognised whereas distinctions based on privileges are challenged. However Sieyès is considerably more specific about the nature of privilege in contemporary society, the organisation required to combat it, and the political feasibility of different institutional relationships after its overthrowal.

The main obstacle to universal liberty and therefore to representative government is the existence of privileges in society, which are seen as artificial social inequalities, contrary to natural rights and impeding human independence. Sieyès, like Condorcet, condemns such distinctions as opposed to liberty and equality. 'Without exception all privileges have the effect either to exempt from the law, or to give an exclusive right to something which is not forbidden by the law. Privilege consists in being outside common law.'[113] Privileges are necessarily contradictory to natural law since they transgress its main tenet, which is that no one's freedom should impinge on that of others. Thus the privilege granted to one – whether it be a title, the exemption from a duty or the conferring of a right – is a direct infringement on the liberty of others. 'We have observed also that everything which is not forbidden by the law pertains to civil liberty and belongs to everyone. To give an exclusive privilege to someone out of that which belongs to everyone is to damage all for the sake of some.'[114]

All such artificial inequalities are irrational since, even if they are derived from tradition, the useful services rendered by ancestors cannot justify the privileges of their descendents. They are also unjust for they are exemptions from the commitments imposed on all members of society and result in increasing the responsibilities incumbent on some. Similarly artificial distinctions are harmful as they create a distribution of rewards unrelated to merit and endeavour.[115] It is on these three grounds that Sieyès attacks the nobility and the clergy, in other words, the socio-religious structure of France under the *anicen régime*. Artificial inequalities are not only harmful to citizens, they are also fundamentally opposed to national unity. A nation is defined as 'a body of associates living under the same law and represented by the same legislative assembly'.[116] Therefore exemptions from the law destroy the fabric of the nation and the privileges enjoyed by the nobility alienate them from the rest of society.

The main function of privilege is social differentiation, its consequence is social stratification. Even what seemed the most justifiable of privileges – those of an honorific kind granted in recognition of service – result in segregating their holders from the people by giving them special rights. While not opposed to rewarding merit, Sieyès regards the system of honours existing under the monarchy as absurd and unfair. If a real service had been rendered, it can only have benefited the nation and in this case the people should not suffer when their benefactor is rewarded or the initial service is more than negated. Apart from the hardships this system of honours imposes, it does not differentiate men, but stratifies society. 'You ask less to be distinguished *by* your fellow-citizens than you ask to be distinguished *from* your fellow-citizens.'[117] This stratification prevents human relations from being based on free exchanges governed by utility and transforms free associations into domination and subjection. This is because the existence of privileges has robbed some individuals of their liberty, whereas ideally 'all relations between citizens are free; one gives his time or his goods, the other gives his money in exchange; here there is no subordination, but a continual exchange'.[118]

The existence of artificial social inequalities means that the privileged increasingly regard themselves as a group apart and further their own interests at the expense of the general good. 'The moment the Prince elevates a citizen to the ranks of the privileged, he opens the mind of this citizen to a special interest, and more or less closes it to the general interest.'[119] Since the nature of their privileges gives them an exclusive right to rule,[120] the first two estates are at liberty to pursue their interest at the expense of the nation. Thus post-feudal history has largely been that of aristocratic and clerical domination over the government, and all other social institutions. Simultaneously the privileged develop a sense of innate superiority which contributes to the formation of class solidarity among them. They construe this as personal superiority rather than the attribute of their functions. Increasingly therefore they assume the role of a social class engaged in protecting its own interests. To the monarch they pretend to be his defenders against the populace. To the people they claim themselves to be a protection against despotism.[121]

Thus the privileged have all the attributes of a class: economic and political interests, solidarity and consciousness. Their existence has unavoidably led to popular impoverishment, since they consume instead of producing. 'It seems that our unhappy Nation is condemned to work and impoverish itself unceasingly for the privileged class.'[122] 'The productive parts of the nation, engaged in agriculture, industry and commerce, support this class by their labour and at the same time are considered lower in the social hierarchy precisely because they work.'[123] This emphasis on class 'challenges comparison with the "Communist Manifesto" and with Lenin's "What is to be Done?". Like the first, it asserted the claims of the many against the few, of the exploited masses against the exploiting minority.'[124]

The assertion of the Third Estate. It is because the privileged class has violated natural law that the Third Estate is entitled to attack it. Since political participation is open to all as a natural right, the limitation of the right to rule to the privileged cannot be justified. In fact, it is the privileged who ought not to be represented because they are set apart from the rest of the nation by being exempted from the provisions of the law. Moreover, as a numerical minority, they correspond to a mere fragment of popular opinion and could not in any case be representative of the general will. In effect the nation would benefit from the suppression of the privileged estate. 'The so-called usefulness of a privileged order in public service is nothing but an illusion.'[125] The existence of estates invalidates the notion of one people and the possibility of a good government reflecting the general will, because a plurality of wills and interests is implicit in social stratification.

It follows logically from this that it is perfectly pointless to try to determine the ratio or *proportion* in which each Order should participate in the making of the general will. This will cannot be *one* as long as you retain three Orders and three representations. At the very most, these three assemblies could meet together to pass the same resolution, just as three allied nations can express the same wish. But they will never be *one* nation, *one* representation, *one* common will.[126]

It is in this context that Sieyès asserts the claims of Third Estate to be the embodiment of the general will: 'For him political rights were not based on property but were inherent in individuals.'[127] Therefore the Third Estate is not defined along economic lines, but is comprised of all those who are not set apart by privilege. It is synonymous with the nation, since it is ruled by the law without being differentiated by any exemption from its provisions. 'The Third Estate is the whole mass of the non-privileged.'[128] In fact, Sieyès was criticised for including manual workers in this definition.[129] In the later years of the Revolution he published *What is the Third Estate?* under the alternative and revealing title of *What are the People?* He stressed that the workers, even unskilled, are an essential part of every nation. 'You cannot refuse the quality of citizen and the rights of citizenship to this uneducated mass wholly occupied by forced labour.'[130] Since the nation cannot be free unless its will is expressed by a representative government, its liberty is synonymous with the political emancipation of the Third Estate.[131]

The whole thought of Sieyès on the assertion of the people is summed up by the three questions: 'What is the Third Estate? Everything. What has it been up to now in politics? Nothing. What does it ask for? To become something.'[132] By claiming that the Third Estate is everything, he means both that it is the only embodiment of the general will and the only productive section of the community. Historically, it has been active in agriculture, industry, trade and the public service. Therefore it could and should depose the triple aristocracy of the clergy, the sword and the robe. This class conflict is at times interpreted by Sieyès as a confrontation between sterile privilege and production – derived from labour or property. He sees a solidarity of interest between the latter two and rather naively expects the abolition of personal privileges to result in the complete unification of the Third Estate. While the existence of artificial social inequalities had divided this estate against itself through the promotion of some of its leading members to the nobility of the robe, the abolition of privileges would restore its solidarity. In other words, he ignored the possibility of clashes and differences of interest between labour and capital.

Education and the Third Estate. In order to become aware of its rights and capable of assuming its responsibilities, the Third Estate must be enlightened. Like Condorcet, Sieyès is convinced that the diffusion of rationality in society is a pre-condition of good government, defined as representative democracy. There is a reciprocal relationship between education and representation. Education will not be widespread unless a representative government carries out the general will by meeting the popular demand for knowledge. Simultaneously a constitution based on the representative principle, in negating artificial social distinctions, will replace privilege by intellectual superiority as a qualification to rule. Therefore in the short term it will benefit the most educated and ultimately, once a national educational system has been organised, the most able citizens.

Like Condorcet, Sieyès accepts that the right to develop one's innate potential is an indispensable aspect of personal liberty. Therefore he is not opposed to intellectual differentiation in society, since the submission of all to the same law will minimise the harmful effects of natural inegalities. While education thus fulfils the requirements of liberty, it should also seek to restore a spirit of equality in society. 'There can be no equality unless all can acquire accurate ideas on those objects whose knowledge is necessary for every day living.'[133] Instruction is essential to achieve the independence without which man cannot be free. It will have a dual end: to free men from prejudice and therefore give them intellectual independence, and to impart useful skills, whose application in work will relieve from material dependence. Therefore there ought to be a common fund of primary education to make all citizens independent and eradicate artificial inequalities between them. At the same time elementary schooling should be designed to stimulate a sense of solidarity in the nation. The school would thus be the institution which spread reliance on self and respect for others.

'Among the revolutionaries, Sieyès is one of those who attached the most importance to educational matters; one of the first who pondered on the matter and who systematised it.'[134] His main concern is with primary education because he is predominantly interested in preparing workers to participate more fully in representative government. 'Uneducated men whose habits are simple generally have clear minds, their common sense leads them to the truth, but habit has given them prejudices particularly difficult to uproot since their ideas are restricted to a narrow sphere.'[135] Thus the people need instruction to develop their intellectual faculties. They should be taught in a way which will increase their political participation and also improve their contribution to the economy.

Instruction, one must admit, has been nothing up till now but a literary tuition. It is necessary to extend its range, to include physical and moral education, as well as the stimulation of intellect, industrial and manual pursuits as well as artistic ones; because true instruction concerns the whole man and, having sought to perfect the individual, endeavours to improve the species.[136]

While elementary education is to have some vocational aspects, these reflect a concern for individual independence rather than national productivity. This priority is made explicit when Sieyès advocates the creation of spare-time for the instruction of children and adults alike. 'If holidays from work did not exist, it would be necessary to invent them . . . it is obvious . . . that they are mainly to the advantage of those sections of the population who work hardest.'[137]

While Sieyès, in his plan for the Convention, only proposed the creation of a primary state system, leaving secondary education to private initiative, this was merely a provisional solution intended to spare public funds. However, in the long term he envisages that secondary schools would come under state auspices. Certainly he places a high premium on both secondary and adult instruction. 'To have brought up and taught people during childhood and the first years of adolescence, until they can learn a trade, does not exhaust your duty. Men of every age ought also to receive uninterrupted assistance.'[138] Nevertheless, while the government cannot afford to provide secondary schooling in the short run, this should not prejudice the chances of the able poor to obtain it in private institutions. A system of state grants will be available for those who have shown sufficient merit at primary level to continue their education, if their parents cannot cover its cost: 'to the children of poor citizens who have shown the seed of real ability in primary education, enough assistance to enable them to acquire specialised vocational training and to enter lycées or private schools.'[139] Eventually Sieyès hopes to employ some of the clergy's endowments to finance an overall state system.[140] Thus while his immediate proposals fall short of Condorcet's plan, they are no less egalitarian and more directly related to the financial possibilities of the Republic at the time.

To Condorcet the Revolution was fought on rationalistic grounds – 'the war of reason against prejudice',[141] not on behalf of any particular social group. It was this absence of partisanship and this commitment to abstract issues which led to his condemnation by the Jacobins – 'This man who because he has sat among the learned in the Academy imagines that he has the right to give laws to the French Republic'.[142] His thought became part of the mainstream of republican educational philosophy as Jaurès was to acknowledge,[143] but it was Sieyès as a politician advancing the claims of the Third Estate who temporarily succeeded in implementing part of their educational blueprint.

The immediate legal restriction of the clerical monopoly in education reflected a major area of ideological agreement among all sections of the Third Estate. The attempts made to replace it by a state system showed a greater resemblance to the plans of revolutionaries than to the blueprints of the Parliamentarians. The pressing political need to retain the loyalty of the people increased the bargaining power of Sieyès and his followers, enabling them to fight off bourgeois claims for adapting education strictly to its own needs. Thus the revolutionary Assemblies never sanctioned the double standard and the return of clergy to their teaching posts. The short-lived legislation passed was an attempt to base education on natural rights within the limitations of scarce resources.

However, this very limitation precluded the successful assertion of the Third Estate – it could restrict the clergy's use of its monopoly, but could not replace it. The integration of education to the political structure existed on paper rather than in fact; the state had accrued the right (or rather duty) to control it, but the people had not begun to benefit from its exercise. In practical terms this situation arose through the shortage of teachers, but it also reflected a paradox in the theory of natural rights itself. The assumption was made by both Condorcet and Sieyès that such rights will only exist if suitable political conditions are achieved. Hence the contradiction that while the state derives its obligation to educate citizens from the natural law, it is instrumental in making this law operative through education. The revolutionaries only succeeded in bringing about the first step of legitimating state control of instruction in the context of a democratic political system, without being able to secure those institutional arrangements necessary to increase liberty and equality. Thus when the political structure changed during the Empire the principle of state control over education had been established and Napoleon had only to change what the revolutionaries had considered as a duty to the people into a right of the Imperial University.

10. French ideologies legitimating educational domination

THE LEGITIMATION OF BOURGEOIS EDUCATIONAL DOMINATION – NAPOLEON

The Revolution had resulted in a double failure – that of Republican planning and that of Third Estate cohesion. Social antagonisms and political dissensions, culminating in the Reign of Terror, had underscored the need for order in society. The incapacity of successive governments to achieve it, to exercise or even to retain power, made an authoritarian regime appear as a refuge against outbursts of uncontrolled violence. As absolute ruler, Bonaparte, scorning political debate and bent on achieving administrative efficiency, designed the institutions of the Consulate, and later of the Empire as firmly state-integrated. He looked to the educational system in the context of this institutional reform, to supply the state with trained personnel and with docile subjects. Thus he endorsed the Parliamentarians' view that instruction should serve the national interest in promoting citizenship and in inculcating the skills related to state needs. The ideology which informed the creation of the Imperial University was completely divorced from any appeal to individual rights to instruction, and firmly rooted in the pre-revolutionary tradition.

Both the nationalism and the vocationalism of Napoleon's educational ideology were directly conducive to secularism at post-primary level. The group singled out for training in secular citizenship and receiving advanced instruction had not been explicitly identified in the pre-revolutionary blueprints, since the demarcation line between the privileged and the non-privileged orders did not delineate it. The Parliamentarians considered the lower section of the nobility and the upper section of the Third Estate (the *noblesse de robe* and the *bourgeoisie*) as joint beneficiaries of secular instruction. After the Revolution, however, the bourgeoisie was considered by Napoleon – in his distrust of the aristocracy and dismissal of the people – as the class best able to serve the state and most interested in the preservation of social order.

The arguments advanced in favour of bourgeois educational domination were all related to the requirements of the secular state – since the privileged access of the bourgeoisie to secondary and higher establishment was justified by reference to training for future roles in the state hierarchy. The state was thus the end legitimating bourgeois domination and the state system the means ensuring it.

The division within the Third Estate between the bourgeoisie and the people was reflected by the dichotomy between secular and religious instruction in the Imperial University. Not only was primary instruction insufficiently important to warrant the commitment of limited state resources, the stimulation of rationalist thinking among the mass contradicted the ideology of divine right by which Napoleon endeavoured to legitimate his reign. Thus the reliance on the clergy at primary level emphasised the difference between the secularism reserved for the bourgeoisie and the religious instruction subordinated to secular ends, meted out to the people.

Education by the state and for the state

In designing a new educational system, Napoleon consciously departed from the pattern of Republican legislation. To him the experience of the Revolution had shown that freedom in education only benefited the enemies of social order. On his assumption to power, he found France completely disunited, 'the Emperor found in his generation too many unsworn priests, too many royalists and too many republicans'.[1] It is for this reason that the unitary and unifying system envisaged by the Parliamentarians appeared to him especially suited to current needs. He became gradually convinced that only state monopoly over education could lead to the integration he sought.[2]

Teaching is a function of the State, because this is a need of the nation. In consequence, schools should be State establishments and not establishments in the State. They depend on the State and have no resort but it; they exist by it and for it. They hold their right to exist and their very substance from it; they ought to receive from it their task and their rule. Then again, as the State is one, its schools ought to be the same everywhere.[3]

Thus the central aspect of Parliamentarian thought – the direct connection between state domination over schooling and the maintenance of social order – reappears as fundamental in Napoleon's approach to education. Instruction, viewed as formative, is the only guarantee that future generations will prove loyal to the regime. 'Public education is the future and the duration of my work after me.'[4] Hence the related aims of nationalism and citizenship are to be implemented by the state educational system.

The Revolution had seen only the State as teacher, the State as schoolmaster. Napoleon envisages the doctrinaire State, the State as head of education ... The men of the Revolution had mainly considered national education as a duty of the State towards its citizens, Napoleon primarily sees in it the interest of the State and that of its sovereign.[5]

Consequently Napoleon gives to education a responsibility for moulding the moral and political opinions of citizens along the lines laid down by the head of state. 'To instruct is secondary, the main thing is to train and to do so according to the pattern which suits the State.'[6] 'The State will not form a nation until one is taught from childhood whether to be republican or monarchist, Catholic or irreligious.'[7]

Therefore education is never an end in itself, only a means of reinforcing state power. 'He wished to found his despotism on souls, and a public education firmly centralized and given by the State, or under the supervision of the State, appeared to him the most efficient means to shape souls.'[8] Hence the whole of his educational system is designed to maximise the influence of the state over citizens, and to minimise that of any other groups which might intervene between the Emperor and his subjects. Thus the decree of 1808 creating the Imperial University forbids private schools to teach without state authorisation and denies them any title other than 'institutions' or 'pensions'.[9] This illustrates the attempt to eliminate the private sector from education and to make state monopoly absolute. Such a policy embodies Napoleon's determination to erect his university as the ultimate authority in education, and loyalty to his dynasty as the ultimate goal of instruction within a single state system dominated by this ideal. The Imperial University is the name given to this system as a whole, not to a specific establishment. It is both the official statement proclaiming uniformity in instruction throughout the country and the declaration of the government's right to enforce this. While this legislation does not make all schools government property, it places them all under official control, thus ensuring both ideological orthodoxy and geographical uniformity. The latter aim was achieved by standardising curricula throughout the country and making all qualifications national. All schools are to impart the same instruction at the appropriate level and to each level corresponds a specific type of school organisation. The identity of all equivalent establishments throughout the country is thus guaranteed.

While legal provisions sufficed to standardise education on a nation-wide basis, its efficacy for indoctrination could only be engineered by securing the personal adhesion of teachers to the ideology of the state and their willingness to inculcate it to their pupils. Therefore the institutionalisation of the teaching profession was a logical corollary of the creation of the Imperial University. Firstly, teachers, as civil servants, contract statutory obligations towards the state which appoints and dismisses them. They therefore have the same duty as other government officials to endorse and advance the political principles on which the state is based. Secondly, this group has exclusive rights to teach granted and guaranteed by the state and denied to other unauthorised persons.[10] However, such formal bonds do not in themselves represent an assurance of loyalty. In order to secure the reliability of masters and the uniformity of the political instruction given in schools, Napoleon instituted a form of state training. The 'École Normale' was to provide a pipeline through which official ideas could be transmitted directly to future teachers. Eventually it became the main source of recruitment into the Imperial University, ensuring that 'All will have a single goal, that of training virtuous subjects, useful to the State through their abilities and their knowledge, loyal to the government and devoted to its august head through inclination and through duty.'[11]

In organising the teaching profession, the discipline, obedience and solidarity characterising the teaching orders were the features Napoleon sought to recapture. 'Communal life, hierarchy, rigorous discipline, such were in his eyes the reasons which had guaranteed the success of the Jesuits.'[12] He therefore attempted to emulate these characteristics in the teaching body of the Imperial University. 'He used the model of a great secular congregation, a kind of secular Society of Jesus.'[13] He refused to reinstate the Jesuits themselves, doubting their loyalty to his rule, and instead replaced them by a new corporation accepting his own authority rather than that of the Pope and serving it with equal fervour. 'I do not wish to re-establish the Jesuits nor any other corporation which is submitted to a foreign power . . . I wish to train a corporation, not of Jesuits who have their sovereign in Rome, but of Jesuits who have no other ambition than that of being useful and no other interest than the public interest.'[14] Not only is a corporation more homogeneous and better disciplined than an unco-ordinated group of individual teachers, it also provides better prospects of continuity. Thus the teaching body was to be both the instrument of his reign and the perpetuation of the Napoleonic tradition. 'I want a corporation because a corporation never dies.'[15]

However, Napoleon was aware that what was least acceptable to him in religious orders – their allegiance to the Catholic faith, was the most essential bond between their members and the basis of their discipline. He endeavoured to find a counterpart for his own teaching profession and on the whole wished to substitute the enthusiasm engendered by ambition for the zeal inspired by religion. Teaching was founded as an open career in which both recruitment and promotion were awarded on the grounds of merit. Napoleon sees his university as a civilian counterpart to his military hierarchy, with a similar blend of *esprit de corps*, competitiveness and loyalty.[16] Thus the title of *Officier d'académie* was introduced for services rendered to education, on the pattern of the *Légion d'honneur*, the creation of orders and decorations being an integral part of the design whereby ambition is harnessed to state service. The constitution of such a secularised teaching order illustrates the way in which Napoleon wanted to retain some politically useful features of Catholicism while rejecting any elements in religious thought or church organisation which might jeopardise his power.

This attitude is equally apparent in the general rule assigned to religion under the Empire. On the one hand, Napoleon acknowledged the strength of the Catholic church in France and the impossibility of attempting to eradicate it without disruption of social order. On the other, he realised that the clergy could be an independent power in the state and therefore a danger for his rule. As head of state, he saw in the church an incipient challenge to his authority which must be restricted if his position were to be consolidated. However, assuming that the Catholic hierarchy accepted the Emperor as supreme temporal authority and allowed him to define the spiritual sphere, religion could provide a useful agency for increasing social order. Thus while inheriting the Parliamentarian tradition of anti-clericalism, Napoleon accentuated its corollary – faith was socially useful, while the clergy was politically unreliable. Again like the Parliamentarians, it is as a nationalist that he distrusts the temporal power of the church and as an exponent of social order that he supports the integrative power of Catholicism. Therefore compromises with the clergy are prompted by the dictates of social policy rather than by any ideological sympathy. They are always limited by considerations of national prestige.

Thus Napoleon's religious policy in education had a double aim: to control the church in the state and the people in society. Both goals are compatible with the incorporation of some members of clergy in the university, where they will be made harmless by this very integration and where their teaching can be turned to political advantage. Napoleon considered that the clergy would be less dangerous if they were allowed to teach under state control.

One has put forward the view that primary schools run by the brothers (Ignorantins) could introduce a dangerous spirit into the University and we have been advised to leave them outside its jurisdiction; those who suggest it do not appreciate that they are going against their own aim; it is by including the brothers in the University that one will attach them to the civil order; they will no longer be dangerous when they cease to have a foreign or unknown head.[17]

Hence the acceptance of the clergy into the Imperial University was an attempt to make it less politically dangerous because less independent. To implement this policy, the educational monopoly of the state implied the obligation for the members of teaching orders to register with the university and to swear an oath of allegiance.[18]

While the clergy was being tamed in the university, religion was being used in education. Thus in every sense the church was to be subordinated to the power of the state and the needs of government. Napoleon rejected as disruptive a completely secular instruction for the whole of society. 'You must make me pupils who know how to be men . . . you believe that man can be man without God . . . man without God, I have seen him at work since 1793. That man, one does not rule him, one shoots him: I have had enough of that type of man.'[19] It is predominantly at the primary level that religion can be used to reinforce social control and it is in such schools that political conformism and religious orthodoxy can mutually reinforce each other. 'God and the Emperor, there are the two names that one must engrave in the heart of children. It is to this double thought that all the system of national education must address itself.'[20] Not only is it a more difficult task to reconcile citizenship and faith in secondary and higher education, it is downright opposed to state utility to further faith at the expense of reason among the elite.

This duality corresponds to both the political and the Utilitarian aspects in Napoleon's educational philosophy. Indeed instruction is designed to inculcate citizenship and the skills considered by the state as useful to society. In relation to these two aims, there is an obvious distinction between what is held sufficient for the people and what is considered necessary for the elite. The mass is only required to accept the existing political structure – an acceptance made easier by religious legitimation – and to learn a few basic skills unrelated to occupational mobility. On the other hand, the efficiency of the state machinery depends upon the training of personnel qualified to fill diverse positions of responsibility. Their competence requires an advanced education relevant to their future duties. Therefore Napoleon's system of instruction is twofold: it aims to provide skilled cadres for the government and loyal citizens for the state: 'on the one hand a tendency to give education a utilitarian and vocational character; on the other, a tendency to use it for political ends.'[21] Thus he envisages a specialised training for some key occupations and an elementary education for the rest of society. The duties of citizenship, common to all, require a basic fund of knowledge for all, whereas the needs of specialisation restrict any tuition beyond primary level to a limited group. Two forms of education must therefore co-exist and must be the preserve of different populations.

Since state efficiency is Napoleon's overriding goal, the recruitment of the best qualified personnel for his administration dictates a priority in his educational plan. It is secondary and higher instruction which are intended to supply such 'cadres' and which are therefore of paramount importance to him. 'It is secondary education which is the most complete achievement of his university; it is there also that the political character of his work appears most clearly.'[22] This political character results ultimately from the basic proposition that the service of the state requires special skills which must be taught within the Imperial University. The maximum efficiency of the state machinery will only be achieved if such training is given to the most able. Hence nationalism leads to utilitarianism and utilitarianism to meritocracy. It is for these reasons that Napoleon modelled his *lycées*, where secondary education was to be dispensed, on military lines. 'If some military practices have been introduced in the lycées, it is because one has recognized the extent to which these practices were favourable to order without which there are no good studies.'[23] This form of organisation was credited with stimulating patriotism and favouring an efficient tuition.

G

State qualifications and bourgeois entrenchment

The search for efficiency in education led directly to a meritocratic structure in which success at secondary level, entry into higher education and access to positions of responsibility either in the state hierarchy or in the liberal professions were dependent upon proven ability. Contrary to the revolutionary tradition, exemplified by Condorcet and centred on the diffusion of enlightenment for its own sake, the Imperial University saw no value in reason unrelated to utility. Nor did it seek to generalise knowledge unrelated to future occupations. This utilitarian concern is expressed by the importance of diplomas testifying to a certain level of performance and qualifying the holder either for proceeding to the next level of education or for embarking on a predetermined set of careers. The state monopoly in education had as its corollary a unique control over entry not only into the administration, but into professional careers. 'To this end grades were re-established, and turned into State guarantees. Diplomas were no longer mere evidence of study. They were changed into certificates of aptitude. The State put its trade-mark on the products of its schools as the only good and reliable ones.'[24] Since state qualifications became indispensable for a professional life, they represented the key to social mobility. The *baccalauréat*, which concluded secondary and gave right to higher education, was therefore a necessity for individual promotion, since it was a prerequisite for the majority of careers. 'From the start, the baccalauréat was not a mere pedagogical examination, but a social institution, the condition for admission to civil offices.'[25] This interpenetration of educational qualifications and occupational ranking made access to secondary schooling the main determinant of future career. Entry to higher institutions was dependent upon attendance at a *lycée* and performance in it. Therefore the dividing line in social selection ran between the primary and the secondary cycles.

Predominantly designed to satisfy the two needs of the state – for specialisation and for submission, the distinction between primary and secondary schooling acquired the feature of social discrimination, inevitable in a system giving promotion to tested merit without ensuring equality of opportunity at the start. Thereby Napoleon confirmed the special advantages acquired by the bourgeoisie in postrevolutionary society.

It is not completely true that the bourgeoisie exist only in culture and not in law. The lycée made it a legal institution. It even has official certificates, with a ministerial signature, duly stamped, sealed and hallowed by the administration . . . The baccalauréat is the real barrier guaranteed by the State, which is a protection against invasion. One can become bourgeois, it is true; but for that it is first imperative to acquire a baccalauréat. When a family rises from the people to the bourgeoisie, it does not do this in a generation. It succeeds when it has managed to give its children secondary education and to make them pass the baccalauréat.[26]

Similarly Napoleon's attitude to primary education was dictated by state requirements, which determined its length and content, as well as the role assigned to it in the Imperial University. While it was incorporated into the overall system, it was not considered worthy either of great attention or of considerable investments. 'No special allocation of funds was ever made in the budget of the Empire for primary education . . . The State would consent to no sacrifice for the primary schools, the municipalities had to cover the cost of their creations and the pupils to pay the salary of the masters.'[27] Furthermore proposals had been made for classes in the *lycées* to be set apart for the training of primary teachers, but did not appear to have been carried out.[28] This neglect is indicative of the view that if the state has no need of mass instruction, the people have no right to it. Napoleon 'wished to use the masses for manual labour and above all wanted them to obey and to die beneath the flag; one does not need to know how to read and write for that. It was enlightened officers and heads of industry he needed, therefore he left primary instruction to go its own way.'[29]

The primary instruction which could actually be obtained was closely related to a minimal definition of the knowledge required by common people in their current occuptions. Therefore there were two types of subjects: the elements of literacy and the rudiments of religion. Thus the two interrelated themes governing elementary education were the inculcation of basic skills adequate for manual workers and the propagation of an ideology which would make them satisfied with their station in life.

The school, like the Church, becomes an instrument of rule, it must inculcate in children a spirit of universal submission. Thus the State which intends to use the school in the interest of the secular power instituted the monopoly to avoid the proliferation of private schools whose teaching would escape its control; to secure the allegiance of the Church to the new educational policy, it made primary schools religious.[30]

Thus, in spite of an initial reluctance to restore teaching orders to their pre-revolutionary position, the overwhelming advantages their tuition offered for social control and the economy it represented for the state induced Napoleon to entrust the 'Frères de la doctrine chrétienne' with responsibility for primary schools. This was not entirely dictated by considerations of expediency. It resulted both from his nationalistic definition of citizenship, which a loyal clergy would further, and from the premium he placed on social order – which tallied with religious teachings. His criterion of utility involved no necessity for the diffusion of learning to those who could not apply it. Therefore utility supported the existing form of stratification on practical grounds of efficiency, whereas the church did so on theological grounds of submission to divine will. Theology served as an additional reinforcement to an educational policy whose true foundations were secular. The extent to which religion was used for social control is apparent in the Imperial catechism, officially taught in all primary schools and providing a justification for devotion to the head of state.

Because God, in endowing our Emperor with gifts, be it in Peace, be it in war, has established him as our sovereign and made him his own image on earth . . . to honour and to serve our Emperor is to honour and to serve God himself . . . He has restored and conserved public order by his deep and active wisdom; his strong arm defends the State; he is annointed by God through the consecration he has from the Pope, head of the Universal Church.[31]

Civil disobedience is threatened with religious sanctions: 'According to the Apostle Saint Paul, they would be resisting the order established by God himself and would become liable for external damnation.'[32] Conversely, loyalty to the state is equated with obedience to God's will.

By creating the Imperial University, Napoleon not only gave France an education system which survived his reign and important parts of which outlasted the nineteenth century, he also provided the bourgeoisie with the institutional framework in which its educational domination was to prove durable. The dissociation between popular primary instruction, neglected by the state, and the secondary-higher network, state-centred, state-controlled and state-financed, corres- ponded to the aspirations voiced – even before the Revolution – by the leading section of the Third Estate. Thus Napoleon's legislation continued a pre-revolutionary tradition – interrupted during the Republic, when the need to secure popular support compelled succes- sive assemblies to pass radical legislation, ranging from the utopian to the egalitarian. All the bills adopted or debated at the time were concerned with individual rights rather than state needs; education was to be provided by the state to serve the cause of secular enlightenment rather than its own ends. Hence only secularism remained a central theme of educational legislation during the whole revolutionary period; the other tenets of the Parliamentarians were rejected, the vocationalism of the system they advocated being unacceptable as opposed to individual freedom and its integration with social stratification as incompatible with individual equality. Yet they reappeared in the Napoleonic legislation – whereby nationalism and *étatism*, which had been theoretical postulates of the assertive ideologies formulated at the end of the *ancien régime*, were made the main features of the Imperial University. In this respect, the principles underlying the educational monopoly of the state and presiding over educational organisation can be seen as part of an ideology formulated by the Parliamentarians, although the continuity is not unbroken.

In subordinating all other considerations to state efficiency, Napoleon both designed the educational system most conducive to the domination of the bourgeoisie and formulated – in his reflections on, and analysis of his own reforms – an ideology legitimating this domination by reference to state interests. Therefore the state provided the educational means required for bourgeois entrenchment at secondary and higher level and constituted the end justifying this entrenchment. Since only a small educated elite was needed to reach the goal of state efficiency, any emphasis on educational equality was precluded. The assertive ideologies of the revolutionary period, with their concentration on emancipating individuals from societal constraints rather than fitting them for duties to society, could be countered as contrary to the needs of the state, under which those of all citizens were subsumed. Consequently the fundamental differentiation between the training of an elite, whose enlightenment was necessary for the performance of their administrative and professional roles, and the minimal instruction sufficient for the mass, was fully compatible with the introduction of a double standard with regard to religious education. It was in the interest of social order and political stability (equated by Napoleon with dynastic continuity, but later reinterpreted as the acceptance of the political *status quo* – whether monarchic or moderately republican) that the people should be taught to accept their station in life as preordained. This type of indoctrination could best be supplied by clerical primary schools, which not only spared the limited resources of the state (both human and material) for investment at the secondary level, but harnessed the conservative forces of religious education to the service of the secular ruler. Thus an enclave of church-run, but state-controlled primary schooling could not only be accepted in the context of the Imperial University, but was defended by Napoleon for reasons of social order as well as of economy.

The elitarian implications of Napoleon's ideology were as important for legitimating the educational domination of the bourgeoisie as for negating the claims of revolutionary theories which linked popular instruction to the rights of man. These, in the Imperial University as in its founder's thought, were subordinated to the duties of the citizen; since such duties varied, any demands for uniformity of instruction could be rejected as ultimately detrimental to the general interest, embodied by the state and defended by the bureaucracy. In fulfilling these two functions of an ideology – legitimation of the new dominant group and negation of egalitarian challenges to its entrenchment at secondary and higher level – Napoleon's defence of the university was better suited to the requirements of the post-revolutionary period than his eighteenth-century predecessors' ideologies. The definition of state requirements was more clearly linked with incontrovertible general needs – since the efficiency of the administrative and the stability of the political institutions were seen, if only by contrast with the disorder of the revolutionary years, to coincide with the interests of society. This connection was more obvious than the service of the enlightened despot posited by Diderot or the continuity of the national monarchy advocated by the Parliamentarians. In the case of the former, despotic arbitrariness, in that of the latter, traditionalism could impede the identification between an educational elite and the state it was trained to serve. By contrast, the Napoleonic state – by acknowledging a vocational principle in tuition and a meritocratic principle in selection – was committed to a standardised elite recruitment, in which its own educational establishments were the training ground and its own examinations the testing device. The bourgeoisie, by populating these establishments could secure elite membership for its children and by acquiring the formal qualifications they dispensed could justify this privilege by proven merit. Hence the Napoleonic ideology specifies the integration of the educational system not only with the political and bureaucratic structure of the state, but with the system of social stratification. This multiple integration was achieved through the use of meritocratic educational selection. Since entry into the state bureaucracy and the professions was on the basis of manifest ability, a diploma elite replaced the former traditional elite. Since the detection of latent ability was neglected and the social determinants of merits were overlooked, educational chances reflected and perpetuated the post-revolutionary system of stratification. To the differential opportunities of social classes corresponded the dichotomy of primary and secondary establishments, dispensing the instruction deemed appropriate for the people and the bourgeoisie – and ensuring that the political socialisation of pupils fitted them for their future responsibilities, whether as passive citizens or as useful servants of the state. At secondary level, the education given was secular, while at primary the monopoly of teaching staff on which the domination of the Catholic church over instruction had been founded prior to the Revolution was allowed to endure within the Imperial University. However this was in a context of state monopoly and therefore any defence of the remaining sector of religious domination – and *a fortiori* any attempt at *reconquista* – implied a debate on the mutual relations of the spiritual and the temporal power, in order to demarcate their respective spheres.

THE LEGITIMATION OF CATHOLIC EDUCATIONAL DOMINATION

Attacks on the educational domination of the church under the *ancien régime* had been mainly directed against the teaching orders and their allegiance to the papacy. The secular clergy was more acceptable to nationalists since the Gallican tradition emphasised the liberties of the French episcopate in relation to the Holy See and its correlative dependence on the sovereign. It was tolerated by rationalists in the sphere of primary instruction, destined to the sections of society least in need and least capable of enlightenment.

The Revolution – depriving the clergy of its legal status as a privileged order – attempted to carry Gallicanism to its extreme form by dissociating the religious hierarchy from Rome and submitting it to the sole authority of the state. The creation of a schismatic national church was the logical outcome of the views propagated by Diderot and a continuation of the Erastianism postulated by pre-revolutionary educational planning. The experiment failed both to attract a sufficient proportion of the clergy[33] and to commend itself to the Catholic population. Robespierre's attempt to institute the cult of reason and to divorce morality from dogma was even less acceptable to the masses.

Therefore without a restoration of the Catholic church no attempt could be made either to reinforce citizenship by religious instruction or to legitimate political authority and social institutions by reference to divine will. Napoleon acknowledged the conservative role which the clergy could play among the sections of the population, particularly the peasantry, still susceptible to its traditional appeal. However this participation of the church in his policy of national reconstruction required the restoration of its connection with Rome, inseparable from the integrity of its dogma and hence essential to its legitimacy.

To this end Napoleon concluded the Concordate of 1802 which established formal relations between the papacy and post-revolutionary France and recognised Catholicism as 'the religion of the great majority of French people'. The departure from the Gallican tradition was complete, since the bishops were entirely submitted to papal authority, but the control of the state over the clergy was strong. Ecclesiastical appointments required governmental approval, priests were civil servants, remunerated by the state and swearing an oath of loyalty to the Emperor, and the main orders remained banned. While the clergy was used to dispense elementary instruction the existence of the Imperial University presented a major obstacle to any attempt at restoring the former educational position of the church. Religious education was either tolerated (at post-primary level) or even encouraged in primary schools, but it was to further secular ends, defined by the state.

Under the restored dynasty of the Bourbons, Catholicism was again a state religion – until the July Monarchy reverted to the 'majority religion' formula. The position of the clergy within the Royal University may have been stronger, but the survival of the state monopoly over education witnessed to the prevalence of secularist views. The church was made to serve purposes of educational control, in the context of a system inherited from the Empire and in accordance with an ideology which could be traced back to the *ancien régime*.

To believers who rejected Erastianism, this treatment of the church state seemed more harmful than revolutionary persecutions. Those who admitted that martyrdom was part of the priest's calling could not see him turn into a civil servant; they rejected the subordination of the spiritual to the temporal power. The sphere of education provided the most striking example of this subordination and therefore the defence of the church against state encroachments upon its former prerogatives took the form of an attack upon the university monopoly. There were two main grounds on which this campaign could be conducted – the right of the church to dispense education without being controlled by the state and the right of individuals to receive religious instruction. Both were formulated by Lamennais under the Restoration and the July Monarchy.

The right of the church to educate

Demands for the educational autonomy of the church, which could only be achieved by the abolition of the state monopoly, were initially linked under the Restoration with a condemnation of Erastianism. In *Essai sur l'indifférence dans les matières religieuses* (1817), Lamennais describes the enslavement of the Catholic hierarchy by the Imperial government and the exploitation of the clergy by the university as the culminating point of a pernicious tradition which he traces to pre-revolutionary Gallicanism. He condemns Gallicanism as 'a system which consists in believing as little as possible without being a heretic, in order to obey as little as possible without being a rebel',[34] hence as being contrary to religious orthodoxy as well as to ecclesiastical discipline. To restore both and thus to regain the position undermined by compromise with secular power, Lamennais advocates a return to the principle of papal authority. His Ultramontanism is an alternative to the intervention of the state in religious matters and a protection against such interference. Thus in seeking the emancipation of the church from secular ties, he differs from both Maistre and Bonald, to whom papal infallibility was a counterpart of monarchic absolutism and who looked to religion for an ideology of social control. His version of 'French Ultramontanism and the Oxford Movement in England moved on parallel lines. Both were protests against a system tending to confound the Church with the State'.[35]

The state is condemned not only as irreligious by virtue of its revolutionary legacy, but as authoritarian, in accordance with pre-revolutionary tradition. Both these aspects of state policy are evident in the field of education where the Imperial University epitomises the evils of secularism at post-primary level and of Erastianism at primary. 'Of all the ideas of Bonaparte, the most appalling to those who think, the most deeply anti-social, in a word the most characteristic of him . . . is the University . . . embodying his hatred for future generations.'[36] To Lamennais the most totalitarian feature of the imperial policy was the attempt to control the mind by monopolising education. 'I do not know whether there exists a worse evil or one which incorporates a greater number of them than the abusive practice whereby the govern-ment is in complete control of education.'[37] The violence with which he defends freedom of thought is a corollary of his con-viction that instruction can truly mould the mind. Thus he accepts the formative power of education, which can be used for good or evil, and posits that only the church can be trusted with such responsibility.

Historically all states – 'if one excepts a few small Greek republics famous for their immoral institutions'[38] – have recognised that educa-tion pertains to the sphere of the spiritual rather than the temporal power. It has been the province of the church since the establishment of Christianity and can only be degraded by being subordinated to temporal ends. The participation of the clergy in dispensing state-controlled instruction does not remove the stigma of state domination from education, but puts it on the church by making it subservient to secular government. As Montalembert was to claim, in rejecting the attempts of the July Monarchy to use religious indoctrination in primary schools, the church is 'neither the slave, nor the client, nor the auxilliary of anyone. She is queen or she is nothing'.[39]

This formula sums up the arguments in favour of the separation between church and state, of the dissociation between religious education and the secular system. Hence Lamennais is logical in passing 'from a mere condemnation of the Concordate to the principle of a separation between the altar which is sacred and the throne which is cursed'.[40] However, this standpoint would not be defended by claiming that exceptional rights to educate the people should be granted to the church because it rejected the principle of state mono-poly. Objectionable as its ideology was, the Imperial University remained a fact and hostility to it was not an argument likely to mobilise public opinion if it merely emphasised church rights – largely unacceptable in a post-revolutionary society and rejected by the secularised bourgeois elite. To those who did not acknowledge the church as 'queen', it was perfectly impossible to consider education as its natural domain. The defence of individual rights to religious education was a more politically effective approach, since its appeal was not limited to believers. 'The State and the constitution did not allow them to claim any special or acquired right, any kind of divine right, the supporters of the Church appealed to the common rights, to natural rights.'[41]

The right of individuals to religious education

The passage from pure Ultramontanism to liberalism, represents a major shift in the arguments used by Lamennais to defend the church against the state monopoly over education rather than a political conversion.

It is easy (as it is usual) to exaggerate the gulf between the Lamennais of the 'Drapeau Blanc' [royalist paper under the Restoration] and the Lamennais of the 'Avenir' [the liberal paper he edited with Montalembert under the July Monarchy]. In both cases he was seeking the same end – the triumph of religion: the difference lay chiefly in the choice of the means of securing it. The Liberalism against which he fought was not Liberalism in the political sense, but Liberalism as Newman understood it – the setting up in the sphere of religion of free thought and free discussion in the place of revealed truth.[42]

Hence religious Ultramontanism coexisted with political liberalism[43] and the right of the church to dispense education was legitimated by reference to natural rights, including the individual's right to choose his children's education. This second phase in Lamennais's work, initiated by the publication of *Du progrès de la Révolution et de la guerre contre l'Église* in 1828, linked the defence of the church and that of the individual against the despotism of the secular state which threatened both.

To Lamennais the rights of man are God-given. Therefore it is divine will rather than human nature which he invokes to substantiate his theory. Nevertheless, the rights he considers as divinely ordained are in no way different from those which rationalist philosophers derived from human nature. Equality originates from the fact that all are equal in the sight of God. By this he does not imply an identity of ability, but only the innate right to an equality of treatment. Indeed he points out that talents are unevenly distributed in society,[44] but stresses that differences of rank and fortune are purely artificial. Therefore liberty is a corollary of equality, since without it men will never be exempted from social constraints and able to develop the latent aptitudes which provide the only morally acceptable ground for differentiating between them. Thus true equality of treatment can only be achieved in a free society.

An essential aspect of personal liberty is for all individuals to be unconstrained mentally, as well as physically. This means that they must not be prevented in any way from thinking independently on any subjects, including religion. A government monopoly over education or information is thus in direct contradiction with freedom of thought and negates human rationality. 'One wants individual reason to be independent from the law, from God himself; and the government is given the right to enslave the reason of society as a whole by taking over instruction.'[45] Since to instruct is merely to communicate thoughts, education should be as free as thought itself. Historically the two freedoms have always been inseparable: 'Education, which is but the communication of thoughts, has always been as free as thought itself.'[46]

Thus liberty of opinion, as a God-given right, should be protected by any just society and this implies that there must be freedom of association and of the press, as well as of instruction – to ensure the communication and transmission of thought. In this Lamennais echoes the claims traditionally made by Catholics in secular states: 'Of all public liberties, two are particularly dear to Catholics, the two which governments try most frequently to take away from them: freedom of education and of association, two attributes almost equally essential to its calling which the Church claims as a natural right wherever it cannot have them as a privilege.'[47] He sees no contradiction between advocating these freedoms, which would predominantly benefit religious congregations, and his attacks on indoctrination. Indeed, he does not construe religious instruction as an infringement upon free thought, provided that alternative forms of secular schooling are available and that parents' choice between the two types of establishments is unconstrained. Therefore the support he gives to Catholic education is no longer principally motivated by the church's right to propagate its dogma, but by the father's right to choose his children's education.

State intervention in education has always resulted in infringements upon individual rights, limitation of intellectual freedom and maximisation of social inequalities. Napoleon's educational policy epitomises all these abuses. He sought to restrict free thought through indoctrination. 'Education had a tariff, customs controls and forbidden goods.'[48] The Imperial University served to propagate political conformism and the militaristic spirit which Napoleon expected from his future soldiers; it was meant to 'change France into a big military encampment always ready to march when the signal was given . . . and turn all Frenchmen into one passive and submissive body'.[49] Thus a political cult replaced religion, interfering with the liberty of conscience as well as with parental rights. Similarly the application of the vocational principle in the Imperial University reduced freedom by preventing individuals from developing their particular talents or following disinterested pursuits.[50] Thus the content of state education as designed under Napoleon is undesirable in what it teaches – since it indoctrinates – and in what it prevents people from learning – because of its narrow vocationalism.

Secondly, Lamennais denounces the social discrimination inseparable from the structure of the Imperial University. The policy of the Empire was not only to recognise existing social inequalities, but in fact to reinforce them by giving differentiated schooling. Thus artificial distinctions of rank and wealth replace the basic equality of men before God from which their equal right to acquire knowledge is derived.[51] Instead the Imperial University not only excluded the poor from any learning other than elementary, but also prevented other agencies from giving them more advanced instruction. 'I do not reproach the University for shutting its schools to the children of the poor, since this saves them from corruption; but to prevent the creation of other establishments for them, that is the revolting injustice.'[52] In not providing gratuitous education, the Imperial University discriminated against the poor and reinforced the advantages of the rich.[53] In such a system, the government does not give instruction, it sells instruction. 'It does not establish an institution, it makes an investment; it sells to the rich knowledge, morality, Religion, and confers an exclusive right thereby; it establishes the monstrous aristocracy of money.'[54] This policy of educational discrimination is one of the factors contributing to the lack of independence of the people, which made the Third Estate the historical successor to systems of slavery and serfdom.[55] The differentiation between bourgeois and popular education in the system of the Imperial University perpetuates this dependence for one section of the Third Estate. 'Education is one of the first needs of the people and for this very reason it must be freely available like food. If one wanted to feed a nation according to an administrative programme, in spite of the most beautiful theories, it would die of starvation.'[56] To discriminate in education is not only to destroy equality of opportunity, it is to negate freedom of thought.

As a guardian of Christian morality, the church ought by definition to side with the people and to promote egalitarianism. Although in history it has often forgotten its special responsibilities to protect the poor against the rich and the ruled against the rulers, this can be attributed to the pernicious influence of Erastianism. While the Gallican church has been particularly prone to excessive submissiveness in its relations with the state and has therefore been used by temporal sovereigns for purposes of social control, it has at least remained aware of its educational duties. In providing free tuition, the religious orders – least receptive to the dictates of the state and consequently most faithful to the true mission of the church – ministered to the needs of the people. It is characteristic, according to Lamennais, that the education they dispensed should have been accessible to 'all estates, to all members of society without distinction',[57] whereas from the outset the educational establishments run by the state were fee-paying and consequently discriminatory.

Thus, in spite of its Gallicanist errors, the church has provided for centuries an education which did not infringe upon individual rights, since it was gratuitous and since, being based on Christian values, it was conducive to the moral integrity of individuals, as well as to the social solidarity of all classes.[58] This elementary schooling may have been more morally formative than intellectually stimulating, but this is no deprivation for the vast majority of the population. 'It matters little to the happiness of man, and even less to the happiness of society that his intellect should expand beyond certain limits.'[59] Advanced instruction would be inappropriate for most individuals, since it would exceed their intellectual potential, their needs in later life and the wishes of their family. On the other hand, moral formation, such as the church has given for centuries, is precisely that which fathers want for their children, which the average person can easily assimilate and which will prove useful, regardless of occupation or wealth. It is egalitarian by being the lowest common denominator. Hence religious education has been what the people wanted and needed, whereas state education is unrelated to popular requirements, its content being dictated by the narrow temporal ends of occupational training and of political indoctrination. Its vocational aspects contradict equality, its secularism affronts morality, its politicisation negates freedom.

The logical conclusion Lamennais and the liberal Catholics grouped around *L'Avenir* drew from this contrast between the appropriateness of religious education for the people and the inevitable use of state instruction to undermine individual rights, was that the church could not co-operate with the Imperial University without betraying its true calling. To make religion serve secular purposes of social control was to degrade it and to deprive Christians of the independent tuition which they were entitled to expect from the clergy. Thus the union of the church and state under the Concordate was contrary to the freedom of conscience, as well as being an immoral compromise which neither partner could accept without relinquishing a basic principle. 'The Union was profanity for the Church, hypocrisy for the State; it went against both faith and reason.'[60] To advocate separation from the state ensued logically from the two tenets that establishment is fatal to the integrity and independence of the church, and that the state is necessarily inimical to individual rights. Thus both the Ultramontanism and the liberalism underpinning Lamennais's plea for religious education, both his defence of the church's right to give instruction and of the individual right to receive it, led to the advocacy of disestablishment. Thus 'the principle of separation between Church and State is the basic principle of the religious policy put forward in l'Avenir'.[61]

The condemnation of this central tent of Catholic liberalism by the papal encyclical *Mirari vos* in 1832 was bound to result in a complete transformation of the ideology upheld to legitimate Catholic educational domination. *L'Avenir* disappeared and its editorial team disintegrated. Lamennais rebelled against the papacy, increasingly differentiated Christian ethics from the activities of the clergy, and ultimately condemned religious authoritarianism for being equally pernicious to individual rights as secular absolutism. He remained consistent in his rejection of the unholy alliance between church and state in education. By contrast, Montalembert accepted the doctrinal decision of the encyclical and constituted the Catholic parliamentary party which was to defend the clergy's right to teach and the individual right to receive religious education throughout the July Monarchy. This campaign relied on the arguments formulated by Lamennais in his early works and in *L'Avenir*, but stopped short of demanding disestablishment and of condemning all secular states. It merely attacked the university monopoly as illiberal and advocated 'neither theocracy nor Gallicanism; but freedom, the mutual independence of the temporal and of the spiritual'.[62]

Catholic liberalism and bourgeois educational domination

The educational policy of Montalembert's party revealed the contradictions inherent in an ideology in which Ultramontanism and liberalism were imperfectly blended. After the condemnation of disestablishment as doctrinally unsound, the arguments previously advanced to advocate this drastic solution to the problem of demarcating the religious from the secular in education, were used to support demands for an increase in the share conceded by the state to the clergy within the university. The earlier attempt to legitimate and regain religious educational domination gave way to a plea for greater clerical participation in the secular system. In fact the *loi Falloux* of 1850 which was the culminating point of this policy was considered as a political triumph for Catholicism, because it relaxed the formal obstacles to the admission of clerics into the teaching profession by reducing the qualifications demanded from them and by giving seats in state educational councils to members of the Catholic hierarchy.[63] Yet it contradicted the tenets of anti-Erastianism and of the individual right to an educational choice unhampered by state intervention. In other words, the principle on which this legislation was founded was incompatible with the ideology by reference to which religious educational domination had been legitimated by the Catholic party. Far from offering an alternative to state indoctrination, the church participated in it by undertaking to provide popular primary instruction and was rewarded by concessions at secondary level, without any relinquishment of the secularist principle embodied in the university monopoly. This increase in the participation of the clergy in the educational system represented 'a gift from the State, a right granted by the State to the Church, not for her sake, but for its own, because it needed the Church, her dogma, her action on the masses, her help in the struggle against the social peril'[64] which the Revolution of 1848 had made clear to the bourgeoisie.

The acceptance of this gift granted by the state meant that the Catholic opposition to its educational monopoly as an encroachment on church rights and on individual rights had been abortive. The ideology, negating the secularism on which bourgeois domination over education was founded and legitimating the competing educational claims of the church, incorporated a blueprint for action – based on disestablishment. Once this had been condemned by the Vatican, the Catholic party could only fight a rearguard action. The relative success of its policy – bargaining with the secular state rather than challenging its educational system – was due to the prevalence of a concern for social control over anti-clericalism in the ideology of the bourgeoisie, whose educational domination had been fully realised under the July Monarchy and whose fear of social unrest had been stimulated in 1848. In fact the supporters of religious education within the university referred to this bourgeois ideology – rather than to that of *L'Avenir* – in the debate preceding the adoption of *loi Falloux*. They explicitly accepted social control as a function of the church on behalf of bourgeois interests:

Who is it who defends order and private property in the countryside? Is it the (secular) schoolteacher? who has been pampered by the property owners, by the bourgeois for so long? Let us say it, it is the priest . . . the priest represents order, even for those who do not believe, even for those who have no use for religion . . . [the clergy] represents at the same time the moral order, the political order and the material order.[65]

By thus linking the educational function of the clergy with the defence of property and of citizenship in a secular state, Montalembert acknowledged the triumph of Napoleonic ideology over Catholic liberalism and offered the services of the clergy to further the domination of the bourgeoisie in education.

11. Conclusion

By the middle of the nineteenth century, assertive groups seeking to gain control over education and to replace traditional forms of religious domination were fully successful in France, while their English counterparts were still engaged in an unresolved conflict with the Anglican church. In the two countries different kinds of educational change took place in the first half of the century, leading to the establishment of a state educational system in France and in England to a diversification of educational provisions and practices but not to changed structural relationships with other social institutions. It now remains to be seen on a comparative basis how far different forms of interaction between dominant and assertive groups account for educational change. It has been shown that the type of education existing in both countries at the end of the eighteenth century offered great formal similarities. If the differences exhibited by mid-century are to be interpreted as divergences, then it must be demonstrated that educational change is not merely responding to the same pressures but at different rates. Clarification of this issue necessarily precedes a reassessment of the three assumptions, queried on theoretical grounds in the introduction, in the light of comparative data – the simplicity of institutional relations in the pre-industrial period; some aspect of industrialisation accounting for the transition from simplicity to complexity; and the processes of industrialisation and institutional secularisation being concurrent.

DOMINATION AND ASSERTION AND EDUCATIONAL CHANGE IN ENGLAND AND FRANCE

In presenting the differences between the two countries with regard to one social institution – education – abstractions and generalisations are necessarily being made across the whole range of educational establishments. Such constructed types as those presented below have the inevitable characteristic of exaggerating certain broad features and minimising certain specific differences in order to clarify the major dissimilarities. These characterisations of English and French education in the mid-nineteenth century necessarily cannot be exhaustive; it is unavoidable in a comparative study that they should amplify striking differences rather than points of similarity. However, if these eight dimensions can be accepted as essential for the formal description of education as a social institution, they define at least the minimal elements for which any theory of institutional change must account. Since a constructed type is not descriptive, a theory may be capable of explaining such differences without accounting for all variation between the two systems studied. Nevertheless, the usefulness of a theory of institutional development can be assessed operationally in relation to its capacity for explaining differences along the stated dimensions. It is, of course, possible to argue that the types should have been differently constructed and that other dimensions should have been selected. This does not prevent the dimensions chosen from corresponding to actual differences or from being in need of explanation.

CHARACTERISTICS OF EDUCATIONAL INSTITUTIONS	ENGLAND	FRANCE
Organisation	Voluntary	State
Administration	Local	Centralised
Financing	Mainly privately organised	Mainly state organised
Goal	Character formation	Career orientation
Structure	Hierarchical, unintegrated	Hierarchical, integrated
Teaching profession	Untrained individuals	Trained corps
Pupil selection	Social	Meritocratic
Curricula	Unstandardised	Standardised

ORGANISATION

In England, until 1833, educational establishments were organised on a purely voluntary basis. Their whole range – from dame and charity schools at primary level, owned and run by private individuals, through endowed and public schools, founded, financed and regulated by individual bequests, to the university colleges, originating in foundations and continually asserting their independence – was outside state intervention or control. Reforms or expansion occurring in each sector were, until the passage of the First Reform Bill, fully dependent upon private initiative and voluntary subscription. Thus the creation of the British and Foreign School Society and of the National Society for Promoting the Education of the Poor, at primary level, the opening of mechanics' institutes for adult education, that of denominational or experimental private schools at secondary level, and finally the foundation of London University – all represented private enterprise. Significantly, the first state grant in aid of primary education confirmed this trend which was then expanded into 'the voluntary principle'. Treasury grants were to be distributed through the National Society and the British and Foreign School Society without comprehensive governmental directives concerning the utilisation of such funds, the educational standards to be maintained or the subjects to be taught. The control of schools remained the prerogative of the subscribers, both to the original two societies and to those which developed subsequently. State intervention was limited to the appointment of inspectors, after 1839, and even then the societies could veto any particular inspector. The fact that the church of England at the peak of its Tractarian revival combated governmental interference in educational matters, in defence of the traditional supremacy of Anglicanism, strengthened voluntarism. The dissenters were equally opposed to state intervention which they felt to be antagonistic to religious liberty because of the existence of the established church. This 'religious difficulty' prolonged the voluntary system in primary education, while secondary and higher remained wholly private.

In France, the necessity of a state system was proclaimed by successive revolutionary Assemblies. The legislative provisions for primary instruction (1793), for secondary *écoles centrales* (1795), and for *grandes écoles* to provide specialised higher education (1794) implemented this principle without, however, creating a complete network. It was the Imperial University, founded by Napoleon in 1806, which fully embodied the monopoly of the state over education. The private establishments which survived were not allowed (after 1808) to function without state authorisation and the examination system compelled them to follow official curricula. Religious schools did not escape this rule and, while the church was allowed considerable latitude in primary schooling, this was due to governmental indifference and desire for economy. Popular instruction was abandoned to the church for reasons of expediency without being formally excluded from the control of the Imperial University. The latter years of the

Empire merely marked an intensification of state monopoly over secondary and higher education, with the nationalisation of many religious schools and increased state powers over the remaining private institutions. The system of the Imperial University survived the fall of Napoleon and retained its virtual monopoly over post-primary education. Its influence over primary schooling was strengthened under the Restoration, when attendance was made compulsory (1816), and with the creation by the July Monarchy of the *primaire supérieur* (higher-grade schools) in 1833. By an interesting coincidence, the date of 1833 marks both the consolidation of state control over all branches of French education and the formal recognition of voluntarism in England.

ADMINISTRATION

The corollary of English voluntarism was that educational administration was locally based. Thus the university colleges, the boards of school governors and trustees, and the committees of the mechanics' institutes, as well as the independent bodies managing experimental and denominational schools, witnessed to the diversity of administrative patterns and to the concentration of decision-making at the local level. In fact, only one central administrative body existed at the time – the Committee of the Privy Council on Education – founded in 1839, and concerned with the allocation of state grants rather than with school management. While this Committee of Council was the distant forerunner of the Board of Education (1889), its attempts at intervention during the first half of the nineteenth century met with firm opposition from the voluntary bodies.

The educational blueprints of the French revolutionary period showed a lack of consensus about state responsibility in education. While this uncertainty was reflected by legislative instability throughout the period, in practice all teaching institutions at all levels were under the control of the Minister of the Interior. A high official of the ministry (*directeur général*) was responsible for educational affairs and it is in this capacity that, under the Consulate, Fourcroy superintended the reform which culminated in the Imperial University. The model inspiring this reform was military centralisation with a hierarchy of delegated responsibilities linking upwards to the head of state. The legislation of 1806 created a centralised educational administration – a unitary structure with powers of control over all teaching establishments and the exclusive legal right to grant degrees and diplomas. This monopoly of conferring degrees, including the *baccalauréat*, the preliminary qualification for entry into higher education and the professions, placed the French state in a unique position, since alone it controlled academic selection at all levels. It was thus the first European country to replace the former administration of education through religious bodies by a separate, highly integrated organisation, distinct from the teaching profession and differentiated from other parts of the civil service. At the head of the university was a *grand maître* (director), appointed and dismissed by the Emperor himself and personally responsible to him. This director was assisted by a council of the university with powers of supervision over the whole educational system. The territory of France was divided in 1808 into *académies*, the regional subdivisions through which education was administered. The advantages of this centralised structure were perceived and retained by subsequent regimes after the fall of the Empire. Although the Imperial University was abolished in 1814, it was resurrected under Napoleon's *Cent Jours* and survived the Restoration of 1815, under the name of Royal University. The office of *grand maître* was then abolished and his functions entrusted to the Minister of the Interior; however, it was soon recreated (1822), its holder being a bishop until 1830. The July Monarchy did not alter this administrative structure, but merely emphasised its secular character. However, it should be remembered that, since Napoleon's Concordate, members of the Catholic clergy were civil servants and therefore the role they played in education under the Restoration had not interrupted the tradition of state control over educational administration. This tradition was to remain unbroken throughout the nineteenth century and is still strong in the twentieth.

FINANCING

Until 1833 all funds devoted to educational purposes in England were private. When governmental grants for primary education began on that date, £20,000 were voted by Parliament and this amount was annually reviewed. Its generosity can be assessed by reference to the same sum having been spent that year on the upkeep of the royal stables. It was increased to £30,000 in 1839, albeit by a small majority vote. Even in the schools receiving state aid – whose object was limited to the provisions of buildings and facilities – private subscriptions represented two-thirds of the cost of upkeep. The primary schools remaining outside the grant-aid framework were wholly supported by fees and voluntary subscriptions. The minimal nature of state contributions is illustrated by the fact that working-class parents in Bristol were paying over £15,000 a year for their children's education in 1834 – over half the amount of the governmental grant to the whole country. In addition, one should take into account the considerable funds from private sources donated to teaching establishments at all levels; the capital accumulated for the foundation of London University by the sale of £100 shares amounted to £150,000, while lesser undertakings, such as the establishment of a hall of science for popular adult education cost about £5,000. Naturally, private financing played an even bigger part in secondary and higher education, since endowed and public schools were maintained by fees and the revenue of bequests, as were university colleges. In this context, state aid to education can be seen as a negligible part of the total expenditure.

While all French revolutionary educational plans (with the exception of Mirabeau's) had advocated gratuity at primary level and a system of scholarships for individuals progressing to secondary and higher establishments, the Assemblies of the time always faced too many financial difficulties to provide the degree of state support implied by those proposals. It is because of the inadequacy of the resources available to municipal and departmental administrations that the network of primary schools and *écoles centrales* was never fully developed. This financial problem was solved under the Empire. Whilst state expenditure on education did not substantially increase, a great step forward was made in the utilisation of public resources and for the first time the state made itself fully responsible for the financial organisation of education. Seven different sources of revenue were drawn upon by the imperial state:

(1) the income derived from bonds subscribed in particular by the purchasers of confiscated property during the Revolution;

(2) fees paid by graduates for their examination costs;

(3) one-twentieth of all the amounts paid as fees by the pupils attending any type of school at secondary or higher level;

(4) all the assets of former teaching establishments, including endowments;

(5) from 1811 onwards, the municipalities were made responsible for the upkeep of faculty, *lycée* and *collège* buildings;

(6) a state loan of 1 million francs covered the initial expenditures resulting from the creation of educational establishments;

(7) compulsory municipal contributions, the bigger towns being forced to create grants.

While the share of the state in financing education remained comparatively small and was largely restricted to the maintenance of the central educational administration and the country-wide academic administration, the principle had been firmly established that the state should be responsible for ensuring that educational expenditures would be covered.

GOALS

The traditional ascriptive nature of English education meant that instruction confirmed rather than determined the existing system of social stratification. Its task was mainly twofold: either imbuing the upper class with a sense of their future role as a social and political elite, or conditioning the lower classes to a passive acceptance of their station in life. While ascriptive educational selection is not necessarily non-vocational, the main roles for which education prepared the elite at the time, those of churchmen, statesmen and resident landowners, were not held to require specialised training. Conversely, at the bottom of the social hierarchy, even literacy appeared of dubious utility for a population which was still predominantly agricultural. The only exceptions to this non-vocational rule were the commercial schools patronised by the wealthier section of the middle class. All other secondary establishments were aimed at producing Christian gentlemen, albeit with varying degrees of emphasis on Christian virtues versus social graces. The predominance of clerics among teachers at all levels intensified concern for character rather than intellect and morality rather than knowledge.

French revolutionaries were committed to the philosophy of the enlightenment whose central postulate was that knowledge would unfailingly lead to virtue. Therefore they did not see intelligence and character as alternatives. Hence the encyclopaedic curricula of the *écoles centrales*, devoid of a vocational bias. While general ideas were to be propagated in these secondary establishments, and, less generously, at primary level, higher education was to provide for the application of knowledge to the professions. Thus vocationalism was embodied in the specialised schools created by the Convention, such as Polytechnique and Normale. Subsequently, Napoleon's concentration on state efficiency and professional competence strengthened the connection between academic qualifications and careers. Not only was the *baccalauréat* designed as a pre-condition for entry into the civil service and the professions, but also the educational and the administrative hierarchies were fully articulated. To each degree actually corresponded an occupational outlet. It was only primary education which remained non-vocational and the creation of *primaire supérieur* under the July Monarchy was an attempt to universalise vocationalism.

STRUCTURE

In England, a hierarchical structure of educational institutions had been inherited from the eighteenth century: these could broadly be classified into the three groups of primary, secondary and higher institutions. However, they could in no way be said to constitute a system, since there was no articulation between stages. On the contrary, each level tended to be terminal for the pupils who attended the corresponding establishments. Thus, children from primary schools only exceptionally progressed to anything which could be termed secondary education. The dominant secondary institutions, the endowed and public schools, never required primary-school attendance before enrolment, but tended to rely on previous private tuition at home. Nor was secondary-school attendance a prerequisite for university entrance. While the strongest degree of institutional integration in England at this time was the bond between the public schools and the universities, it only implied that certain college places were reserved for the pupils of some of these schools and not that tuition in a formal establishment was an absolute requirement. Many cases of private pre-university instruction at home or by local tutors or curates appear in the literature of the time. Thus no ladder – in the sense of a necessary progression from one institution to the next – existed during the first half of the nineteenth century and correspondingly the curricula of the various levels were not interrelated. Indeed, the assumption was that such a syllabus corresponded to an autonomous (and hence terminal) course of studies. Therefore, primary schooling aimed at imparting literacy; commercial schools – clerical skills; endowed and public schools – classical scholarship sufficient for entry into the minor professions; and universities – the degree of culture held necessary for professionals and clerics. The ascriptive nature of English society was reflected and perpetuated by this educational structure, its hierarchical nature mirrored vertical stratification and its non-integration, the lack of social mobility.

During the revolutionary period, French educational blueprints were divided between those which interpreted equality as synonymous with the provision of a minimal standard of elementary instruction for all citizens and those which defined equality of opportunity as the creation of an educational ladder. The second interpretation implied that passage from one level to the next would be conditioned by merit alone. As a result, legislation either catered for the primary level only or foresaw a complete integration between primary, secondary and higher education – although the lack of financial resources prevented the network from ever becoming nation-wide. The Imperial University was a conscious attempt to produce a system with the characteristics of geographical universality and uniformity, as well as full vertical co-ordination. Although the lowest echelons of this pyramid – the primary schools – were largely left to the church, they were not necessarily considered as terminal institutions, since state grants were provided for the most able pupils to proceed to secondary education. Moreover, this reliance on the church was a solution of expediency until state resources were equal to the total integration of a national secular system. Under the Restoration, the law of 1816 confirming state control over primary schools, achieved this goal, but did not solve the problem of the increasing number of pupils who sought additional tuition without having the ability or the wish to enter secondary establishments. For them the July Monarchy created the higher-grade schools (*primaire supérieur*) which made the system fully integrated, although primary and secondary education were not strongly connected. Obviously, the advantages of birth and environment favoured the privileged classes. However, the hierarchical integration of education not only reflected the meritocratic aspects of an egalitarian ideology, but actually made social mobility possible – for some individuals. This is not to assert that integration by itself equalised opportunities – it is incapable of doing so – but merely that where it exists together with the notion of selection by merit, and where education is relevant to social promotion, manifest ability has a greater chance of being recognised and rewarded.

TEACHING PROFESSION

The essential qualification for teaching in England at the beginning of the nineteenth century was moral certification by an Anglican bishop.

This privilege of the established church operated at all levels and accounted for the overwhelming predominance of clerics as teachers in secondary and higher education. For many posts the lack of orders was an actual bar to appointment. With the increased political importance of education as an issue before Parliament and in the press, the unsatisfactory nature of current pedagogical standards became more and more apparent. The lack of state contributions to secondary and higher education made it impossible for official criticisms to have force. As far as the state was concerned a complete liberty to teach existed at these levels – although the church was able to enforce moral criteria, no agency was competent to insist on academic qualifications. Therefore moral standards obviously predominated over intellectual. However, at primary level the state's minimal financial involvement enabled it to advocate the training of teachers and the inspection of schools. The Committee in Council formulated in 1839 a scheme for a teacher-training establishment, but was forced to abandon it by the 'religious difficulty'. Similarly, its plans for school inspection were diluted by the fact that the two societies administering the schools' grant acquired a right of veto. While no overall training scheme was acceptable to all denominations, attempts by some of them took place, but it would be fair to state that over the whole period there was infinitely less concern for pedagogical standards than for doctrinal orthodoxy. While the personal efforts of Kay-Shuttleworth resulted in setting up one establishment for teacher training, which received state aid in 1842, there was no overall governmental action which would have been required to turn teaching into a profession. It remained the pursuit of the amateur whose only credentials were moral and doctrinal acceptability to either church or chapel.

The overriding concern of French revolutionary Assemblies was to dislodge members of the clergy from their traditional position as educators at all levels. This desire was prompted by a rejection of the Catholic ideology both on philosophical and political grounds, and to a lesser degree by a concern for raising teaching standards. An official certificate of civic virtue was therefore required – under the law of 1793 – for primary-school teachers. Similar requirements existed before appointment to *écoles centrales*. Although these provisions show that ideological considerations predominated at the time in the reform of the teaching profession, the foundation of the École Normale in 1794 witnessed to a parallel interest in raising pedagogical competence. This first attempt at teacher-training proved short-lived, but, as many other revolutionary endeavours – was resumed under the Empire. The imperial decree of 1808 organising the university refounded the École Normale for secondary teachers initially in arts subjects only, but rapidly expanded to cover mathematical and scientific studies. This creation reflects a desire to generalise teacher training and at the same time to promote specialisation. Indeed, the pupils of École Normale were to attend lectures and pass examinations in the faculties corresponding to their future subject-matter. Academic success regulated the level at which entrants to the profession would be allowed to teach – for example, a *baccalauréat* enabled one to teach only the first three forms of secondary schools; a *licence* the next two; and a doctorate the two top forms of students presenting themselves for the *baccalauréat*. These requirements were obligatory for all new entrants, while the problem of teachers already practising was solved by equating their number of years of experience with a particular qualification. This was seen as a temporary solution whose duration would be limited by the life-span of those who were already teaching before the Napoleonic reform. Training was intended to apply to all members of the teaching profession, although considerations of expediency led to a concentration on the secondary level. Indeed, training courses in the *lycées* for future primary-school teachers were contemplated as an integral part of the programme. Such a preoccupation with pedagogical standards need not logically imply the formation of a highly integrated corps of individuals imbued with common goals and ranked in a single hierarchy. However, the fact that the teaching hierarchy was modelled on military ranks, that all teachers were employed by the state as civil servants, and thus had common, non-pedagogical duties and responsibilities, and the deliberate fostering of an *esprit de corps* among new entrants, transformed a set of qualified individuals into a group with shared values, obligations and expectations. This corresponded to Napoleon's explicit policy of creating a secular corporation equally faithful to the service of the state in education as religious teaching orders had been to that of the church. The Restoration, without abandoning the concept of a state-controlled teaching profession, marked a retreat to moral rather than academic criteria for entry. Thus the law of 1816 placed the primary-school teacher under the academic supervision of the university and the moral control of the mayor and parish priest. Correspondingly, the secondary-teacher-training École Normale was abolished in 1822 as lacking in religious spirit. However, teachers remained civil servants under the Restoration and therefore the main achievement of the Empire in consolidating the profession did not disappear. With the advent of the July Monarchy, the École Normale was immediately re-established (1830) and considerable attempts were made to impose secular pedagogical criteria at primary level. Teacher-training for *primaire* and *primaire supérieur* was organised by the law of 1833, which thus extended the obligatory nature of training to the whole of the profession.

PUPIL SELECTION

It was social self-selection rather than any other criteria which determined attendance at all educational levels in nineteenth-century England. School fees tended to regulate this selection – their level was determined by the social class of the prospective patrons and maintained the exclusive character of each degree of instruction. The stratification of establishments was reinforced by status. Thus while the upper classes could obviously afford the cost of elementary education for their children, considerations of prestige led them to incur the greater expense of private tutors. Similarly, the wealthy section of the middle class, able to afford either public school or university fees, would usually find themselves debarred on either social or religious grounds. The existence of the Test Acts reinforced the social bias of higher education. This combination of objective and subjective barriers resulted in a concordance between the social and educational hierarchies. The compartmentalisation of educational levels and the lack of integration between institutions mirrored the closed nature of English society. Thus the best instruction available to the working class was provided by charity schools, imparting literacy, and possibly the artisans' finishing school – the mechanics' institute. The middle class could only aspire at secondary level to the commercial, the experimental or the endowed school. The public school directly linked to Oxbridge largely remained the preserve of the upper class during this period. Individual exceptions, made possible by the existence of the Scottish universities and of such institutions as Birkbeck College, merely confirmed the rule.

In France, revolutionary egalitarianism was universally interpreted as postulating the creation of a common primary education accessible to all citizens. However, there was a divergence of views between the extreme left, particularly vocal under the Convention, who considered that the provision of any additional degrees of instruction would be a source of new inequalities – and a majority who deemed them not only necessary, but compatible with equality of opportunity. In the latter view, selection by merit guaranteed that individuals had equal chances. The provision of scholarships for deserving pupils in the law of 1795 creating *écoles centrales* exemplified this trend. While to Napoleon considerations of efficiency outweighed those of equality, selection by merit could serve both purposes and was therefore retained as the method of transition between educational levels. Subsequent regimes inherited this system of selection and in fact extended it, as in the case of the higher-grade school (*primaire supérieur*) whose intake was creamed off from the primary school population. This is not to assert that educational opportunity was immune from the influences of social stratification – the existence of fees introduced financial obstacles to educational mobility and the consideration given to manifest talent rather than latent aptitude made for a class bias, since there was no allowance for environmental disadvantages. The extent to which the *baccalauréat* came to be monopolised by the bourgeoisie illustrated the social bias of meritocratic selection. However, while influenced by class origin, educational promotion was partially independent from it, particularly when merit was most evident. Therefore it could act as an avenue of social mobility, albeit for a limited number of individuals and at a comparatively slow pace.

CURRICULA

The traditional emphasis on the predominantly classical character of English nineteenth-century education should not be confused with a standardisation of curricula at secondary and higher level. The absence of any form of state control or central co-ordination by the university authorities permitted wide variations between colleges and schools. Many endowed establishments were bound in syllabus by the needs of their various foundations. Where provisions were less stringent, the initiative of the headmaster was sufficiently wide to determine such large issues as the incorporation or exclusion of scientific subjects. Furthermore, the range of interpretation of classicism was broad – some, like Thomas Arnold, equated it with the study of comparative social institutions, while others restricted the course to teaching ancient languages. This diversity clearly shows that university entrance examinations imposed few definite requirements upon secondary schools, and candidates frequently resorted to cramming tutors. In higher education, the autonomy of colleges meant that the lectures centrally provided by the university authorities were viewed as optional extras to tutorials rather than as the definition of a curriculum. In such a context, classicism was the lowest common denominator between the diverse forms of instruction which could more aptly be named the liberal education – the title preferred by contemporaries.

A constant feature of French educational legislation from the Revolution onwards was the establishment of fixed curricula by the acts creating a certain type of instruction. This concern for identity at each level corresponded to a determination that local particularisms should be eradicated. Thus the main target of the Convention in its primary-school policy was to eliminate dialects and provincial traditions. For the Republic to be one and indivisible, its citizens had to be imbued with a common culture. This element of uniformity was not only dictated by egalitarianism, but also by nationalism. The commitment of revolutionary Assemblies to spreading enlightenment had its full outlet at post-primary level, particularly in planning the *écoles centrales* and *écoles spéciales*. Far from detecting a contradiction between political democracy and cultural authoritarianism, republican leaders saw the latter as a means to achieve the former. Thus educational standardisation at each level predated Napoleon's reform, although it is usually attributed to the Imperial University – of which it was indeed a dominant characteristic. The centralised organisation, the integrated structure and the meritocratic selection of this system were inseparable from standardised curricula. The monopoly of conferring degrees held by the university extended this standardisation downwards into the *lycées*, which had to prepare pupils for the *baccalauréat*, an examination taking place before faculty professors, not secondary-school teachers. It also extended it outwards, into the schools authorised (and not run) by the state, since their pupils were equally subject to the examination system. This connection between the monopoly of degree-granting and the central setting of curricula remained a permanent feature of French education.

It is obvious, on the dimensions considered, that a greater amount of educational change characterised France than England in the first half of the nineteenth century. It was argued earlier that the integration of education with religion in the late eighteenth century lead to considerable institutional similarities between the two countries; in the following fifty years, it was France which underwent the greater departure from this pattern. The differential amount of change occurring in the two countries appears to reflect the relative success of their respective assertive groups in challenging religious domination over education and destroying this type of structural relationship.

However, while the amount of change taking place can be attributed to the differential success of national assertive groups, the kind of change brought about cannot receive the same type of explanation. This would be tantamount to assuming that both English and French assertive groups sought identical ends. Although there were certain educational reforms that both the bourgeoisie and middle class advocated, their differences are equally striking and reflect the specific interests of the two groups. For example, while both sought a more vocational instruction, for the former this was to be oriented to professional–administrative careers and for the latter to productive employment. Educational change in England must not be seen as merely following the same 'path' as in France, but as proceeding at a slower rate. Thus the early nineteenth century was not only a time of *differential* rates of educational change in England and France, but also of *diverging* patterns being imposed with relative degrees of success. Hence a problem remains of distinguishing differences due to degree of success of assertive groups from those due to their divergent educational aims and interests.

The nature and interests of the two assertive groups – professional/bureaucratic in France and entrepreneurial/non-conformist in England – led both to attack the educational domination of the established churches, but to try to replace this form of integration with very different structural relations. Consonant with their interest the former sought to integrate education with the administrative bureaucracy and the latter with the economy. Both endorsed the aim of retaining the subsidiary integration of education with social stratification, but wished to relate it to the new tripartite class structure, not to the two–class feudal agricultural model which religious education had reinforced in each country. The extent to which the new structural relationships were established reflects the degree of success of the two groups and the policies of assertion employed. However, these two groups differed fundamentally since their assertion was not derived from the same elements. In the case of the French bourgeoisie their *Instrumental Activities* stemmed from their control of the state machinery, whose legislative powers were used to devaluate the church's monopoly of educational facilities through the confiscation of school buildings and the prohibition of teaching orders. Their *Bargaining Power* in relation to education was based on their hegemony in the revolutionary legislative Assemblies and subsequently on their control of key administrative positions under the Empire and the July Monarchy. Their rationalistic *Ideology* stressed secular nationalism and administrative efficiency. Conversely, the *Instrumental Activities* of the English middle class devalued the former Anglican educational monopoly by the creation of alternative institutions, made possible by their new-founded economic wealth. Their *Bargaining Power* consisted in their capacity as entrepreneurs to organise voluntary subscription for all levels of instruction and to profit from their unique position of being able to educate their own employees. Their *Ideology* united the principles of classical economics with the tenets of Utilitarian ethics. Hence the assertive policies of the French bourgeoisie depended on their political and that of the English middle class upon its economic role and interests.

In France, the political nature of bourgeois assertion meant that ultimately complete educational *restriction* could be achieved, such that the previous Catholic monopoly of educational facilities had been devalued and that any enduring church activities in this field could only occur if sanctioned by the state. This policy was in the long run equally successful at all levels of the educational system. On the contrary, in England the middle class could only attempt to *substitute* for the Anglican educational monopoly and hence only devalued it without eliminating it. The increasing expenditures involved in challenging this monopoly at the secondary and higher levels account for its greater endurance than in primary schools.

The types of instrumental activities adopted by the two assertive groups were more a matter of necessity than choice. As a basically professional group, the French bourgeoisie through lack of resources never attempted a policy of substitution, even at an experimental level. From the Enlightenment onwards, they consistently accepted that the powerful monopoly of the church could only be damaged through a policy of restriction initiated by the state. The expulsion of the Jesuits marked the beginning of this policy before the bourgeoisie gained control of the state legislative machinery. In England, the virtual exclusion of the middle class from political participation and their early failure to initiate a policy of state restriction on an extra-parliamentary basis, coincided with the possession of sufficient wealth to begin widespread substitution. Thus the pattern of assertive activities differed in the two countries – the bourgeoisie began by restriction and progressed to substitution, whilst the middle class moved from a policy of substitution to one of restriction.

Having stressed the different goals and means of the assertive groups, their relative degrees of success in deposing the dominant religious groups can be assessed in relation to their respective aims. The events taking place in both countries tend to confirm the initial hypothesis that it is only when a dominant group has been successfully replaced that the relationships between education and other social institutions are altered. Thus when the French bourgeoisie gradually gained control over all levels of education under the July Monarchy, it succeeded in adapting instruction to the requirements of the ad- ministrative bureaucracy and political structure in the context of the contemporary system of social stratification. On the other hand, challenge to the dominant group in England which did not lead to its replacement resulted in certain concessionary forms of internal educational change, but left structural relations unaltered. Any increased integration of education with the economy was in direct proportion to middle class substitutive activities and therefore limited and not nation-wide.

To attribute specific educational changes to differential success of the assertive groups, it is necessary to show that such changes were sought by both groups. Despite their differences in aims and on structural relationships desired, both groups recognised that their attainment implied an education which was state-*organised*, *-adminis- tered and -financed*. Through its legislative activities the bourgeoisie succeeded in organising and consolidating a state educational system, centrally administered and financed, whilst the substitutive activities of the middle class merely diversified pre-existing forms of provisions. In terms of organisation, the activities of dissenting and secular groups intensified the voluntary nature of English education – instead of leading to an increase in state responsibility at primary level, it resulted in state recognition of voluntarism. Administration, under the volun- taristic principle, of necessity remained fragmented and basically local, tied as it was to the production of subscriptions. In their common pursuit of these three objectives, the two assertive groups sought totally different ends as they did in their mutual advocacy of *vocationally*-oriented instruction within state educational establish- ments.

It is not suggested that had both assertive groups succeeded, English and French education would have been very similar on these four dimensions. The different structural relationships sought by them would have meant that each was employed to a different end in the two countries, leading to a corresponding fund of internal variation. For example vocationalism would have been biased towards preparation for economic roles in England and to administrative–professional ones in France. Thus the equal success of the bourgeoisie and middle class would have resulted only in formal, not in substantive similarities on these dimensions. It is only in this sense that these specific educational changes can be related to the differential success of the assertive groups.

However, there is another category of educational change, occurring in France and absent in England, which cannot be attributed to the extent of successful assertion, but which depends upon it for implementation. In other words, those changes occurring in France, which if it had gained domination the English middle class would *not* have introduced, must be explained by divergent aims, not differential success. While the establishment of state education in France was a necessary pre-condition for the transformation of its structure into a hierarchically integrated system, of the teaching profession into a trained corps, of pupil selection into a choice based on merit, and of curricula into nationally-standardised programmes, it does not account for the implementation of these reforms. Alternative provisions could have been made without detracting from the control of the bourgeoisie. Therefore the policies actually implemented on these four dimensions reflect the *ideology* of the assertive group rather than its success in gaining control over education. The great differences between French and English education on the dimensions already discussed can be related to the differential degree of success of the assertive groups, the middle class not having yet attained the necessary conditions for the implementation of such policies. However, the *ideology* of the middle class, congruent with its economic interests, distinctly endorsed social selection as against meritocratic recruitment and appeared to favour unstandardised curricula, related to the industrial specialisation of geographical areas and of social strata. While a teaching profession more thoroughly trained – particularly in scientific subjects, would have served the needs of technology and production, there was no suggestion of establishing a teaching corps receiving a common training. Lastly, while the middle class lacked the degree of educational control required to integrate the three levels of education, an unintegrated structure coincided with their blueprints in which no ladder between primary and secondary estsblishments was advocated.

The ideology held by a given dominant group must thus be regarded as a partially independent variable in educational change, since the interests of the group and the structural relations it wishes to establish between education and other social institutions do not dictate the specific blueprint advanced. While the blueprint must be consonant with the group's interests, a plurality of specific internal educational arrangements may be compatible with a given set of structural relationships. In other words, the requirements of bureaucratic efficiency (in the case of France) exhibit a certain range of tolerance towards the educational provisions capable of meeting them. The choice between them – if it is perceived as a choice, which is not always the case – is made as the group's ideology is elaborated. Thus for example the institution of teacher training was necessary for a new secular dominant group if it were to fully devalue the clerical monopoly and redirect education to vocational ends – but the decision to found a single corps of teachers cannot be derived directly from it. This depended on certain ideological postulates concerning the imitation of the Jesuit order. Thus decisions of this kind, about the particular arrangements best able to meet a given end, always depend upon 'judgements of appropriateness' derived from the ideology. It is this interaction between interests and ideology which account for educational differences in two societies, with similar types of groups dominating education and where similar structural relations prevail. In the same way, this interaction between different interest groups and their supportive ideologies leads to divergent forms of educational change in England and France, quite apart from the differential success of their respective forms of assertion.

In relation to the greater success of bourgeois assertion in France than in England, it might now be queried whether in fact success or failure do not depend simply upon the types of instrumental activities employed to challenge a previous dominant group. It might be argued that there is a logical connection between policies of restriction and successful assertion and therefore that such policies are always superior to those of substitution. Since restriction always involves use of the state machinery whereas substitution does not, a corollary to the previous proposition would be that the educational assertion of a political elite would succeed while that of an economic elite would be more doubtful. However, there seem to be difficulties in accepting this as a logical relationship and all of them rest on the concept and role of bargaining power in assertive action.

As was argued in the introduction, the fact that a political elite controls the state legislative machinery does not automatically make it the educationally dominant group in society – this presupposes the desire to control instruction, not universal among governing elites, and the possibility of organising the overthrowal and replacement of the previous dominant group. Through the use of legislation a political elite can succeed in completely devaluing this group's monopoly by legally restricting its exercise, but without sufficient bargaining power or organisation it cannot substitute alternative educational provisions. The French revolutionary Assemblies eliminated the church from education without being able to introduce a complete alternative. Financial limitations preventing the implementation of educational blueprints meant that ultimately, within the Imperial University, the church had to be recalled to supplement the inadequacies of the state. Thus the educational domination of the French bourgeoisie cannot be dated from the time of the Revolution but only came into existence at all levels under the July Monarchy when the increased bargaining power of this group made its policy successful, by organising adequate financing.

Conversely do the activities of the English middle class provide any indication that of necessity assertion through substitution is related to failure? All that can be stated with confidence is that inadequacies in its bargaining power certainly contributed to making substitution weaker than it might have been. Had the active section of this assertive group been numerically and organisationally stronger, its cumulative resources could have gone further in pricing the church out of the educational market. Particularly at primary level, had the entrepreneurial sector collectively exploited the educational provisions under the Factory Act, the religious monopoly could have been devalued at a greater rate. With the lack of state intervention at this level assured by the religious difficulty that middle-class activities had precipitated, successful assertion was at least possible in theory.

However, there seems little doubt that, while there is no logical association between successful assertion and policies of restriction, there is a strong contingency relationship. The advantage an assertive political elite possesses over other groups rests simply on the fact that a policy of restriction is easier to operate, involving less resources, than one of substitution. It enables the monopoly of the previous dominant group to be devalued imperatively and immediately. The provision of alternative facilities may be considerably delayed, but possession of legal authority can be used to organise public educational financing rather than the new dominant group having to own and provide establishments and teachers itself. If the foregoing analysis is correct, then a crucial period of educational change in all countries should coincide with the assumption to power of a political elite endowed with the desire and the possibility of replacing the previous dominant group. The importance of this juncture lies in its endurance, since despite political change or the elaboration of complex and multiple structural relations, the integration of education to the state, once established, is unlikely to be reversed.

The difficulties, both organisational and financial, in operating a policy of substitution in nineteenth-century England were eventually recognised by both middle and working classes. Increasingly both groups sought state intervention, and saw their own enfranchisement as the only way in which the legislative machinery could be employed to devalue the monopoly of the church. It is interesting to note with reference to their respective resources that the working class turned away more decisively from attempting a policy of substitution. Equally significant, however, was the way in which the church, its monopoly threatened but not fully devalued by the substitutive activities of the middle class, also turned towards state intervention to provide it with the legal constraints necessary to protect its domination. In England at least, profound educational conflict seems to have produced a strain towards state intervention as a means, although not to the integration of education to the state as an end. On the part of the assertive groups, it represented an attempt to increase bargaining power, on the part of the dominant group – to augment its means of constraint.

It may be that this strain towards state intervention regularly occurs in situations where deadlock is reached between dominant and assertive groups, but this would require checking by wider comparative analysis. What appears clear, however, from the English situation, is that the attempted use of state intervention by both types of groups does not lead *directly* to the integration of education with the state. The acquisition of political influence following enfranchisement did not enable the middle classes to operate a policy of restriction (as the 1870 Elementary Education Act shows) but mainly to undermine the legal constraints that the church possessed over education (such as repealing of the Test Acts). Similarly the use of political influence by the church enabled it to protect its remaining monopoly, but not to extend it or to gain additional constraints to repulse assertion. England would thus appear to be a good example of a parliamentary democracy in which the slow transition from the possession of political influence to the constitution of the political elite had to be made before the process of integrating education with the state could be initiated.

Education and social structure in the pre-industrial period

An examination of the type of educational change occurring in pre-industrial France and industrialising England provides an adequate basis upon which to assess the proposition that the pre- and post-industrial dichotomy coincided with simple and complex relationships between education and other social institutions. Havinghurst's theory of evolution in socio-educational relations represents a clear example of this view and can usefully be considered with reference to comparative data from the two countries. Starting from 'the proposition that the educational system of a society is shaped and directed by one or more of the four basic social institutions; family, church, state and economy',[1] Havinghurst assigns complex structural relationships either to traditional societies or to industrial economies. Thus between the stage in which family–education–religion are closely integrated and that in which economy–education–state are related in these two types of social structure, simple socio-educational relations prevail. Furthermore, as is common with such theories, the actual emergence of an educational system is held to depend upon economic change. 'As society evolves towards greater technological complexity, and as it achieves a standard of living that permits at least some people to think reflectively about society and its future, it creates a major educational institution, which is a set of schools, colleges, universities.'[2]

Havinghurst posits four different types of relations between social institutions and education, corresponding to stages of social development. In the first type, the family dominates informal education in the simple pre-literate society, in the second, religion (together with the family, where religion is domestically based) dominates formal education in the theocracy - a church- or priest-dominated society. In the third type, under the national state simple structural relations prevail – 'The society is now unified by the state, which reduces or suppresses divisions due to family and church. The state takes responsibility for the educational system.'[3] Finally, in socialist or neo-capitalist societies complex relations emerge with the state and the economy jointly dominating education. Apart from difficulties of applying this sequential order to educational change in England (where stages three and four are confounded), more serious problems arise in the case of France.

Firstly, while education was certainly integrated with the state in France before the beginning of industrialisation, it may be doubted whether this represented a simple socio–educational relationship. After the bourgeois political elite had succeeded in replacing the church as the educationally dominant group, it initiated changes bringing about three new structural relationships between education and other social institutions. Education was integrated with the political structure through the teaching of citizenship and the general use of instruction for political socialisation. It was integrated with the government bureaucracy through the specialised training given for entry to administrative posts, the founding of special establishments for this purpose, the calibration of degrees given at secondary and higher level with entry requirements and, lastly, the incorporation of the teaching profession into the civil service. Finally, it was integrated with the post-revolutionary system of social stratification, both in its bias at the higher levels towards professional–administrative careers to which the bourgeoisie had better access and a stronger leaning than other sections of society and in the founding of primary instruction, which operated largely as a terminal institution for the mass of the lower classes.

Thus difficulties arise from Havinghurst designating the state as a single 'basic' institution and particularly from not differentiating between the state as political structure and as governmental bureaucracy. Where the two develop conjointly in the pre-industrial economy, as in France, socio–educational relationships may be as complex as those characterising advanced societies, with their close association between the state and the economy. In the same way, the development of a national educational system, comprising all three levels, is not the prerogative of societies which have 'evolved toward greater technological complexity', but can occur in pre-industrial societies where the educationally dominant group perceives the need and possesses the means for its establishment.

Hence there appears to be little justification in regarding simple institutional relationships as universally characteristic of pre-industrial societies and complex relations as necessarily located in the post-industrial period. The endorsement of this dichotomy often appears to depend upon an underlying dichotomous view of education itself in which instruction is seen either as an unproductive luxury or a productive necessity. Thus to Drucker 'Until the twentieth century no society could afford more than a handful of educated people; for throughout the ages to be educated meant to be unproductive . . . The educated person was then still a luxury rather than a necessity, and education a preparation for dignified leisure rather than productive life.'[4] The development of education is linked to economic progress precisely because the only way in which education can be an investment is defined as economic. The case of France is important in showing a dominant group organising public investment in education, not to increase economic productivity, but administrative efficiency.

Industrialisation and education

As has been seen, the thesis that simple and complex structural relations between education and other social institutions correspond to the pre- and post-industrial dichotomy cannot take account of educational development in France. Thus the theory that some aspect of the industrialisation process is crucial for the transition from simple to complex relations cannot be held as universal. However, the possibility remains that while industrialisation is not the exclusive determinant of such educational change, it may be one of a plurality of factors which influence education in this way. In other words, it might be argued that the development of complex relations between education and other social institutions in England was in fact due to some aspect of the industrialisation process. It appears, however, that again there are difficulties in accepting even this modified version of the thesis.

Three fairly distinct versions of this thesis have been applied by different writers to educational development in England. Their common denominator is the proposition that industrialisation resulted in an integration of education with the economy, and through it with other social institutions, but they differ about the precise stage of economic development held responsible for structural change. Firstly, and most infrequently, it has been claimed that the earliest stages of industrialisation provided an impetus for educational growth which culminated in the establishment of an educational system. Thus Bantock states that

undoubtedly one of the basic contributory factors was the *coming* of industrialization and the need to have workmen who could read and calculate if only to understand the instructions relating to the machines they were called on to operate . . .
The process of industrialisation . . . the social, economic and political changes
engendered, induced our society in the nineteenth century to undertake an experiment unique in the history of mankind – the setting up of a *system* of education
intended to lead to universal literacy.[5]

Each of the propositions advanced in this statement seem open to doubt. In the first place, many historians have questioned the industrial imperative for the instruction and training of the *lower* classes, par-
ticularly in the early stages of economic development. Thus, stated most strongly, Thompson claims that as industrialisation proceeded, more and more people had less and less to learn in preparation for their working life.[6] Next, it is extremely difficult to claim that the coming of industrialisation induced the establishment of an educational system unless an extremely long time scale is accepted and additional postulates of 'cultural lag' are introduced. Finally, of course, there was nothing unique in the nineteenth-century English provisions for literacy, these were more thorough and gratuitous in France at an earlier date, not to mention the comparative merits of, for example, the 1870 Japanese reforms.

It is factors of this kind, combined with recognition that 'in the rise of British industry . . . formal education of any sort was a negligible factor in its success'[7] which predispose more writers to the second version of the thesis. Thus both Ashby and Ottaway claim that far from the process of industrialisation prompting educational expansion, this impulsion only arose after the 1851 Exhibition with the fear of *losing* economic supremacy. Thus 'it became clear as the century went on that economic forces would demand an improved educational system'.[8] While this version has the advantage of being able to point to attempted reforms seeking to integrate education more closely with the economy, it again involves a considerable time-lag. Ottaway himself acknowledges that 'by the turn of the century the situation was so bad that thousands of well educated German clerks had to be employed in London offices to carry on the work of commerce'.[9] The need to maintain industrial competitiveness was insufficient to bring about changed structural relations and 'in the late nineteenth century England was still educationally a very underdeveloped society'.[10]

The third version of the thesis argues that it was not the rise of industry itself, but the gradual development of technology which finally accomplished the integration of education with the economy. To the extent that writers make a clear distinction between the 'first' and 'second' Industrial Revolutions, their arguments constitute criticisms of the initial thesis and thus cannot be assimilated to it, but this is not always the case. Where the two factors are clearly differentiated, as in Olive Bank's discussion, explanation is also given for the absence of educational adaptation during the first period of industrialisation.

In pre-industrial societies all such skills are taught 'on the job' . . . Even after industrialisation 'on the job' training has retained its importance, until recently, for many of the lower levels of industrial skills. What characterises an advanced industrial society is the extent to which skills at all levels of the occupational hierarchy are increasingly acquired within formal educational institutions.[11]

In other words, the development of skills, frequently postulated as a demand exerted by the process of industrialism upon formal educational institutions, can be met without adaptation occurring in the latter.

Thus while the case of France indicates that industrialisation is not a necessary condition for the development of complex relations between education and social structure, that of England shows that there is no direct or mechanistic association between economic development and educational change at the macro-sociological level. Correspondingly the plurality of mechanisms advanced as engineering the integration of education with the economy, and through it with other social institutions – changing norms and values, class conflict, the need for technical training etc. – may be contributory factors in some cases, but are clearly not deterministic. Such conclusions tend to be supported by modern research indicating relationships between stage of economic development and amount of educational provision, but a lack of association between the type of education available in countries at the same stage.[12] It appears that increase in national wealth facilities expenditure on educational expansion without imposing clear directives on its form and content.

Industrialisation and institutional secularisation

Despite the existence of historical examples of multiple integration between education and other social institutions, including religion in ancient Chinese and Indian societies, many theorists have posited that increased complexity in the structural relations of education in industrial societies is inseparable from the decline and ultimate exclusion of its former integration with the religious institution. Theories of educational secularisation have generally stressed either the spread of rationality, or of industrialism, or a combination of both as the mechanisms responsible for its occurrence. While it is possible to adduce a variety of eighteenth-century thinkers (including Condorcet) who held institutional secularisation exclusively dependent upon the spread of enlightenment, most of their nineteenth-century successors considered that its diffusion would be stimulated by economic development. Thus to Comte the industrial age represented a quest for physical laws whose positive spirit was the exact opposite of reliance on providence, and, while not initiating it, furthered institutional secularisation. Hence there is a comprehensive body of thought which assigns an important role to industrialisation in the process of institutional secularisation.

It is clear that in relation to the decline of religious control over and sacred symbolic content of instruction in England and France, parallel difficulties confront theories of secularisation based on either pure idealism or pure materialism. Those who simply maintain that the spread of enlightenment corresponds to a simultaneous decline in religious prejudice, immediately reflected in social institutions,[13] are compatible with the establishment of a secular educational system in pre-industrial France. However, they offer no explanation of the endurance of religious domination over education in industrial England, unless this were to be attributed to a lesser diffusion of reason among the population. Similarly theories holding institutional secularisation wholly dependent on industrialisation are logically incapable of accounting for secular education in France and have some problems in explaining its delay in England. Such points, however, are not necessarily damaging for a theory which avoids infrastructural-superstructural imputations, concentrating instead, as does Berger, on the 'dialectical relationship between religion and society'.[14]

To Berger the constant structural–cultural interaction gives rise to a socio–psychological phenomenon such that the 'manifestation of secularisation on the level of consciousness ("subjective secularisation", if one wishes) has its correlate on the socio–structural level (as "objective secularisation"'.[15] However, when dealing with specific historical occurrences of secularisation, the dialectic must be traced throughout the different parts of the time sequence. In analysing secularisation in the West, Berger clearly separates the causes of origin of the phenomenon from the cause of continuation. The causes of origin are multiple, but the cause of continuation is single and located in the process of industrialisation. Thus Berger refers to the 'secularising potency of capitalistic–industrial rationalization'[16] which operates through the need for large cadres of trained personnel whose instruction and organisation presupposes 'a high degree of rationalization, not only on the level of infrastructure but also on that of consciousness'.[17] Statements of this kind are not necessarily incompatible with the acceptance that other processes can operate to the same end. However, it is clear that to Berger rationality and industrialisation are so inextricably linked that 'one may say, with only some exaggeration, that economic data on industrial productivity or capital expansion can predict the religious crisis of credibility in a particular society more easily than data derived from the "history of ideas" of that society'.[18]

In other words, the structural imperatives of industrial production tend to be considered as both necessary and sufficient conditions for institutional secularisation. Certainly Berger admits that this process may be delayed in those social institutions, like the family, which are least involved in the production process, but education cannot be considered one of them, in view of the training functions assigned to it. Yet he appears well aware of the imperfections of this view when used to interpret history. The pre-industrial secular French state and educational system are admitted to run counter to the 'tendency toward the secularisation of the political order that goes naturally with the development of modern industrialism'.[19] Similarly the delayed secularisation of English education cannot be attributed to the differential impact of industry or cultural lag used to account for continued religious practice in the family.

Hence this third and more limited assumption, that one form of institutional relationship – the integration of education with religion – is precluded by industrialism and by this process rather than others, shares the difficulties encountered by the previous two propositions. Educational secularisation neither appears to be dependent upon economic development nor to be a direct consequence of it, since the former view over-restricts the types of institutional relationships in which the integration of education with religion is excluded, while the latter over-emphasises the necessity of this exclusion under certain economic conditions. Instead the secularisation of education appears as the result of complex processes less closely associated with the infrastructure, and the increase of rationalism in instruction responsive to aims less narrow than those of production. While the impact of industrialisation on educational change at the macro-sociological level has been exaggerated, the rationalising influence of bureaucratisation has remained largely unexplored.

Notes

Authors' Note. Unless otherwise stated all translations from French sources are provided by the authors.

Chapter 1 : Introduction

1 J. Floud and A. H. Halsey, 'The Sociology of Education', *Current Sociology*, VII (1958), 170.
2 *Ibid.* p. 169.
3 *Ibid.* p. 187.
4 For a fuller discussion, see M. Scotford Archer and M. Vaughan, 'Education, Secularization, Desecularization and Re-secularization', in D. Martin and M. Hill (eds.), *A Sociological Yearbook of Religion in Britain* (London, 1970).
5 P. L. Berger, *The Social Reality of Religion* (London, 1969).
6 T. Parsons, 'The School Class as a Social System: Some of its Functions in American Society', in A. H. Halsey, J. Floud and C. A. Anderson (eds.), *Education, Economy and Society* (London, 1967), p. 434.
7 M. D. Shipman, *Sociology of the School* (London, 1968), p. 3.
8 *Ibid.* p. 9.
9 *Ibid.*
10 R. H. Turner, 'Modes of Social Ascent through Education: Sponsored and Contest Mobility', in Halsey *et al.*, *Education, Economy and Society*, p. 122.
11 *Ibid.* p. 128.
12 *Ibid.* p. 122.
13 Shipman, *Sociology of the School*, p. 10.
14 K. Marx, *Critique of Political Economy* (Stone ed., New York, 1904), pp. 11–12.
15 K. Marx, *German Ideology* (Pascal ed., London, 1938), p. 39.
16 R. Aron, *Main Currents in Sociological Thought*, I (London, 1968), 160.
17 G. Leff, *The Tyranny of Concepts* (London, 1961), pp. 130–1.
18 A. MacIntyre, *Secularization and Moral Change* (Oxford, 1967), p. 20.
19 Marx, *German Ideology* (p. 39): 'The ideas of the ruling class are in every epoch the ruling ideas: i.e. the class which is the ruling material force of society is at the same time its ruling intellectual force. The class which has the means of material production at its disposal, has control at the same time over the means of mental production, so that thereby, generally speaking, the ideas of those who lack the means of mental production are subject to it.'
20 A. H. Halsey, 'The Changing Function of Universities', in Halsey *et al.*, *Education, Economy and Society*, p. 458.
21 *Ibid.* p. 457.
22 *Ibid.* p. 458.

Chapter 2: Domination and Assertion

1 H. H. Gerth and C. Wright Mills (eds.), *From Max Weber: Essays in Sociology* (London, 1967), pp. 426–7.
2 *Ibid.* p. 426.
3 *Ibid.* p. 243.
4 *Ibid.* p. 241.
5 *Ibid.* p. 243.
6 *Ibid.*
7 Cf. Max Weber, *Basic Concepts in Sociology* (London, 1962), p. 117: 'By *domination* is meant the opportunity to have a command of a given specified content obeyed by a given group of persons.'
8 Gerth and Wright Mills, *From Max Weber*, p. 181.
9 J. Freund, *The Sociology of Max Weber* (London, 1968), pp. 154–5.
10 Gerth and Wright Mills, *From Max Weber*, pp. 190–1.
11 Weber, *Basic Concepts in Sociology*, p. 119.
12 Cf. Gerth and Wright Mills, *From Max Weber*, p. 183: 'Communal action refers to that action which is oriented to the feeling of the actors that they belong together. Societal action, on the other hand, is oriented to a rationally motivated adjustment of interest.'
13 Cf. R. Bendix, *Max Weber. An Intellectual Portrait* (London, 1960), p. 296, n. 16.
14 *Ibid.* p. 297.
15 *Ibid.* p. 267.
16 M. Kolinsky, *Ideology, Organization and Conflict in Social Movements* (Univ. of Birmingham mimeographed publication, 1968), p. 10.
17 F. Clarke, *Education and Social Change* (London, 1940), p. 6.

Chapter 3: Change in English Primary Education

1 Cf. J. H. Adamson, *English Education, 1789–1902* (Cambridge, 1964), p. 18.
2 Cf. H. B. Binns, *A Century of Education, Being the Centenary History of the British and Foreign School Society (1808–1908)* (London, 1908).
3 Select Committee on the Education of the Lower Orders in the Metropolis, appointed 1816, but terms of reference eventually included the whole country.
4 Cf. Binns, *Century of Education*.
5 Cf. H. C. Barnard, *A Short History of English Education (1760–1944)* (London, 1955).
6 Hannah More, quoted in M. T. Hodgen, *Workers' Education in England and the United States* (London, 1925), p. 30.
7 Cf. Binns, *Century of Education*.
8 Cf. G. Wallas, *The Life of Francis Place* (London, 1898), ch. 4.
9 Devised by A. Bell and described by him in *An Experiment in Education made at the Male (Orphan) Asylum in Madras, suggesting a System by which a School or Family may teach itself under the superintendence of the Master or Parent*, 2nd ed. (London, 1809).
10 Cf. M. Tylecote, *The Mechanics' Institutes of Lancashire and Yorkshire before 1851* (Manchester, 1957).
11 Cf. Wallas, *Life of Francis Place*, p. 268.

12 *Ibid.* p. 161.
13 Cf. A. Aspinall, *Politics and the Press, 1780–1850* (London, 1949).
14 Cf. C. Knight, *Passages of a Working Life* (3 vols., London, 1864–73).
15 Cf. R. K. Webb, *The British Working Class Reader, 1780–1848* (London, 1955), p. 142f.
16 G. M. Trevelyan, *English Social History*, 2nd ed. (London, 1946), p. 543.
17 Quoted by J. de Montmorency, *State Intervention in English Education* (Cambridge, 1902), p. 330.
18 *Ibid.* pp. 325–57.
19 J. Kay-Shuttleworth, 'The Moral and Physical Condition of the Working Classes of Manchester in 1832', in *Four Periods of English Education* (London, 1862), p. 39.
20 Trevelyan, *English Social History*, p. 401.
21 *Ibid.* p. 518.
22 Quoted by Wallas, *Life of Francis Place*, p. 20.
23 Trevelyan, *English Social History*, p. 479. In 1824, 1,500 workmen subscribed a guinea per year to the London Institute (p. 486).
24 *Mechanics' Magazine*, 11 October 1823.

Chapter 4: Change in English Secondary and Higher Education

1 Adamson, *English Education*, p. 44.
2 According to the Schism Act of 1713.
3 Except in Scottish universities.
4 V. Knox, *Remarks on the tendency of certain clauses in a Bill now pending in Parliament to degrade Grammar Schools*, 2nd ed. (London, 1821), p. 256.
5 Cf. W. F. Hastings, 'The Education of English Catholics (1559–1800)', London University thesis (unpublished), 1923.
6 Adamson, *English Education*, pp. 47–8.
7 Under the Clarendon Code in the seventeenth and eighteenth centuries.
8 Cf. F. Pritchard, *Methodist Secondary Education* (London, 1949), p. 187f.
9 Cf. H. C. Maxwell-Lyte, *A History of Eton College* (London, 1899), p. 388f.
10 B. Darwin, *The English Public School* (London, 1929), p. 8.
11 S. Butler, *Life and Letters of Samuel Butler* (2 vols., London, 1896), I, 38.
12 Cf. Darwin, *English Public School*, p. 136.
13 E. Thring, *Education and School* (Cambridge, 1864), p. 94.
14 Cf. K. E. Kirk, *The Story of the Woodard Schools* (London, 1937).
15 W. R. Ward, *Victorian Oxford* (London, 1965), p. xiii.
16 Whereby only those who subscribed to the Thirty-nine Articles were allowed entry to Oxford or graduation in Cambridge.
17 M. Pattison, *Memoirs* (London, 1885), pp. 74–5.
18 Cf. J. Sparrow, *Mark Pattison and the Idea of a University* (Cambridge, 1967), ch. 3.
19 *Quarterly Journal of Education*, VII, no. 14 (April 1834).
20 Sir William Hamilton, 'On the State of the English Universities', in *Edinburgh Review*, LIII, no. 106 (1831), 386f.
21 *Westminster Review*, XV, no. 29 (July 1831).
22 Harriet Grote, *The Personal Life of George Grote*, 2nd ed. (London, 1873), p. 56.

23 A. Bain, *James Mill* (London, 1882), p. 357.
24 Ward, *Victorian Oxford*, p. 80.
25 Hamilton, 'On the State of the English Universities', p. 384.
26 *Ibid.*
27 *Ibid.* p. 386.
28 Published in 1831, and followed by *The Legality of the Present Academical System of the University of Oxford Reasserted* (1832).
29 Cf. W. Whewell, *On the Right Principles of English University Education* (London, 1837).
30 W. Sewell, *Thoughts on the Admission of Dissenters to the University of Oxford* (Oxford, 1834), p. 96.
31 Cf. J. H. Newman, *Idea of a University* (London, 1893).
32 Pattison, *Memoirs*, p. 101.
33 G. Faber, *Jowett* (London, 1957), p. 195.
34 *Ibid.* p. 190.
35 *Ibid.* p. 197.
36 *Ibid.*
37 Cited by Faber, *Jowett*, p. 198.
38 Sewell, quoted by Ward, *Victorian Oxford*, p. 158.
39 Faber, *Jowett*, p. 197.
40 Cf. Ward, *Victorian Oxford*, p. 150f.

Chapter 5 : Assertive Ideologies in English Education

1 Cf. P. Hazard, *La Pensée européenne au 18ᵉ siècle de Montesquieu à Lessing* (Paris, 1946), I, 240.
2 Cf. M. Weulersse, *Le Mouvement physiocratique en France (1756–1770)* (Paris, 1910).
3 F. Quesnay, 'Droit naturel', in E. Daire (ed.), *Les Physiocrates* (Paris, 1846), p. 55.
4 P. Le Mercier de la Rivière, 'L'Ordre naturel et essentiel des sociétés politiques', in Daire, *Physiocrates*, p. 615.
5 Cf. N. Baudeau, 'L'Introduction à la philosophie économique', in Daire, *Physiocrates*, p. 820.
6 Cf. Mercier de la Rivière, 'L'Ordre naturel', p. 617.
7 *An Inquiry into the Nature and Causes of the Wealth of Nations* (Cannan ed., 2 vols., London, 1904), vol. 2, bk 4, ch. 9, p. 176.
8 *Ibid.* vol. 1, bk 2, ch. 3, pp. 323–4.
9 Cf. *ibid.* vol. 1, bk 7, ch. 1, p. 6.
10 *Ibid.* vol. 2, bk 5, ch. 1, p. 267.
11 *Ibid.* vol. 2, bk 5, ch. 1, p. 273.
12 B. Simon, *Studies in the History of Education, 1780–1870* (London, 1960), p. 139.
13 D. Ricardo, *The Principles of Political Economy* (Gonner ed., London, 1891), p. 179.
14 Cf. E. Halévy, *Le Radicalisme philosophique* (Paris, 1904), p. 54: 'By a historical accident (Ricardo) happens to be the representative, the theoretician and the spokesman of an occupationally optimistic class: the great English industrialists who dream of the economic conquest of the world.'

15 Cf. T. Malthus, *First Essay on Population* (Bonar ed., London, 1926), p. 79: 'I cannot by means of money raise a poor man and enable him to live much better than he did before, without proportionably depressing others in the same class.'

16 *Ibid.* p. 95: 'To remove the wants of the lower classes of society is indeed an arduous task. The truth is that the pressure of distress on this part of a community is an evil so deep seated that no human ingenuity can reach it.'

17 *Ibid.* p. 368. Nevertheless the same numerical restriction should not apply to the more enlightened section of society: 'Though we cannot possibly expect to exclude riches and poverty from society, yet if we could find out a mode of government by which the numbers in the extreme regions would be lessened, and the numbers in the middle regions increased, it would be undoubtedly our duty to adopt it.'

18 Bain, *James Mill*, pp. 88–9: Bentham 'made use of the Deity, as Napoleon wished to make use of the Pope, for sanctioning whatever he himself chose, in the name of Utility, to prescribe'. This is seen in his comment 'the divine will cannot require anything inconsistent with general Utility' (J. Bentham, *Church of Englandism, and its Catechism examined* (London, 1818). See also *Not Paul but Jesus* (London, 1823). Bentham cautiously proclaimed himself a deist, while maintaining the position of an anti-clerical.

19 James Mill, 'On Education', in F. A. Cavenagh, *James and John Stuart Mill on Education* (Cambridge, 1931), p. 60.

20 *Ibid.* p. 5: 'Nor can education assume its most perfect form till the science of the human mind has reached its highest point of improvement.'

21 *Ibid.* p. 23: 'It thus appears that the science of ethics . . . must be carried to perfection, before the best foundation is obtained for the science of education.'

22 *Ibid.* p. 53.

23 *Ibid.* p. 23.

24 *Ibid.*

25 *Ibid.* p. 29: 'Those peculiarities, if any such there be, which sink a man below, or elevate him above the ordinary state of aptitude to profit by education, have no operation in the case of large numbers, or bodies.'

26 *Ibid.*

27 *Ibid.* p. 58.

28 In domestic education 'the habits, which are then contracted, are the most pervading and operative of all' (*ibid.* p. 43).

29 In social education 'inducements, operating upon us continually, have an irresistible influence in creating habits, and in moulding, that is, educating into a character conformable to the society in which we move' (*ibid.* p. 71).

30 *Ibid.* p. 61.

31 *Ibid.* p. 62.

32 *Ibid.*

33 *Ibid.* p. 66.

34 Letter to Brougham quoted by Bain, *James Mill*, p. 364.

35 *Ibid.* p. 365.

36 *Ibid.* p. 321.

37 According to Bain, *James Mill*, the franchise arrangements of the 1832 Reform Bill represented James Mill's ideal. Education of the lower orders must always

precede enfranchisement and hence 'he differed from the Cobbetts and the Hunts, in taking securities against ignorance and brutality' (p. 446).

38 *The Works of J. Bentham* (Bowring ed., Edinburgh, 1838–43), VIII, 24.

39 Cf. J. Bentham, *Traités de législation civile et pénale* (London, 1858), pt I, ch. 11.

40 Cf. J. S. Mill, *On Liberty*, 2nd ed. (London, 1859), p. 194: '. . . to produce children beyond a very small number, with the effect of reducing the reward of labour by their competition, is a serious offence against all who live by the remuneration of their labour'.

41 F. Engels, *The Condition of the Working Class in England in 1844* (London, 1892), p. 114.

42 The way in which J. S. Mill designated the middle class itself: cf. Cavenagh, *J. and J. S. Mill on Education*, p. 174.

43 Simon, *Studies in the History of Education*, p. 278.

44 P. Holbach, *Système social* (Amsterdam, 1773), I, 12.

45 A. Helvétius, *Œuvres* (4 vols., The Hague, 1773), II, 183.

46 D. Fleisher, *William Godwin: a Study in Liberalism* (London, 1951), p. 63.

47 W. Godwin, *Enquiry Concerning Political Justice and its Influence on Morals and Happiness* (London, 1793 ed.), bk 2, p. 473.

48 *Ibid.* bk 1, p. 49.

49 W. Godwin, *The Enquirer* (London, 1797), p. 24: 'Genius is wisdom; the possession of a great store of ideas, together with the facility in calling them up, and the peculiar discernment in their selection or rejection.'

50 *Ibid.* p. 36.

51 *Political Justice* (1796 ed.), bk 1, p. 51.

52 *Ibid.* bk 1, p. 244.

53 Cf. Fleisher, *William Godwin*, p. 87: 'The ultimate goal of this long process is anarchism; an intermediate political stage is democracy.'

54 *Political Justice* (1793 ed.), bk 1, p. 158.

55 Cf. J. A. Preu, *The Dean and the Anarchist* (Florida, 1959).

56 *Political Justice* (1793 ed.), bk 1, p. 215.

57 W. Godwin, *Thoughts on Man, his Nature, Productions and Discoveries* (London, 1831), p. 373.

58 *Political Justice* (1798 ed.), bk 6, p. 302.

59 *Ibid.* bk 6, p. 300.

60 *Political Justice* (1793 ed.), bk 1, p. 35.

61 T. Hodgskin, *Labour defended against the claims of Capital or the Unproductiveness of Capital with Reference to the present Combinations amongst Journeymen* (Cole ed., London, 1922), p. 89.

62 *Ibid.* p. 92.

63 *Ibid.* p. 102.

64 E. Halévy, *L'Évolution de la doctrine utilitaire de 1789 à 1815* (Paris, 1901), p. 235: 'The tradition of Helvétius is perpetuated . . . by Robert Owen, to whom it was transmitted by William Godwin.'

65 Title-page of R. Owen's *A new view of Society*, 1st ed. (London, 1813).

66 R. Owen, *The Life of Robert Owen (by himself)* (London, 1857), I, 285.

67 R. Owen, *Report to the county of Lanark of a plan for removing public distress* (Glasgow, 1832), p. 46.

68 E. Dolléans, *Robert Owen* (Paris, 1905), pp. 25–37.

69 Four of the six points of the Charter appeared in J. Cartwright's *Take your Choice* in 1776. Cf. E. Dolléans, *Le Chartisme (1830–1848)* (Paris, 1912).
70 F. E. Gillespie, *Labour and Politics in England (1850–1867)* (Durham, N. Carolina, 1927), p. 17.
71 W. Lovett, quoted by R. H. Tawney, *The Radical Tradition* (London, 1964), p. 21.
72 W. Lovett and J. Collins, *Chartism: a new organisation of the people* (London, 1840), p. 67.
73 *Ibid.* p. 63.
74 *Ibid.* p. 70.
75 *Ibid.* p. 73.
76 *The Life and Struggles of W. Lovett* (Tawney ed., London, 1920), I, 134.
77 *Ibid.* I, 99.
78 *Ibid.* II, 384.
79 *Ibid.* I, 139.
80 *Ibid.* II, 439f.
81 Lovett and Collins, *Chartism*, p. 73.
82 *Life and Struggles of Lovett*, introduction by R. H. Tawney, p. xxvii.
83 Cf. Dolléans, *Le Chartisme*.
84 Cf. A. R. Schoyen, *The Chartist Challenge: a Portrait of George Julian Harney* (London, 1958), p. 55.
85 *Northern Star* (24 March 1838).
86 Cf. J. B. O'Brien, *Life and Character of Maximilian Robespierre* (London, 1837), p. 276f.
87 *Northern Liberator* (28 December 1838).
88 *The Red Republican* (June–December 1850) (Harney, editor).
89 *Northern Star* (12 September 1846).

Chapter 6: Defensive Ideologies of Anglican Domination

1 A. O. J. Cockshut, *Anglican Attitudes* (London, 1959), p. 15.
2 *Ibid.* p. 47.
3 Cf. D. Voll, *Catholic Evangelicalism* (London, 1963).
4 G. Faber, *Oxford Apostles* (London, 1954), p. 81.
5 Fernande Tardivel, *J.H.Newman, éducateur* (Paris, 1937), p. 95.
6 Newman, *Idea of a University*, p. 114.
7 *Ibid.* p. 120.
8 *Ibid.* p. 104.
9 *Ibid.* p. 152.
10 *Ibid.* p. 120.
11 *Ibid.* p. 108.
12 *Ibid.* p. x.
13 J. H. Newman, *University Sketches* (Tierney ed., Dublin, 1952), p. 10.
14 Newman, *Idea of a University*, p. 20.
15 *Ibid.* p. 42.
16 *Ibid.* pp. 72–3.
17 *Ibid.* p. 36.
18 *Ibid.* p. 25.

19 *Ibid.* p. 42.
20 *Ibid.* p. 72.
21 *Ibid.* p. 53.
22 *Ibid.* p. 97.
23 *Ibid.* p. 431.
24 *Ibid.* p. 434.
25 *Ibid.* pp. 432–3.
26 *Ibid.* p. 454.
27 R. L. Archer, *Secondary Education in the Nineteenth Century* (Cambridge, 1921), p. 40.
28 *Ibid.*
29 M. Tierney, intro. to Newman, *University Sketches*, p. xvii.
30 Newman, *Idea of a University*, p. 227.
31 *Ibid.* p. 215.
32 *Ibid.* p. 216.
33 *Ibid.* p. ix.
34 T. W. Bamford, *Thomas Arnold* (London, 1960), p. 57.
35 R. W. Church, *The Oxford Movement : twelve years (1833–1845)* (London, 1891), p. 6.
36 Bamford, *Thomas Arnold*, p. 65.
37 T. Arnold, *Principles of Church Reform* (London, 1833), p. 88.
38 Cf. S. T. Coleridge, *On the Constitution of Church and State* (London, 1852).
39 J. Fitch, *Thomas and Matthew Arnold and their Influence on English Education* (London, 1897), p. 141.
40 Arnold, *Principles of Church Reform*, p. 125.
41 T. Arnold, quoted by Fitch, *Thomas and Matthew Arnold*, p. 140.
42 T. Arnold, *Miscellaneous Works* (London, 1845), p. 372. (Letter to the *Sheffield Courant*, published as 'The Education of the Middle Classes'.)
43 Arnold, Second Letter to the *Sheffield Courant*, 1832, published as 'The Social Condition of the Operative Classes', in *Miscellaneous Works*, p. 421.
44 Arnold, Sermon XXIII, in *ibid.*
45 A. P. Stanley, *Life and Correspondence of Thomas Arnold* (London, 1846), p. 79.
46 Letter to a Sheffield Friend (6.12.1837).
47 Bamford, *Thomas Arnold*, p. 152.
48 Arnold, Seventh Letter to the *Sheffield Courant*, published as 'The Social Condition of the Operative Classes', in *Miscellaneous Works*, p. 481.
49 Arnold, Tenth Letter to the *Sheffield Courant*, ibid. p. 431.
50 Quoted by J. J. Findlay, *Arnold of Rugby* (Cambridge, 1898), p. 199.
51 Stanley, *Life and Correspondence of Thomas Arnold*, p. 83.
52 T. Arnold, *Sermons* (6 vols., London, 1878), vol. 5, no. 8 ('Education and Instruction').
53 Stanley, *Life and Correspondence of Thomas Arnold*, p. 83.
54 Quoted by Findlay, *Arnold of Rugby*, p. 35.
55 *Ibid.*
56 Letter to W. Empson, 1837, quoted by Findlay, *ibid.* p. 34.
57 Fitch, *Thomas and Matthew Arnold*, p. 132.
58 *Ibid.* p. 33.
59 Quoted by Bamford, *Thomas Arnold*, p. 122.

60 Fitch, *Thomas and Mattehw Arnold*, p. 75.
61 *Ibid*. p. 128.
62 *Ibid*.
63 *Ibid*.
64 Letter to the *Sheffield Courant*, 1831, in *Miscellaneous Works*, p. 475.
65 *Ibid*.
66 Quoted by Findlay, *Arnold of Rugby*, p. 203.
67 *Ibid*. p. 201.
68 J. H. Newman, *Apologia pro Vita sua* (London, 1878), p. 214.
69 Faber, *Oxford Apostles*, pp. 397–8.
70 Simon, *Studies in theHistory of Education*, p. 289.

Chapter 7 : Change in French Primary Education

1 Religious schools were not uniformly free, though the contribution of the local community varied. Sometimes a religious order ran the school, while in other places the local priest did so, or the bishop of the region certified a lay teacher. Cf. A. Léaud and E. Glay, *L'École primaire en France, ses origines, ses différents aspects au cours des siècles, ses victoires, sa mission dans les démocraties* (Paris, 1934); and A. Babeau, *L'Instruction primaire dans les campagnes avant 1789* (Paris, 1875).
2 Cf. M. Gontard, *L'Enseignement primaire en France de la Révolution à la loi Guizot (1789–1833)* (Lyon, 1959), p. 52f.
3 Voltaire, *Correspondance* (Garnier ed., Paris, 1883), no. 6296.
4 Gontard, *L'Enseignement primaire en France*, p. 187.
5 G. de Mirabeau, *Travail sur l'éducation publique* (found in his papers by Cabanis) (Paris, 1791).
6 A. Duruy, *L'Instruction publique et la Révolution* (Paris, 1882), p. 74f.
7 Cf. C. Hippeau, *La Révolution et l'éducation nationale* (Paris, 1883).
8 M. Lepelletier de St Fargeau, *Plan d'éducation nationale (présenté aux Jacobins par son frère* (Paris, 1793), p. 7.
9 *Ibid*. p. 36.
10 G. Compayré, *Histoire des doctrines de l'éducation en France* (Paris, 1879), p. 349.
11 Following a plan of Bouquier's, compulsory, free and useful primary instruction was introduced on 29 Frimaire An II (19.12.1793) which was in force until the Ninth Thermidor. After the fall of Robespierre, Lakanal became president of the Committee of Public Instruction of the Convention and a project was voted on 27 Brumaire An III (17.11.1794) establishing a primary school per thousand inhabitants, with separate sections for the two sexes; school attendance was theoretically compulsory and any citizen (including former priests) was allowed to teach. The last educational law of the Convention was the decree of 3rd Brumaire An IV (25.10.1795), based on a plan by Lakanal and Daunou, according to which primary education would be neither compulsory nor gratuitous, and its content would be limited to reading and writing. Schools could be opened either by local authorities or by individuals, without limitation. Cf. J. C. Dawson, *Lakanal the Regicide* (Alabama, 1948); and J. Gros, *Lakanal et l'éducation nationale* (Paris, 1912).

12 A. Delfau, *Napoléon Ier et l'instruction publique* (Paris, 1902), p. 7.
13 Cf. A. Chevalier, *Les Frères des écoles chrétiennes et l'enseignement primaire après la Révolution (1797-1830)* (Paris, 1887).
14 A. Aulard, *Napoléon Ier et le monopole universitaire* (Paris, 1911), p. 242.
15 Chevalier, *Les Frères des écoles chrétiennes*, p. 164f.
16 R. Sevrin, *Histoire de l'enseignement primaire en France sous le Révolution, le Consulat et l'Émpire* (Paris, 1932), p. 25.
17 Cf. Chevalier, *Les Frères des écoles chrétiennes*, p. 369.
18 Comte de Lasteyrie, *Nouveau système d'éducation et d'enseignement ou enseignement mutuel appliqué aux langues, aux sciences et aux arts* (Paris, 1819).
19 Teachers were to be examined by university inspectors (*inspecteurs d'académie*) and granted a certificate of proficiency; a certificate of morality, issued by the mayor and the parish priest, was also required. They were under the joint supervision of mayor and priest. Special provisions were made for Protestant schools and for those run by religious orders, whose members were granted certificates of proficiency by the university upon producing a letter from their superior. The state undertook to give a permanent grant towards the cost of primary education.
20 Gontard, *L'Enseignement primaire en France*, p. 305.
21 *Ibid.* p. 358.
22 The ordinance of 1824 was reactionary in inspiration and increased the administrative and disciplinary power of the church over primary-school teachers. That of 1828 marked a return to the system of 1816 (*ibid.* p. 363f.). At the end of the Restoration, there were some 27,000 religious primary schools.
23 There was to be one primary school per *commune* and primary school teachers were to be divided into three categories, with pension rights attached.
24 Cf. A. Emile-Sorel, *Conférence sur Guizot* (Rouen, 1914), p. 16.
25 E. Labrousse, G. Bourgin, E. Dolléans, *La Pensée ouvrière sur l'éducation* (Paris, n.d.), p. 27.
26 V. Cousin, *Défense de l'université et de la philosophie*, 3rd ed. (Paris, 1844), p. 6.
27 O. Gréard, *Éducation et instruction* (2 vols., Paris, 1887), I, 140.
28 *Ibid.* I, 59.
29 According to this law there was to be a primary school per *commune* and a higher grade (*primaire supérieur*) school in the main town of each *département* and each town of 6,000 inhabitants or more. In the latter some scholarships were granted by competitive examination. The cost of primary education was covered by municipal and departmental funds, with state subventions in the case of need. Inspection was performed by local committees including the mayor and the parish priest.
30 F. Guizot, *Essai sur l'histoire et sur l'état actuel de l'instruction publique en France* (Paris, 1816), p. 4f.
31 Cf. P. Janet, *Victor Cousin et son oeuvre* (Paris, 1885), about Cousin's studies of the Prussian and the Dutch educational systems as a basis for reform in France. Cf. also V. Cousin, *De l'instruction publique dans quelques pays de l'Allemagne et particulièrement en Prusse*, 3rd ed. (2 vols., Paris, 1840).
32 J. Simon, *Victor Cousin*, 4th ed. (Paris, 1910), p. 107.

Chapter 8: Change in French Secondary and Higher Education

1 F. Ponteil, *Histoire de l'enseignement en France, 1789–1964* (Paris, 1966), p. 21.
2 There were ten *collèges de plein exercise* in Paris in 1789 (cf. Gréard, *Éducation et instruction*, vol. I).
3 There were approximately 600 colleges in all, 124 of them run by the Jesuits. Cf. A. Dansette, *Religious History of Modern France* (3 vols, Freiburg, 1961), vol. I.
4 The Jesuits' attachment to Latin reflected their conviction that national languages favoured the propagation of heresies and their opposition to Gallicanism.
5 F. Vial, *Trois siècles d'histoire de l'enseignement secondaire* (Paris, 1936), p. 48.
6 Ponteil, *Histoire de l'enseignement*, p. 34f.
7 *Ibid.* p. 43.
8 C. Falcucci, *L'Humanisme dans l'enseignement secondaire en France au 19e siècle* (Toulouse, 1939), p. 56.
9 Ponteil, *Histoire de l'enseignement*, p. 32.
10 *Ibid.* p. 46.
11 Mirabeau, *Travail sur l'éducation publique*, p. 12.
12 These were to be boarding schools for pupils from ten years of age, teaching Greek and Latin for two years, eloquence and poetry for two years, physics and philosophy for two years (*ibid.* p. 53).
13 In which studies were to last three years and cover grammar, classical and modern languages, mathematics and science, universal history and economics (*ibid.* p. 108f.).
14 Schools of engineering, civil engineering, naval schools, medical schools and law schools, temporarily maintained.
15 Cf. Duruy, *L'Instruction publique et la Révolution*, p. 74f.
16 Cf. Condorcet, *Rapport et projet de décret sur l'organisation générale de l'instruction publique* (Paris, 1792), p. 17f.
17 N. Hentz, Deputy for the Moselle, *Sur l'instruction publique*, speech made before the Convention in 1792, p. 1.
18 Cf. the blueprints presented by Romme, 20 October 1793 and Bouquier enacted on 29 Frimaire An II (19 December 1793).
19 Law of 7 Ventôse An III (25 February 1795).
20 Law of 3 Brumaire An IV (25 October 1795).
21 Falcucci, *L'Humanisme dans l'enseignement secondaire*, p. 82.
22 S. F. Lacroix, *Essais sur l'enseignement en général et sur celui des mathématiques en particulier* (Paris, 1805), p. 64.
23 Vial, *Trois siècles d'histoire de l'enseignement secondaire*, pp. 93–4.
24 *Ibid.*
25 Ponteil, *Histoire de l'enseignement*, p. 91.
26 J. Quincherat, *Histoire de Sainte-Barbe* (3 vols., Paris, 1864), III, 162.
27 M. Cournot, *Des Institutions d'instruction publique en France* (Paris, 1864), p. 271.
28 Cf. L. Liard, *L'Enseignement supérieur en France, 1789–1889* (2 vols., Paris, 1888), II, 18f.
29 École Polytechnique, Museum, Langues orientales, three schools of medicine and three of pharmacy – corresponding to two main requirements, the need to preserve rare forms of knowledge, and to foster skills essential to public well being. Cf. G. Pinet, *Histoire de l'École Polytechnique* (Paris, 1887).

30 Liard, *L'Enseignement supérieur en France*, II, 1.

31 *Ibid.* II, 12. The main projects were drawn up by Chaptal and Fourcroy.

32 Ponteil, *Histoire de l'enseignement*, p. 104.

33 The members of the teaching profession became civil servants whose training was to be given by the state and whose hierarchy corresponded to that of the army. After the creation of École Normale in 1808, prospective teachers were admitted to it from the *lycées* by competitive examination and had, on graduation, to undertake ten years of service to the state. The head of this profession and of the Imperial University had the title of *grand maître* and was personally responsible to the Emperor.

34 There were three main degrees: *baccalauréat* (successful completion of secondary studies), *licence* (successful completion of university course) and *doctorat* (successful completion of a thesis). These could be granted either by the faculties of *lettres* (arts) or of *sciences*. The remaining faculties – medicine, law and after 1808 theology – only granted degrees higher than the *baccalauréat*. Within the present boundaries of France there were 22 faculties of *lettres*, 9 of *sciences*, 8 of law, 3 of medicine and 7 of Catholic theology. Even when located in the same town, the various faculties were not inter-related.

35 Aulard, *Napoléon Ier et le monopole universitaire*, p. 305.

36 Private schools had to send their pupils to the *lycées* for some courses, they were not allowed to have a special uniform or to receive boarders after the age of nine.

37 Aulard, *Napoléon Ier et le monopole universitaire*, p. 369. According to Dansette (*Religious History of Modern France*, I, 147), at the end of the Empire, 18,000 pupils attended church secondary schools as against 35,000 in *lycées* and *collèges*.

38 A Committee of Public Instruction took over the powers of the *grand maître* and overall control pertained to the Minister of the Interior.

39 17 faculties of *lettres* and 3 faculties of science were abolished.

40 The Ordinance of 27 February 1821 defined religion as the basis of education. In 1822 a bishop became head of the university. Religious practice was expected from members of the teaching profession, those who did not conform being dismissed.

41 Faculties in Paris and the provinces were suspended for re-organisation and their syllabuses expurgated of subjects associated with secularism (e.g. economics, politics). École Normale was closed in 1822 because in the terms of the Ordinance of 6 September 1822 it was *entièrement detachée de la religion* (completely separated from religion).

42 Cf. L. Grimaud, *Histoire de la liberté d'enseignement en France depuis la chute de l'ancien régime jusqu'à nos jours* (Grenoble, 1898), p. 250f. The following plans were submitted to Parliament: Guizot in 1836, Cousin in 1840, Villemain in 1841 and again in 1844, Salvandy in 1846. All of these failed, either because the Cabinet fell (in 1836 and 1840) or because of parliamentary opposition – largely prompted by the fear of clericalism and of the Jesuits.

Chapter 9: Assertive French Educational Ideologies

1 Gallicanism designated a doctrine defending the liberties of the Catholic church of France and emphasising the role of the Council at the expense of papal

authority. It makes a strong distinction between spiritual and temporal power of Rome. Its main tenets were embodied in the declaration of the French clergy in 1682, drawn up by Bossuet and entitled, 'Declaration des quatre articles'.

2 Cf. Ponteil, *Histoire de l'enseignement*, p. 32, on the Jesuits' attempts to strengthen their educational position.

3 Diderot, 'Plan d'une université pour le gouvernement de Russie ou d'une éducation publique dans toutes les sciences, 1775–76', in *Œuvres complètes* (Assezat–Tourneux ed., Paris, 1875), III.

4 On the eve of the Revolution, there were thirteen, due to the creation of a Parliament in Nancy in 1775. Cf. M. Langrod, 'Stanislas Leszczynski, souverain nominal, philosophe politique et administrateur bienfaisant en Lorraine' (unpublished thesis, University of Paris, 1954).

5 D. Mornet, *La Pensée philosophique au 18e siècle* (Paris, 1956), p. 61.

6 Cf. J. Oestreicher, *La Pensée politique et économique de Diderot* (Paris, 1936).

7 Diderot, quoted by Oestreicher, *ibid.* p. 36.

8 Diderot, 'Plan d'une université', p. 510.

9 *Ibid.* p. 38.

10 Cf. Diderot, quoted by M. Tourneux, *Diderot et Catherine II* (Paris, 1899), p. 298: 'un pays est menacé des plus grands désastres, où, toute la théologie n'est pas réduite à deux pages'.

11 Diderot, 'Plan d'une unversité', p. 517.

12 Diderot, quoted by Mornet, *La Pensée philosophique*, p. 103.

13 Cf. H. Gillot, *Denis Diderot* (Paris, 1937), p. 41.

14 Diderot, 'Plan d'une université', p. 38.

15 G. Compayré, *Histoire des doctrines de l'éducation*, p. 205.

16 Cf. E. Caro, *La Fin du 18e siècle* (2 vols., Paris, 1880), I, 268–72.

17 Diderot, *Œuvres complètes*, I, 12.

18 Diderot, 'Plan d'une université', p. 441.

19 Cf. Caro, *La Fin du 18e siècle*, pp. 255–6.

20 Diderot, quoted by Caro, *ibid.* p. 254.

21 Cf. Diderot, 'Plan d'une université', p. 417f.

22 Cf. Compayré, *Histoire des doctrines de l'éducation*, p. 203.

23 Cf. Tourneux, *Diderot et Catherine II*, p. 366.

24 *Ibid.* pp. 332–3.

25 Diderot, 'Plan d'une université', p. 418.

26 *Ibid.* p. 443. Even elementary knowledge should be proportional to future occupation in life.

27 Compayré, *Histoire des doctrines de l'éducation*, pp. 204–5.

28 Another project was presented by Guyton de Morveau to the Parliament of Burgundy in 1764, whereas La Chalotais advanced his in 1763 and Rolland in 1768. Guyton's blueprint is both less original and less elaborate than the other two. Cf. L. B. Guyton de Morveau, *Mémoire sur l'éducation publique, avec le prospectus d'un collège* (n.p., 1764).

29 Président B. G. Rolland, *Compte-rendu aux chambres assemblées des différents mémoires envoyés par les universités sises dans le ressort de la cour* (Paris, 1786), p. 26.

30 La Chalotais, quoted by J. Delvaille, *La Chalotais: éducateur* (Paris, 1911), p. 131.

31 La Chalotais, *Compte-rendu* (1762), quoted by Delvaille, *ibid.* p. 122.

32 Compayré, *Histoire des doctrines de l'éducation*, p. 249.

33 L. R. de La Chalotais, *Essai d'éducation nationale ou plan d'études pour la jeunesse* (Paris, 1763), pp. 12-13.

34 La Chalotais, quoted by Delvaille, *La Chalotais: éducateur*, p. 111.

35 Rolland, *Compte-Rendu*, p. 38.

36 La Chalotais, *Essai d'éducation nationale*, p. 17.

37 Cf. Compayré, *Histoire des doctrines de l'éducation*, p. 274: 'The complete dependence of education on the State was then considered as an elementary and essential principle.'

38 La Chalotais, *Essai d'éducation nationale*, p. 12.

39 Rolland, *Compte-Rendu*, p. 20.

40 Delvaille, *La Chalotais: éducateur*, p. 95.

41 Rolland, *Compte-Rendu*, p. 16.

42 Cf. Compayré, *Histoire des doctrines de l'éducation*, p. 274: 'The spirit of unity which will later be the guiding principle of the Revolution and of the Empire is already the principle of the parliamentarians.'

43 Rolland, *Compte-Rendu*, p. 24.

44 La Chalotais, quoted by Delvaille, *La Chalotais: éducateur*, p. 164.

45 La Chalotais, *Essai d'éducation nationale*, p. 132.

46 La Chalotais, quoted by Delvaille, *La Chalotais: éducateur*, p. 140.

47 Rolland, *Compte-Rendu*, p. 70.

48 *Ibid.* p. 75.

49 La Chalotais, quoted by Delvaille, *La Chalotais: éducateur*, p. 108.

50 Rolland, *Compte-Rendu*, p. 20.

51 *Ibid.* p. 76.

52 La Chalotais, *Essai d'éducation nationale*, pp. 26-7.

53 *Ibid.* p. 4.

54 *Ibid.* p. 26.

55 Voltaire, quoted by Delvaille, *La Chalotais: éducateur*, p. 118.

56 H. C. Barnard, *The French Tradition in Education* (Cambridge, 1922), p. 235.

57 La Chalotais, *Essai d'éducation nationale*, p. 26.

58 *L'Émile*, book I, in *Collection complète des Œuvres de J. J. Rousseau*, VII (Paris, 1782), 44.

59 Barnard, *French Tradition in Education*, p. 233.

60 Condorcet quoted by J. S. Shapiro, *Condorcet and the rise of Liberalism* (New York, 1934), p. 202.

61 F. Vial, *Condorcet et l'éducation démocratique* (Paris, n.d.), p. 13.

62 F. Alengry, *La Philosophie politique de la Révolution française dans son expression la plus élevée: Condorcet* (Paris, 1938), p. 9.

63 Vial, *Condorcet et l'éducation démocratique*, p. 14.

64 *Ibid.*

65 F. Alengry, *Condorcet – guide de la Révolution française* (Paris, 1904), p. 747.

66 Vial, *Condorcet et l'éducation démocratique*, p. 14.

67 *Ibid.* p. 21.

68 M. J. A. de Condorcet, *Sur l'instruction publique* (Paris, 1792) ('Sur la nécessité de l'instruction publique'), p. 447.

69 *Ibid.*

70 *Ibid.* p. 439.
71 Condorcet quoted by J. Bouissounouse, *Condorcet, le philosophe dans la Révolution* (Paris, 1962), p. 201.
72 Condorcet quoted by Vial, *Condorcet et l'éducation démocratique*, p. 15.
73 *Ibid.*
74 Condorcet, *Sur l'instruction publique* ('Premier mémoire'), p. 171.
75 *Ibid.* p. 173.
76 *Ibid.*
77 *Ibid.* p. 174.
78 Vial, *Condorcet et l'éducation démocratique*, p. 17.
79 Condorcet, *Sur l'instruction publique*, p. 170.
80 Shapiro, *Condorcet and the rise of Liberalism*, p. 137.
81 Bouissounouse, *Condorcet, le philosophe dans la Révolution*, p. 194.
82 Condorcet, quoted by Vial, *Condorcet et l'éducation démocratique*, p. 30.
83 Alengry, *Condorcet – guide de la Révolution française*, p. 770.
84 *Ibid.* p. 744.
85 *Ibid.* p. 700.
86 *Ibid.* p. 748.
87 A. Aulard, *Christianity and the French Revolution* (Boston, 1927), p. 40.
88 Condorcet, quoted by Vial, *Condorcet et l'éducation démocratique*, p. 29.
89 Condorcet, *Sur l'instruction publique* ('Premier mémoire'), pp. 214–15.
90 *Ibid.* pp. 211–12.
91 Condorcet, quoted by Vial, *Condorcet et l'éducation démocratique*, p. 29.
92 G. Compayré, *Introduction au Rapport Condorcet sur l'organisation générale de l'instruction publique* (Paris, 1883), p. viii.
93 Condorcet, quoted by Vial, *Condorcet et l'éducation démocratique*, p. 51.
94 *Ibid.* p. 52.
95 Bouissounouse, *Condorcet, le philosophe dans la Révolution*, p. 191.
96 Vial, *Condorcet et l'éducation démocratique*, p. 29.
97 H. Bigot, *Les Idées de Condorcet sur l'instruction publique* (Poitiers, 1912), p. 42.
98 Condorcet, *Sur l'instruction publique* ('Premier mémoire'), p. 170.
99 *Ibid.* p. 189.
100 *Ibid.* ('Sur la nécessité de l'instruction publique'), p. 442.
101 Condorcet quoted by Vial, *Condorcet et l'éducation démocratique*, p. 22.
102 *Ibid.* p. 38.
103 *Ibid.* p. 24.
104 Condorcet, quoted by Vial, *ibid.* p. 40.
105 Shapiro, *Condorcet and the rise of Liberalism*, p. 175.
106 L. Cahen, *Condorcet et la Révolution française* (Paris, 1904), p. 328.
107 Condorcet, *Rapport et projet de décret*, p. 31.
108 Condorcet quoted by Vial, *Condorcet et l'éducation démocratique*, p. 39.
109 *Ibid.*
110 Condorcet, *Sur l'instruction publique* ('Second mémoire'), p. 275.
111 *Ibid.* ('Premier mémoire'), p. 189.
112 On the election of Sieyès to the Estates General of 1789 as a representative of the Third Estate, cf. for example, A. Neton, *Sieyès (1748–1836)* (Paris, 1900).
113 E. J. Sieyès, *Essai sur les privilèges* (Paris, 1788), p. 2.
114 *Ibid.* p. 5.

115 Cf. P. Campbell, 'Introduction' to *What is the Third Estate?* (London, 1963), p. 11.
116 E. J. Sieyès, *Qu'est-ce que le Tiers État?* 3rd ed. (Paris, 1789), p. 13.
117 Sieyès, *Essai sur les privilèges*, p. 13.
118 *Ibid.* p. 27.
119 *Ibid.* p. 14.
120 Sieyès points out (*ibid.* p. 26) that while officially a monarchy, France has in fact been ruled by the court, that is, by the top section of the aristocracy except during short periods of royal despotism.
121 *Ibid.* p. 25.
122 *Ibid.* p. 43.
123 Sieyès, *Qu'est-ce que le Tiers État?*, p. 83.
124 Campbell, 'Introduction' to *What is the Third Estate?*, p. 25.
125 Sieyès, *Qu'est-ce que le Tiers État?*, p. 9.
126 *Ibid.* pp. 145–6.
127 G. G. Van Deusen, *Sieyès: his Life and his Nationalism* (New York, 1932), p. 82.
128 P. Bastid, *Sieyès et sa pensée* (Paris, 1939), p. 333.
129 Cf. *ibid.* and F. D. de Montlosier, *Mémoires* (2 vols., Paris, 1832), I, 189.
130 Sieyès, *Qu'est-ce que le Tiers Etat?*, p. 14.
131 It has been claimed that the distinction posited by Sieyès between active and passive citizens, only the former having the right of vote, would not have led to the enfranchisement of all members of the Third Estate. However, since the financial contribution required for active citizenship equalled one day's earnings of an agricultural worker, it could not be interpreted as a property qualification and was not socially discriminatory.
132 Sieyès, *Qu'est-ce que le Tiers État?*, p. 10.
133 Condorcet, Sieyès, J. M. Duhamel, *Journal d'instruction sociale* (Paris, 1793), p. 9.
134 Bastid, *Sieyès et sa pensée*, p. 490.
135 Condorcet, Sieyès, Duhamel, *Journal d'instruction sociale*, p. 7.
136 *Ibid.* p. 83.
137 *Ibid.* p. 149.
138 *Ibid.* p. 85.
139 *Ibid.* p. 87.
140 Cf. E. J. Sieyès, *Projet d'un décret provisoire sur le clergé* (Paris, 1790).
141 Alengry, *La Philosophie politique de la Révolution française*, p. 7.
142 Quoted in Shapiro, *Condorcet and the rise of Liberalism*, p. 104.
143 Bouissounouse (*Condorcet, le philosophe dans la Révolution*, p. 195) quotes Jaurès stating 'the same Condorcet who in 1790 demanded the vote for all before the Hotel de Ville, demanded thought for all before the Legislative Assembly'.

Chapter 10: French Ideologies Legitimating Educational Domination

1 Delfau, *Napoléon Ier et l'instruction publique*, p. 14.
2 Cf. Aulard, *Napoléon Ier et le monople universitaire*, p. 363.
3 L. Liard, *L'Enseignement supérieur en France*, II, 35.

4 Napoleon, quoted by Delfau, *Napoléon Ier et l'instruction publique*, p. 13.
5 Liard, *L'Enseignement supérieur en France*, II, 68–9.
6 *Ibid.* p. 69.
7 *Correspondance de Napoléon Ier* (34 vols., Paris, 1858–69), X, letter dated 16 February 1805, no. 8328.
8 Quoted by Aulard, *Napoléon Ier et le monople universitaire*, p. 365.
9 Cf. L. Deries, *Les Congrégations religieuses au temps de Napoléon* (Paris, 1929).
10 Cf. Grimaud, *Histoire de la liberté d'enseignement*.
11 Napoleon quoted by Aulard, *Napoléon Ier et le monopole universitaire*, p. 155.
12 Delfau, *Napoléon Ier et l'instruction publique*, p. 79.
13 E. Durkheim, *L'Évolution pédagogique en France* (2 vols., Paris, 1938), II, 172.
14 Napoleon at the meeting of the *Conseil d'état* on 1 March 1806, quoted by P. Pelet de la Lozère, *Opinions de Napoléon Ier sur divers sujets de politique et d'administration recueillies par un membre de son Conseil d'Etat* (Paris, 1833).
15 Napoleon, quoted by Pelet de la Lozère, *Opinions de Napoléon* (meeting of 11 March 1806).
16 Cf. Delfau, *Napoléon Ier et l'instruction publique*, p. 82.
17 Napoleon at the meeting of the *Conseil d'état* of 21 May 1806, quoted by Pelet de la Lozère, *Opinions de Napoléon Ier*.
18 Cf. M. Gontard, *L'Enseignement primaire en France*, p. 236f.
19 Napoleon quoted by E. Rendu, *Monsieur Ambroise Rendu et l'Université de France* (Paris, 1861), p. 28.
20 Fontanes, quoted A. Rendu, *Essai sur l'instruction publique* (3 vols., Paris, 1819), III, 4.
21 Delfau, *Napoléon Ier et l'instruction publique*, p. 72.
22 *Ibid.* p. 59.
23 Fourcroy in 'Exposé des Motifs', *Archives parlementaires*, 2nd series, IX, 414.
24 Liard, *L'Enseignement supérieur en France*, II, p. 39.
25 Delfau, *Napoléon Ier et l'instruction publique*, p. 62.
26 E. Goblot, *La Barrière et le niveau* (Paris, 1930), p. 126.
27 Delfau, *Napoléon Ier et l'instruction publique*, pp. 40–1.
28 Cf. Aulard, *Napoléon Ier et le monople universitaire*, p. 239.
29 J. Simon, *Réforme de l'enseignement populaire* (Paris, 1874).
30 Gontard, *L'Enseignement primaire en France*, p. 240.
31 P. Lanfrey, *Histoire de Napoléon Ier* (5 vols., Paris, 1867–75), III, 457.
32 Aulard, *Napoléon Ier et le monople universitaire*, p. 190.
33 Out of 27,000 or 28,000 priests, 22,000 refused to participate in the constitutional clergy: Dansette, *Religious History of Modern France*, I, 89.
34 Lamennais quoted by C. S. Phillips, *The Church in France 1789–1849. A Study in Revival* (New York, 1966), p. 224.
35 *Ibid.* p. 260.
36 F. de Lamennais, *De l'Université Impériale*, in *Œuvres*, V (Paris, 1844), 359.
37 F. de Lamennais, *Du droit du gouvernement sur l'éducation*, in *Œuvres*, V, 399.
38 *Ibid.* p. 390.
39 C. de Montalembert, *Du devoir des catholiques dans la question de la liberté d'enseignement* (Paris, 1842), p. 48.
40 A. Trannoy, *Le Romantisme politique de Montalembert* (Paris, 1943), p. 69.
41 Phillips, *The Church in France*, 222–3.

42 A. Leroy-Beaulieu, *Les Catholiques libéraux, l'Église et la libéralisme de 1830 à nos jours* (Paris, 1885), p. 80.

43 *Ibid.* p. 111.

44 Cf. C. Carcopino, *La Doctrine sociale de Lamennais* (Paris, 1942), p. 60f.

45 F. de Lamennais, *De l'éducation considerée dans ses rapports avec la liberté*, in *Œuvres*, V, 501.

46 Lamennais, *Du droit du gouvernement sur l'éducation* (Paris, 1817), p. 5.

47 A. Leroy-Beaulieu: *Les Catholiques libéraux*, p. 129.

48 Lamennais, *De l'Université Impériale*, p. 362.

49 *Ibid.* p. 360.

50 Cf. *ibid.* p. 369.

51 Cf. F. de Lamennais, *Le Livre du peuple* (Paris, 1838).

52 Lamennais: *De l'Université Impériale*, pp. 563-4.

53 Cf. J. Poisson, *Le Romantisme social de Lamennais* (Paris, 1931), p. 338.

54 Lamennais, *Du droit du gouvernement sur l'éducation* (1817), p. 13.

55 Cf. F. de Lamennais, *De l'esclavage moderne* (Paris, 1840).

56 Lamennais, *Du droit du gouvernement sur l'éducation* (1817), p. 14.

57 *Ibid.* pp. 7-8.

58 F. de Lamennais, *De l'éducation du peuple*, in *Œuvres*, V, p. 384f.

59 Lamennais, *Du droit du gouvernement sur l'éducation* (1817), p. 11.

60 A. de Lamartine, *L'État, l'Église et l'enseignement* (Macon, 1843), p. 8.

61 Trannoy, *Le Romantisme politique de Montalembert*, p. 157.

62 C. de Montalembert, *Du devoir des catholiques dans les élections* (1846) in *Œuvres*, IV (Paris, 1860), 418.

63 Cf. Leroy-Beaulieu, *Les Catholiques libéraux*, p. 145f.

64 H. Michel, *La loi Falloux* (Paris, 1906), p. 270.

65 C. de Montalembert, *Discours sur la loi organique de l'enseignement presentée par M. de Falloux* (Paris, 1850).

Chapter 11 : Conclusion

1 R. J. Havinghurst, *Comparative perspectives on Education* (Boston, 1968), preface.

2 *Ibid.* p. xii.

3 *Ibid.* p. xv.

4 P. F. Drucker, 'The Educational Revolution', in Halsey, Floud and Anderson (eds.), *Education, Economy and Society*, p. 16.

5 G. H. Bantock, *Culture, Industrialization and Education* (London, 1968), p. 12.

6 E. P. Thompson, *The making of the English Working Class* (London, 1963), passim.

7 E. Ashby, 'On Universities and the Scientific Revolution', in Halsey *et al.*, *Education, Economy and Society*, p. 466.

8 A. K. C. Ottaway, *Education and Society* (London, 1953), p. 62.

9 *Ibid.* p. 65.

10 D. V. Glass, 'Education and social change in modern England', in Halsey *et al.*, *Education, Economy and Society*, p. 393.

11 Olive Banks, *Sociology of Education* (London, 1968), p. 19.

12 Cf. F. Harbison and C. A. Myers, *Education, Manpower and Economic Growth* (Princeton, 1964).

13 For example, 'All institutions to Condorcet owed their existence to "opinion": the bad ones to "prejudice", or perverted opinion; and the good ones to "reason", or enlightened opinion', Shapiro, *Condorcet and the rise of Liberalism*, p. 137.

14 Berger, *Social Reality of Religion*, p. 127.

15 *Ibid.* p. 126.

16 *Ibid.* p. 131.

17 *Ibid.*

18 *Ibid.* p. 151.

19 *Ibid.* p. 129.

Bibliography

Adamson, J. H. *English Education, 1789–1902*. Cambridge, 1964.
Alengry, F. *Condorcet – guide de la Révolution française*. Paris, 1904.
  La Philosophie politique de la Révolution française dans son expression la plus élevée : Condorcet. Paris, 1938.
Archer, M. Scotford and Vaughan, M. 'Education, Secularization, Desecularization and Resecularization,' in D. Martin and M. Hill (eds.) *A Sociological Yearbook of Religion in Britain*, no. 3, London, 1970.
Archer, R. L. *Secondary Education in the Nineteenth Century*. Cambridge, 1921.
Arnold, T. *Principles of Church Reform*. London, 1833.
  Miscellaneous Works. London, 1845.
  Sermons. London, 1878.
Aron, R. *Main Currents in Sociological Thought*. Vol. I, London, 1968.
Ashby, E. 'On Universities and the Scientific Revolution', in A. H. Halsey, J. Floud and C. A. Anderson (eds.), *Education, Economy and Society*. London, 1967.
Aspinall, A. *Politics and the Press, 1780–1850*. London, 1949.
Aulard, A. *Napoléon Ier et le monopole universitaire*. Paris, 1911.
  Christianity and the French Revolution. Boston, 1927.
Babeau, A. *L'Instruction primaire dans les campagnes avant 1789*. Paris, 1875.
Bain, A. *James Mill*. London, 1882.
Bamford, T. W. *Thomas Arnold*. London, 1960.
Banks, O. *Sociology of Education*. London, 1968.
Bantock, G. H. *Culture, Industrialization and Education*. London, 1968.
Barnard, H. C. *The French Tradition in Education*. Cambridge, 1922.
  A Short History of English Education (1760–1944). London, 1955.
  Education and the French Revolution. Cambridge, 1969.
Bastid, P. *Sieyès et sa pensée*. Paris, 1939.
Baudeau, N. 'L'Introduction à la philosophie économique,' in E. Daire (ed.), *Les Physiocrates*. Paris, 1846.
Bell, A. *An Experiment in Education made at the Male (Orphan) Asylum in Madras, suggesting a System by which a School or Family may teach itself under the superintendence of the Master or Parent*. 2nd ed., London, 1809.
Bendix, R. *Max Weber. An Intellectual Portrait*. London, 1960.
Bentham, J. *Church of Englandism and its Catechism examined*. London, 1818.
  Not Paul but Jesus. London, 1823.
  Traités de législation civile et pénale. London, 1858.
  Works, ed. J. Bowring. Edinburgh, 1838–43.

Berger, P. L. *The Social Reality of Religion*. London, 1969.

Bigot, H. *Les Idées de Condorcet sur l'instruction publique*. Poitiers, 1912.

Binns, H. B. *A Century of Education, Being the Centenary History of the British and Foreign School Society 1808–1908*. London, 1908.

Birchenough, C. *History of Elementary Education*. 3rd ed., London, 1938.

Bouissounouse, J. *Condorcet, le philosophe dans la Révolution*. Paris, 1962.

Brown, P. A. *The French Revolution in EnglishHistory*. London, 1923.

Burston, W. H. *James Mill on Education*. Cambridge, 1969.

Butler, S. *Life and Letters of Samuel Butler*. 2 vols., London, 1896.

Cahen, L. *Condorcet et la Révolution française*. Paris, 1904.

Campbell, P. 'Introduction' to *What is the Third Estate?* London, 1963.

Carcopino, C. *La Doctrine sociale de Lamennais*. Paris, 1942.

Caro, E. *La Fin du 18ᵉ siècle*. 2 vols, Paris, 1880.

Cartwright, J. *Take your Choice*. London, 1776.

Cavenagh, F. A. *James and John Stuart Mill on Education*. Cambridge, 1931.

Chevalier, A. *Les Frères des écoles chrétiennes et l'enseignement primaire après la Révolution (1797–1830)*. Paris, 1887.

Church, R. W. *The Oxford Movement; twelve years (1833–1845)*. London, 1891.

Clarke, F. *Education and Social Change*. London, 1940.

Cockshut, A. O. J. *Anglican Attitudes*. London, 1959.

Coleridge, S. T. *On the Constitution of Church and State*. London, 1852.

Compayré, G. *Histoire des doctrines de l'éducation en France*. Paris, 1879.
Introduction au rapport Condorcet sur l'organisation générale de l'instruction publique. Paris, 1883.

Condorcet, M. J. A. de. *Rapport et projet de décret sur l'organisation générale de l'instruction publique*. Paris, 1792.
Sur l'instruction publique. Paris, 1792.

Condorcet, M. J. A. de, Duhamel, J. M. and Sieyès, E. J. *Journal d'instruction sociale*. Paris, 1793.

Cournot, M. *Des Institutions d'instruction publique en France*. Paris, 1864.

Cousin, V. *De l'instruction publique dans quelques pays de l'Allemagne et particulièrement en Prusse*. 3rd ed., 2 vols, Paris, 1840.
Défense de l'université et de la philosophie. 3rd ed., Paris, 1844.

Dansette, A. *Religious History of Modern France*. 3 vols., Freiburg, 1961.

Darwin, B. *The English Public School*. London, 1929.

Daunou, P. C. F. *Essai sur l'instruction publique*. Paris, 1793.

Dawson, J. C. *Lakanal the Regicide*. Alabama, 1948.

Delfau, A. *Napoléon Ier et l'instruction publique*. Paris, 1902.

Delvaille, J. *La Chalotais: éducateur*. Paris, 1911.

Deries, L. *Les Congrégations religieuses au temps deNapoléon*. Paris, 1929.

Diderot, D. 'Plan d'une université pour le gouvernement de Russie ou d'une éducation publique dans toutes les sciences, 1775–76', in *Œuvres complètes* (Assezat-Tourneux ed.). 3 vols., Paris, 1875.

Dolléans, E. *Robert Owen*. Paris, 1905.
Le Chartisme (1830–1848). Paris, 1912.

Drucker, P. F. 'The Educational Revolution', in A. H. Halsey, J. Floud and C. A. Anderson (eds.) *Education, Economy and Society*. London, 1967.

Durkheim, E. *L'Évolution pédagogique en France*. 2 vols, Paris, 1938.

Duruy, A. *L'Instruction publique et la Révolution*. Paris, 1882.

Emile-Sorel, A. *Conférence sur Guizot*. Rouen, 1914.

Engels, F. *The Condition of the Working Class in England in 1844*. London, 1892.

Everett, C. *Jeremy Bentham*. London, 1966.

Faber, G. *Oxford Apostles*. London, 1954.
Jowett. London, 1957.

Falcucci, C. *L'Humanisme dans l'enseignement secondaire en France au 19e siècle*. Toulouse, 1939.

Fellows, O. *Diderot Studies*. 3 vols., Syracuse, 1961.

Findlay, J. J. *Arnold of Rugby*. Cambridge, 1898.

Fitch, J. *Thomas and Matthew Arnold and their Influences on Englih Education*. London, 1897.

Fleischer, D. *William Godwin: a Study in Liberalism*. London, 1951.

Floud, J. and Halsey, A. H. 'The Sociology of Education'. *Current Sociology*, VII, 1958.

Fontainerie, F. de la. *French Liberalism and Education in the 18th century*. New York, 1932.

Freund, J. *The Sociology of Max Weber*. London, 1968.

Gerth, H. H. and Mills, C. W. *From Max Weber: Essays in Sociology*. London, 1967.

Gide, C. and Rist, C. *A History of Economic Doctrines*. London, 1915.

Gillespie, F. E. *Labour and Politics in England (1850–1867)*. Durham, N. Carolina, 1927.

Gillot, H. *Denis Diderot*. Paris, 1937.

Glass, D. V. 'Education and social change in modern England', in A. H. Halsey, J. Floud and C. A. Anderson (eds.), *Education, Economy and Society*. London, 1967.

Goblot, E. *La Barrière et le niveau*. Paris, 1930.

Godechot, J. *Institutions de la France*. Paris, 1951.

Godwin, W. *Enquiry Concerning Political Justice and its influence on Morals and Happiness*. London, 1793, 1796, 1798 (eds.).
The Enquirer. London, 1797.
Thoughts on Man, his Nature, Productions and Discoveries. London, 1831.

Gontard, M. *L'Enseignement primaire en France de la Révolution à la loi Guizot, 1789–1833*. Lyons, 1959.

Granger, G. G. *La Mathématique sociale du marquis de Condorcet*. Paris, 1956.

Gréard, O. *Éducation et instruction*. 2 vols., Paris, 1887.

Grimaud, L. *Histoire de la liberté d'enseignement en France depuis la chute de l'ancien régime jusqu'à nos jours*. Grenoble, 1898.

Gros, J. *Lakanal et l'éducation nationale*. Paris, 1912.

Grote, H. *The Personal Life of George Grote*. 2nd ed., London, 1873.

Guizot, F. *Essais sur l'histoire et sur l'état actuel de l'instruction publique en France*. Paris, 1816.

Guyton de Morveau, L. B. *Mémoire sur l'éducation publique, avec le prospectus d'un collège*. n.p., 1764.

Halévy, E. *L'Évolution de la doctrine utilitaire de 1789 à 1815*. Paris, 1901.
Thomas Hodgskin (1787–1869). Paris, 1903.
Le Radicalisme philosophique. Paris, 1904.

Halsey, A. H. 'The Changing Function of Universities', in A. H. Halsey, J. Floud and C. A. Anderson (eds.), *Education, Economy and Society*. London, 1967.

Hamilton, W. 'On the state of the English Universities'. *Edinburgh Review*, LIII, no. 106, 1831.

Hammond, J. L. and B. *The town Labourer*, (1760–1832). London, 1936.

Harbison, F. and Myers, C. A. *Education, Manpower and Economic Growth*. Princeton, 1964.

Hastings, W. F. 'The Education of English Catholics (1559–1800)'. London University thesis (unpublished), 1923.

Havinghurst, R. J. *Comparative perspectives on Education*. Boston, 1968.

Hazard, P. *La pensée européenne au 18e siècle de Montesquieu à Lessing*. Vol. I, Paris, 1946.

Helvétius, A. *Œuvres*. 4 vols., The Hague, 1773.

Hentz, N. *Sur l'instruction publique*. Paris, 1792.

Hippeau, C. *La Révolution et l'éducation nationale*. Paris, 1883.

Hodgen, M. T. *Workers' Education in England and the United States*. London, 1925.

Hodgskin, T. *Labour defended against the claims of capital or the unproductiveness of capital with reference to the present combinations amongst journeymen* (G. D. H. Cole ed.). London, 1922.

Holbach, P. *Système social*. Amsterdam, 1773.

Janet, P. *Victor Cousin et son œuvre*. Paris, 1885.

Jaubert, L. *La gratuité de l'enseignement secondaire*. Bordeaux, 1938.

Jones, M. G. *Hannah More*. Cambridge, 1953.

Judges, A. V. *Pioneers of English education*. London, 1952.

Kay-Shuttleworth, J. *Four Periods of English Education*. London, 1862.

Kelly, T. *George Birkbeck Pioneer of adult education*. Liverpool, 1957.

Kirk, K. E. *The Story of the Woodard Schools*. London, 1937.

Knight, C. *Passages of a Working Life*. 3 vols., London, 1864–73.

Knox, V. *Remarks on the tendency of certain clauses in a Bill now pending in Parliament to degrade Grammar Schools*. 2nd ed., London, 1821.

Kolinsky, M. *Ideology, Organization and Conflict in Social Movements*, University of Birmingham mimeographed publication, 1968.

Koung, Y. *Théorie constitutionelle de Sieyès*. Paris, 1934.

Labrousse, E. Bourgin, G. and Dolléans, E. *La Pensée ouvrière sur l'éducation*. Paris, n.d.

La Chalotais, L. R. de. *Essai d'éducation nationale ou plan d'études pour la jeunesse*. Paris, 1763.

Lacroix, S. F. *Essais sur l'enseignement en général et sur celui des mathématiques en particulier*. Paris, 1805.

Lamartine, A. de, *L'État, L'Église et l'enseignement*. Macon, 1843.

Lamennais, F. de. *Du droit du gouvernement sur l'éducation*. Paris, 1817.

Le Livre du Peuple. Paris, 1838.

De l'esclavage moderne. Paris, 1840.

De l'éducation considerée dans ses rapports avec la liberté, in *Œuvres* v, Paris, 1844.

De l'éducation du peuple, in *Œuvres*, v, Paris, 1844.

De l'Université Imperiale, in *Œuvres*, v, Paris, 1844.

Lanfrey, P. *Histoire de Napoléon Ier*. 5 vols., Paris, 1867–75.

Lasteyrie, Comte de. *Nouveau système d'éducation et d'enseignement ou enseignement mutuel appliqué aux langues, aux sciences et aux arts.* Paris, 1819.

Léaud, A. and Glay, E. *L'École primaire en France, ses origines, ses différents aspects au cours des siècles, ses victoires, sa mission dans les démocraties.* Paris, 1934.

Lebrun, I. *De l'instruction publique sous Napoléon Ier et de l'université.* Paris, 1814.

Leff, G. *The Tyranny of Concepts.* London, 1961.

Leif, J. and Rustin, G. *Histoire des institutions scolaires.* Paris, 1954.

Léon, A. *Histoire de l'enseignement en France.* Paris, 1967.

Lepelletier de St Fargeau, M. *Plan d'éducation nationale.* Paris, 1793.

Leroy-Beaulieu, A. *Les Catholiques libéraux, l'Église et le libéralisme de 1830 à nos jours.* Paris, 1885.

Liard, L. *L'Enseignement supérieur en France, 1789–1889.* 2 vols., Paris, 1888.

Lough, J. 'Helvétius and d'Holbach', in *Modern Language Review*, XXXIII, no. 3, 1938.

    Diderot, Selected Philosophical Writings. Cambridge, 1953.

Lovett, W. and Collins, J. *Chartism: a new organisation of the people.* London, 1840.

    The Life and Struggles of W. Lovett (R. M. Tawney ed.). London, 1920.

MacIntyre, A. *Secularization and Moral Change.* Oxford, 1967.

Malthus, T. *First Essay on Population* (Bonar ed.). London, 1926.

Marx, K. *Critique of Political Economy* (Stone ed.). New York, 1904.

    German Ideology (Pascal ed.). London, 1938.

Maxwell-Lyte, H. C. *A History of Eton College.* London, 1899.

Mercier de la Rivière, P. Le. 'L'Ordre naturel et essentiel des sociétés politiques', in E. Daire (ed.), *Les Physiocrates.* Paris, 1846.

Michel, H. *La loi Falloux.* Paris, 1906.

Mill, J. 'On Education', in F. A. Cavenagh, *James and John Stuart Mill on Education.* Cambridge, 1931.

Mill, J. S. *On Liberty.* 2nd ed. London, 1859.

    Professor Sedgwick's Discourse on the Studies of the University of Cambridge in *Works*, IV, 'Dissertations and Discussions', Series I, London, n.d.

Mirabeau, G. de. *Travail sur l'éducation publique.* Paris, 1791.

Montalembert, C. de. *Du devoir des catholiques dans la question de la liberté d'enseignement.* Paris, 1842.

    Discours sur la loi organique de l'enseignement presentée par M. de Falloux. Paris, 1850.

    Du devoir des catholiques dans les élections, in *Œuvres*, IV, Paris, 1860.

Montlosier, F. D. de. *Mémoires.* 2 vols., Paris, 1832.

Montmorency, J. de. *State Intervention in English Education.* Cambridge, 1902.

Mornet, D. *La Pensée philosophique au 18e siècle.* Paris, 1956.

Neton, A. *Sieyès (1748–1836).* Paris, 1900.

Newman, J. H. *Apologia pro Vita sua.* London, 1878.

    Idea of a University. London, 1893.

    University Sketches (M. Tierney ed.), Dublin, 1952.

O'Brien, J. B. *Life and Character of Maximilian Robespierre.* London, 1837.

Oestreicher, J. *La Pensée politique et économique de Diderot.* Paris, 1936.

Ottaway, A. K. C. *Education and Society.* London, 1953.

Owen, R. *A new view of Society*. London, 1813.
  Report to the county of Lanark of a plan for removing public distress. Glasgow, 1832.
  The life of Robert Owen by himself. London, 1857.
Parsons, T. 'The School Class as a Social system: Some of its Functions in American Society', in A. H. Halsey, J. Floud and C. A. Anderson (eds.), *Education, Economy and Society*. London, 1967.
Pattison, M. *Memoirs*. London, 1885.
Pelet de la Lozère, P. *Opinions de Napoléon Ier sur divers sujets de politique et d'administration recueilleis par un membre de son Conseil d'État*. Paris, 1833.
Phillips, C. S. *The Church in France, 1789–1849. A study in Revival*. New York, 1966.
Pinet, G. *Histoire de l'École Polytechnique*. Paris, 1887.
Piobetta, J. B. *Le Baccalauréat de l'enseignement secondaire*. Paris, 1937.
Podmore, F. *Robert Owen, A Biography*. 2 vols., London, 1906.
Poisson, J. *Le Romantisme social de Lamennais*. Paris, 1931.
Ponteil, F. *Histoire de l'enseignement en France, 1789–1964*. Paris, 1966.
Pouthas, C. H. *Guizot pendant la Restauration. Préparation de l'homme d'État (1814–1830)*. Paris, 1923.
Prentout, H. *L'Enseignement secondaire eu France au 19e et 20e siècles*. Paris, 1921.
Preu, J. A. *The Dean and the Anarchist*. Florida, 1959.
Pritchard, F. *Methodist Secondary Education*. London, 1949.
Prost, A. *L'Enseignement en France (1800–1967)*. Paris, 1968.
Quesnay, F. 'Droit naturel', in E. Daire (ed.), *Les Physiocrates*. Paris, 1846.
Quincherat, J. *Histoire de Sainte-Barbe*. 3 vols., Paris, 1864.
Rémond, R. *Lamennais et la démocratie*. Paris, 1948.
Rendu, A. *Essai sur l'instruction publique*. 3 vols., Paris, 1819.
Rendu, E. *Monsieur Ambrosie Rendu et l'Université de France*. Paris, 1861.
Ricardo, D. *The Principles of Political Economy* (Gonner ed.). London, 1891.
Rolland, Président B. G. *Compte-rendu aux chambres assemblées des différents mémoires envoyés par les universités sises dans le ressort de la cour*. Paris, 1786.
Rousseau, J. J. *L'Émile*, Book I, in *Collection Complète des Œuvres de J. J. Rousseau*. VII, Paris, 1782.
Sainte Beuve, C. de. *Galerie de portraits littéraires*. Paris, 1893.
Schoyen, A. R. *The Chartist Challenge. A Portrait of George Julien Harney*. London, 1958.
Sevrin, R. *Histoire de l'enseignement primaire en France sous la Révolution, le Consulat et l'Empire*. Paris, 1932.
Sewell, W. *Thoughts on the Admission of Dissenters to the University of Oxford*. Oxford, 1834.
Shapiro, J. S. *Condorcet and the rise of Liberalism*. New York, 1934.
Shipman, M. D. *Sociology of the School*. London, 1968.
Sieyès, E. J. *Essai sur les privilèges*. Paris, 1788.
  Qu'est-ce que le Tiers État? 3rd ed. Paris, 1789.
  Projet d'un décret provisoire sur le clergé. Paris, 1790.
Silver, H. *Robert Owen on Education*. Cambridge, 1969.
Simon, B. *Studies in the History of Education, 1780–1870*. London, 1960.

Simon, J. *Réforme de l'enseignement populaire.* Paris, 1874.
Victor Cousin. 4th ed., Paris, 1910.
Smith, A. *An Inquiry into the Nature and Causes of the Wealth of Nations* (Cannan ed.). 2 vols., London, 1904.
Sparrow, J. *Mark Pattison and the Idea of a University.* Cambridge, 1967.
Stanley, A. P. *Life and Correspondence of Thomas Arnold.* London, 1846.
Sturt, M. *The Education of the People. A History of Primary Education in England and Wales in the 19th century.* London, 1967.
Tardivel, F. *J. H. Newman, éducateur.* Paris, 1937.
Tawney, R. H. *The Radical Tradition.* London, 1964.
Thomas, V. *The legality of the present academical system of the University of Oxford asserted against the new calumnies of the Edinburgh Review.* Oxford, 1831.
The legality of the present academical system of the University of Oxford reasserted. Oxford, 1832.
Thompson, E. P. *The Making of the English Working Class.* London, 1963.
Thring, E. *Education and School.* Cambridge, 1864.
Thureau-Dangin, P. *L'Église et l'État sous la Monarchie de Juillet.* Paris, 1880.
Tourneux, M. *Diderot et Catherine II.* Paris, 1899.
Trannoy, A. *Le Romantisme politique de Montalembert.* Paris, 1943.
Trevelyan, G. M. *English Social History.* 2nd ed., London, 1946.
Turner, R. H. 'Modes of Social Ascent through Education: Sponsored and Contest Mobility', in A. H. Halsey, J. Floud and C. A. Anderson (eds.), *Education, Economy and Society.* London, 1967.
Tylecote, M. *The Mechanics Institutes of Lancashire and Yorkshire before 1851.* Manchester, 1959.
Van Deusen, G. G. *Sieyès: His Life and his Nationalism.* New York, 1932.
Vaughan, M. 'The Grandes Écoles', in R. Wilkinson (ed.), *Governing Elites. Studies in Training and Selection.* New York, 1969.
Vial, F. *Trois siècles d'histoire de l'enseignement secondaire.* Paris, 1936.
Condorcet et l'éducation démocratique. Paris, n.d.
Voll, D. *Catholic Evangelicalism.* London, 1963.
Voltaire. *Correspondance* (Garnier ed.). Paris, 1883.
Wallas, G. *The Life of Francis Place.* London, 1898.
Ward, M. *Young Mr.Newman.* London, 1948.
Ward, W. R. *Victorian Oxford.* London, 1965.
Weber, Max. *Basic concepts in Sociology.* London, 1962.
Webb, R. K. *The British Working Class Reader (1780–1848).* London, 1955.
Weill, T. *Histoire de l'enseignement secondaire en France (1802–1920).* Paris, 1921.
Weulersse, M. *Le Mouvement physiocratique en France (1756–1770).* Paris, 1910.
Whewell, W. *On the right principles of English University Education.* London, 1837.

Index

Royal University, 125-6, 144, 192, 206; *see also* Imperial University
Rugby (school), 50, 111, 114
Russell, J., 58

schools of industry, 33, 36
secularism, 33, 36, 41, 44, 46, 48, 69, 94-5, 116, 121, 126, 131, 135, 145-9, 151-5, 159, 160, 165, 179-80, 189, 191, 198-200, 227-30
Sewell, W., 55, 57
Sheffield Courant, 108
Shipman, M. D., 4-6, 8
Shrewsbury (school), 50
Sieyès, E. J., 122, 132, 139, 160-1, 171-8
Smith, A., 63-6; *see also* classical economics and Physiocrats
Society for the Diffusion of Useful Knowledge, 39, 89, 112
Stanley, A. P., 57-8, 115
Sunday schools, 36-7, 41

Tait, A. C., 58, 115
Talleyrand, C. M. de, 122, 138-40
Tawney, R. H., 90
Ten Hours Bill (1847), 40
Test Acts, 45, 52, 55-8, 213, 222
Thomas, V., 55
Thring, E., 51
Tory Party, 44, 54
Tractarianism, *see* Oxford Movement

Trade Union (Grand National Consolidated), 44
Turgot, A. R. J., 61, 63; *see also* classical economics and Physiocrats
Turner, R., 6-7

Ultramontanism, 146, 193, 195, 199
University College, London, 46, 111; *see also* London University
Utilitarianism, 28, 34, 39-44, 46, 48, 53-5, 58, 63, 68-80, 88, 93, 95, 106, 127-8, 158, 217

vocationalism, 18, 43, 76, 122, 128-30, 149-51, 156-7, 170, 177, 179, 186-7, 190, 208, 209, 210, 216
Voltaire (alias F. M. Arouet), 79, 146, 158, 165
voluntarism, 34, 35, 42, 50, 203-5, 218

Weber, M., 1, 16-24
Wellington (school), 50
West London Lancastrian Association, 38
Westminster Review, 54
Whig Party, 37-42, 44, 54, 56
Whitbread, S., 38
Woodard schools, 51
Working Men's Association, 88; *see also* London Working Men's Association